Katy Simpson
with Nick Thorner

Foundation IELTS MASTERCLASS

Teacher's Pack

Great Clarendon Street, Oxford, OX2 6DP, United Kingdom

Oxford University Press is a department of the University of Oxford.
It furthers the University's objective of excellence in research, scholarship,
and education by publishing worldwide. Oxford is a registered trade
mark of Oxford University Press in the UK and in certain other countries

© Oxford University Press 2015

The moral rights of the author have been asserted

First published in 2015

2019 2018 2017 2016 2015

10 9 8 7 6 5 4 3 2 1

No unauthorized photocopying

All rights reserved. No part of this publication may be reproduced, stored
in a retrieval system, or transmitted, in any form or by any means, without
the prior permission in writing of Oxford University Press, or as expressly
permitted by law, by licence or under terms agreed with the appropriate
reprographics rights organization. Enquiries concerning reproduction outside
the scope of the above should be sent to the ELT Rights Department, Oxford
University Press, at the address above

You must not circulate this work in any other form and you must impose
this same condition on any acquirer

Links to third party websites are provided by Oxford in good faith and for
information only. Oxford disclaims any responsibility for the materials
contained in any third party website referenced in this work

ISBN: 978 0 19 470532 5

Printed in China

This book is printed on paper from certified and well-managed sources

ACKNOWLEDGEMENTS

The authors and publisher are grateful to those who have given permission to reproduce the following extracts and adaptations of copyright material: p.12 Adapted extract from "Private Tutoring: how prevalent and effective is it?" by Judith Ireson, London Review of Education, Vol. 2 (2), July 2004.Reproduced by permission ofTaylor and Francis Ltd and Judy Ireson. p.54 Adapted extract from "What's the Earth's biggest threat to biodiversity?" by Jonathan Atteberry, HowStuffWorks.com, 25 August 2010. Reproduced by permission of Discovery Access. p.123 Adapted extract from "Causation vs. Correlation", www.stats.org. Reproduced by permission of Statistical Assessment Service (STATS) at George Mason University.

Sources: p.27 www.uky.edu, p.91 http://news.nationalgeographic.com; www.pratt.duke.edu, p.122 www.badscience.net

Contents

Course overview		4
Speaking DVD information		7
Unit 1	Education & learning	8
Unit 2	Health & medicine	22
Unit 3	Society & family	35
Unit 4	Population & the environment	49
Unit 5	Culture & entertainment	61
Unit 6	Careers & success	72
Unit 7	Nature & biology	85
Unit 8	Producers & consumers	97
Unit 9	Media & travel	108
Unit 10	Science & progress	119
Grammar File answer key		130
Vocabulary File answer key		132
Study Skills File answer key		135
Writing File answer key		136
IELTS Practice Test answer key		136
IELTS Practice Test audioscript		141

Course overview

About *Foundation IELTS Masterclass*
Foundation IELTS Masterclass provides materials which give candidates at IELTS band 4.5–5.5 appropriate preparation and practice for the IELTS exam. In addition to offering students extensive guidance and exam training, it also contains interesting, lively, and informative materials that will build world knowledge and give students the confidence to discuss issues commonly dealt with in the exam.

About the exam
The IELTS exam consists of four papers: Listening, Reading, Writing, and Speaking. Candidates receive a score for each paper. The individual scores are averaged and rounded to produce an Overall Band Score. Candidates receive scores on an Overall Band Score from 1 (Non User) to 9 (Expert User).

Course components
The course comprises:
- Student's Book
- Online Practice
- Teacher's Book with Speaking DVD

The Student's Book
The Student's Book contains:
- 10 topic-based units. Each unit begins with an infographic or image with related questions to engage students with the unit topic and encourage them to think critically. There are four skills-based lessons – Speaking, Listening, Reading, and Writing – focusing on skills development and exam practice for each of the four IELTS papers, with additional grammar- and vocabulary-building activities.
- An *Exam challenge* section at the end of each unit gives students further exam practice
- *Exam tip* boxes alongside exam skills sections
- *Grammar File* with exercises
- *Vocabulary File* with exercises
- *Study Skills File* with exercises
- *Writing File* with model answers
- Overview of *Exam tips*
- Audioscript

Each unit contains:
Unit opener: This section presents the overall theme of the unit by engaging students' interest in the new topic, activating general knowledge, introducing related vocabulary, and providing opportunities for both general fluency practice and specific exam practice for Speaking.

The use of graphics and statistics on these pages is designed to provide a direct, accessible route into the units' themes and to generate quick discussion, without the need for lengthy textual input. Since little language support is needed to engage with the content, students may also wish to discuss these pages before class starts or in preparation for the lesson. The pages, along with infographics on other pages, also provide opportunities for describing numerical or visual data, which teachers may find useful when helping students prepare for Writing Task 1.

Speaking: Each speaking section starts with a lead-in (*Topic focus*) that engages students with the lesson topic, by introducing key concepts or issues, and activating existing knowledge. These sections include practice of one or several Part 1, 2, and 3 tasks from the Speaking paper. Through the course, students gain experience in organizing their responses and in handling different types of discourse, such as giving personal information, expressing opinions, describing cause and effect, extending responses, and varying language. The speaking lessons train students to consider all areas of the IELTS assessment, by developing the grammar, vocabulary, pronunciation, and fluency skills ('exam skills') required to perform a specific exam task. Students then apply learning in all four areas in a final output task. Several speaking sections include opportunities for students to listen to examples of candidates doing a speaking task and to compare their own ideas with those of the candidates. Audioscripts of these recordings are located at the back of the Student's Book and in the Teacher's Book within the unit notes.

Listening: Each listening section starts with a lead-in (*Topic focus*) that prepares students for exam practice either by activating existing knowledge or developing language and skills. These sections focus on one examination task type from the Listening paper and develop a range of listening sub-skills, such as separating connected speech. Throughout the course, students listen to a wide range of texts and learn to complete tables, sentences, and notes; label plans, maps, and diagrams; and choose options from a list. As in the exam, the recordings are scripted and there is a variety of native speaker accents for the exam practice tasks. Audioscripts for all recordings are located at the back of the Student's Book and in the Teacher's Book within the unit notes. These sections finish with discussion activities (*What do you think?*) that enable students to react to the listening texts and activate the language covered in that section. After the listening section there is a Study skills section where students focus on a range of skills that will help them to prepare for the IELTS exam. This is expanded on in the Study skills file at the back of the Student's Book.

Writing: Each writing section starts with a lead-in (*Topic focus*) that prepares students for exam practice either by activating existing knowledge or developing language and skills. These sections prepare students for the two tasks. For Task 1, students are encouraged to view tasks according to the three language functions they are most commonly required to perform. They learn how to describe trend data, compare sets of data, and describe processes. Training on describing maps and plans is available in the Writing file. For Task 2, students are encouraged to view essay writing as a process of response to a task. The lessons appear consecutively and require students to analyse essay questions, brainstorm ideas, plan their essay, structure paragraphs, and write conclusions. This approach is designed to steer students away from a reliance on learnt essay models and towards thoughtful, relevant responses. Further support can be found in the Writing file at the back of the Student's Book.

Reading: Reading sections start with a lead-in (*Topic focus*) that prepares students for exam practice either by activating existing knowledge or developing language and skills. Each Reading section trains students to deal with a particular task from the Reading paper. Through the course students develop the vocabulary and grammar needed for the Reading paper. Exam practice tasks are clearly labelled and are usually accompanied by a tip box with advice on how to approach the task. These sections finish with discussion activities (*What do you think?*) that enable students to react to the reading texts and activate the language covered in that section.

Reading passages offer stimulating, thought-provoking ideas that are designed to engage students, and they reflect a variety of discourse types including arguments, discussions, historical narratives, and informative texts.

Exam challenge: Each unit ends with an *Exam challenge*. These pages are designed to allow students to review the skills and language developed during the unit and to rehearse them within a more authentic exam context. During the listening and reading activities, students are directed to do specific sections of a practice test that correspond to the skills they have been learning. In doing so, students can familiarize themselves with exam rubrics and procedures, and develop a habit of applying recent learning as they tackle exam papers. In the reading, speaking, and writing tasks, students are also encouraged to do all tasks under the time constraints they will face in the exam.

Features

Grammar File: A link at the beginning of each grammar section guides students to the grammar reference section on pages 113–120 of the Student's Book. This reference provides concise explanations and further examples of the grammar points covered in each unit as well as practice exercises. This section can be used for general revision purposes.

Vocabulary File: A link at the beginning of each vocabulary section guides students to the vocabulary reference section on pages 121–130 of the Student's Book. This reference provides further vocabulary exercises. This section can be used for general revision purposes.

Study Skills File: This section gives students an opportunity to reflect on their learning. The activities encourage them to reflect on how they can improve their learning of grammar and vocabulary, and better develop their reading, writing, speaking and listening skills. Students could be encouraged to work through the sections towards the beginning of the course so that they can establish best study practice right at the start.

Writing File: This file (pages 136–144) provides a model answer for each of the tasks in Part 1 and Part 2 of the writing paper with accompanying notes on how to approach each task type and how to structure a response, as well as further practice exercises.

Exam tips: The *Exam tips* section (pages 145–148) includes the tips that accompany the exam skills sections in each unit. These tips provide guidance on how to approach each of the task types in the IELTS exam.

IELTS Practice Test: Students are directed to specific questions in the Practice Test from the Exam challenge sections at the end of each unit (see above). At the end of the course, it might be helpful for students to work through the Practice Test as a whole.

Audioscript: Audioscripts, excluding those for the IELTS Practice Test, on pages 164–173 enable students to follow the recordings or to note how specific language items are used in context. Note that the audioscript for the IELTS Practice Test on pages 149–163 of the Student's Book is on pages 141–144.

Online Practice

If your students have purchased the Student's Book with Online Practice Pack, they get a unique unlock code on the card at the back of their book that gives access to *Foundation IELTS Masterclass* Online Practice and an online IELTS Academic practice test. There are over 50 exercises in the Online Practice which allow students to continue to develop the language, skills, and sub-skills they need for the IELTS exam outside of class time. There are exercises to consolidate and extend the grammar and vocabulary work done in the Student's Book, plus further exam training for Speaking and Writing, and exam practice tasks for all four papers.

The Online Practice is also available separately. For information go to www.oxfordenglishtesting.com.

Using the Online Practice

The Online Practice can be:

- teacher managed via a free Learning Management System (follow the instructions for Option 1 or Option 2 on the card at the back of the Student's Book)

OR

- used by individual students for self-study (refer your students to the instructions for Option 3 on the card at the back of the Student's Book).

Teacher-managed Online Practice

If teaching with the Student's Book in class, we recommend choosing this option so you can assign exercises and tasks from the Online Practice and the online practice test via the free Learning Management System (LMS), where it's easy to:

- manage what exercises and tasks your students do and when they do them

- see your students' results in an online markbook so you can identify areas of class or individual weakness, allowing you to focus on what students really need to work on
- read, comment on, and mark your students' extended writing tasks online with an option to return work to students for them to improve and resubmit. A marking guide and sample answers are provided
- listen to, comment on, and mark your students' recorded responses to speaking tasks online.

You can choose whether to assign the exercises and tasks in the Online Practice with 'no help' (for assessment) or 'with help' (for supported learning). For exercises and tasks you set 'with help', students are allowed to:

- mark their answers, try anything they got wrong again, see the correct answers with explanatory feedback
- look up the meaning of words in questions and texts in the integrated online *Oxford Advanced Learner's Dictionary*, 8th Edition; this saves time and helps students improve their vocabulary
- read tips and strategies to help them prepare for the exam
- see sample answers for the writing tasks, and audioscripts and useful language for the speaking tasks

If you assign exercises with 'no help', these support features will be disabled.

You could choose the sections or exercises of the Online Practice you wish students to do, and assign them first with 'no help', i.e. with all support features disabled. This will allow you to assess how well prepared your students are at any stage of the course. You can then assign any problematic exercises again 'with help', i.e. with all support features enabled, so that individual students can benefit from the learning support features. You can assign the whole Online Practice in one go, or a unit, or a selection of sections or exercises.

If you choose to use the LMS, we recommend following instructions for **Option 1** on the card in the Student's Book. If you would prefer to register students yourself, you will need to collect their cards with unlock codes and follow the instructions for **Option 2**.

Self-study Online Practice

You may prefer your students to work through the material in the Online Practice and online IELTS practice test at their own pace, using the 'self-study' option. Students will need an email address to register. They will need to follow the instructions for **Option 3** on the card in the Student's Book.

For this option, students will have access to all the learning support features (see table below), but you will not be able to track their progress, see their results, or do any marking online.

Note!

It is very important that you tell your students which access option you want to use. For more information about online practice, online practice tests and the LMS go to www.oxfordenglishtesting.com.

Students have 18 months to complete the Online Practice and online IELTS practice test from the time they register.

Online Practice content

There are six sections:

Vocabulary: 10 exercises that review vocabulary from each unit of the Student's Book and 10 exercises that review key academic vocabulary.

Grammar: 15 exercises that review core grammar structures covered in the Student's Book.

Listening: One recorded text for each of the four sections of the IELTS listening exam with 2–3 tasks per text, as in the exam but at a lower level than the exam to build students' confidence.

Reading: Three IELTS-type reading texts with three IELTS task types per text, as in the exam but at a lower level than the exam to build students' confidence.

Writing: Two exam-skills practice exercises for each of the two IELTS writing tasks.

Two IELTS-type tasks for each of the writing sections with sample answers*, including comments on language and content. (*See *Teacher-managed Online Practice* above.)

Speaking: Three exam-skills practice exercises.

Two tasks for each section of the Speaking exam with speak-and-record facility.

Online IELTS practice test

The unlock code that students get for the Online Practice (when purchased with the Student's Book) also includes access to a complete oxfordenglishtesting.com IELTS Academic practice test. If you are using the LMS option, you can assign this test to your students as a whole test, or by paper or part using *Test mode* (= 'no help'/no key) so that you can assess how well prepared your students are, or in *Practice mode* (= 'with help'/with key) for practice and familiarization with the exam task types. Note that this test is not graded to the level of the Student's Book – it reflects the level of the IELTS exam. Additional online IELTS practice tests are available. For information go to oxfordenglishtesting.com.

Teacher's Book

This Teacher's Book contains procedural notes and a full answer key, including suggested answers, for the activities in the Student's Book. It also includes the audioscripts for the listening sections with answers highlighted, as well as optional activities for classroom use.

It includes the answer key (pages 130–140) and audioscript (pages 141–144) for the IELTS Practice Test at the back of the Student's Book.

Website

You will find additional resource materials to further support the Student's Book online at oup.com/elt/exams.

Speaking DVD information

How to use the DVD

The Speaking DVD is designed to familiarize teachers and students with the format and requirements of the Speaking paper. The material can be used alongside *Foundation IELTS Masterclass*, but since it is not intrinsically tied to the course, it will make a useful complement to any IELTS course.

Although the video does not show any actual exam situations, the format of the test is scripted according to IELTS and Cambridge English Language Assessment guidelines, and the 'candidates' are real students who have either taken or are preparing for the IELTS exam in the UK. Different students are shown doing different parts of the test, except in the complete test, which features the same student throughout. Teachers should make it clear to their students that their Speaking test is recorded for examiners to mark – the interlocutor does not do the marking. Note that the 'candidates' shown on this DVD would cover a range of IELTS scores for Speaking, likely to be between 4.0 and 6.0.

The DVD can be used at any point during the course for training, and will make a useful revision tool. It is recommended that teachers watch the complete video before showing all or part of it to their students. They can then choose to show their students the whole video, or individual sections. The suggested activities below can be done individually or in small groups as appropriate. The interviews shown are not intended as model answers – students should be encouraged to suggest how they themselves could have given a better answer 'in the same situation' and also identify what the 'candidates' shown in the video do well.

Suggested activities

1 After viewing the *Introduction to the Speaking paper*, ask questions like:
   - *How long does the test last for?*
   - *How many examiners are there and what do they do?*
   - *Does the examiner tell students how they have done at the end of the exam?*, etc.
2 Show candidates the examples for each part and ask if the candidates followed the advice that the examiner gives in the tips.

Show the complete test but not the Examiner's commentary. Ask students to act as the examiner while they are watching. They can then watch the examiner's commentary and compare their assessment of the candidates. This will help students to focus on what they need to improve in their own performances.

The Speaking DVD contains the following videos:

Introduction to the Speaking paper
An examiner explains the format of the test and timings.

Part 1: Overview and tips + Example
An examiner explains what happens in Part 1 and offers candidates some tips to help their performance. This is followed by an example of a real student doing a Part 1 task.

Part 2: Overview and tips + Example
An examiner explains what happens in Part 2 and offers candidates some tips to help their performance. This is followed by an example of a real student carrying out the relevant tasks.

Part 3: Overview and tips + Example
An examiner explains what happens in Part 3 and offers candidates some advice to help their performance. This is followed by an example of a real student carrying out the relevant tasks.

How candidates are assessed
An examiner explains what the assessment criteria are, and these are illustrated with clips from footage of the 'mock exams'. This section includes:
- Overview of assessment criteria
- Fluency and coherence
- Lexical resource
- Grammatical range and accuracy
- Pronunciation

Complete test with commentary and analysis
A complete test showing a student carrying out an uninterrupted test. This is followed by an examiner's part-by-part assessment of their performance according to the assessment criteria and a final summary of their performance.

Note: The sections can be viewed in any order. Teachers may, for example, like to show students the complete test first to orientate them and then go back to each part separately as they are dealt with in class.

For more information about the assessment criteria for speaking visit the IELTS website at: www.ielts.org.

UNIT 1   Education & learning

Introduction page 7

Featured topic vocabulary
Nouns: *literacy rate, ratio, enrolment, decade, destination, earning potential*
Adverb: *globally*
Adjectives: *global, higher (education), tertiary, primary, secondary, average*

Optional lead-in
Before students open their books, you may like to introduce the topics covered in the infographic by doing the following:
a Write these questions on the board:
• *What percentage of young people aged 15–24 do you think can read and write?* (90%)
• *Which country do you think is most popular for international students?* (the USA)
• *How many school teachers do you think there are around the world?* (about 60 million)
b Group students in fours and ask them to guess what the answers are. Write the groups' guesses on the board.
c Ask students to open their books and find which group guessed the closest answer.

What do you think?

Before speaking, students may require clarification of:
- *literacy*: the ability to read and write
- *enrolment*: officially registering / joining a course, school, etc.
- *decade*: a period of ten years
- *earning potential*: the salary you might be able to get in the future

See background note below for clarification of types of education.

Ask students to discuss the questions in pairs. Tell them to give reasons for their answers and give examples when appropriate. It needs to become automatic for students to extend their answers in the speaking part of the exam. To generate more ideas, encourage students to think about the *Wh-* questions as they answer (*who, what, why, when, where*, etc.). After discussing, get feedback by nominating students to share their ideas with the class.

Background note:

- primary: first stage of compulsory education, usually when a child is 5 / 6 to 11 / 12 years of age
- secondary: the stage immediately after primary; usually 11 / 12 to 16–18 years of age
- tertiary: this third stage is often used to refer to university, but includes a wide range of post-secondary institutions
- higher education: refers to undergraduate and postgraduate studies

Optional activity
For homework, ask students to choose the sub-topic from the infographic that they are most interested in and research statistics related to their country. For example, they may wish to investigate how many teachers there are in their country. Students might like to prepare their own 'infographic' to present in class.

SPEAKING Giving personal information page 8

EXAM FOCUS: PART 1

Lesson aims
1 Develop students' ability to give extended responses in Speaking Part 1.
2 Improve students' accuracy using gerunds and infinitives in speaking.
3 Enable students to speak confidently on the topic of school and university subjects with a range of related vocabulary.
4 Raise students' awareness of the role of word stress in pronunciation.

Key language
University and school subjects: *psychology, geology, chemistry, geography, literature, biology, medicine, engineering, economics, physics, management, history*
Verbs: *enjoy, prefer, would like to, hope to, hate*

Featured topic vocabulary
Nouns: *pupil, curriculum, stream, homework, exam*
Adjectives: *primary, secondary, state, private, compulsory, academic, vocational, talented*

Topic focus

1 This exercise presents new vocabulary in context.

Focus students' attention on the picture and ask what the situation is (a classroom) and how the student might feel (engaged / interested). If possible, show students where Finland is on a world map. Ask students to work alone before comparing with a partner.

The words in bold should not be pre-taught. After reading, you may like to get students to use their dictionary to check the meaning of the words in bold by allocating one word per pair. Tell students to share the meaning of their word with the class. Check students understand the vocabulary by asking:

- *pupils*: What's another word for 'pupil'? (student) Can you be a pupil at university? (No, 'pupil' is for schoolchildren.)
- *primary school / secondary school*: Which one is for older children? (secondary school – NB In the UK, children go to primary school from around the age of 5 to 11, and secondary school from 11 to 16, when they take their GCSEs. They can choose to go on to college, from 16 to 18, where students in an academic stream normally sit their A-levels.)
- *curriculum*: What subjects were part of the curriculum at your school?
- *state school / private school*: Which one do you pay for? (private school) Which one does the government pay for? (state school) Do you have both state and private schools in your country?
- *compulsory*: Can you choose to do a compulsory subject or not? (no) What subjects were compulsory at your school?
- *academic stream / vocational stream*: Can you think of any jobs where vocational studies might be more useful than academic studies? (possible answers: hairdresser, car mechanic, plumber)
- *talented*: Is it a noun, verb, or adjective? (adjective, but students may confuse it with a verb because of the *-ed* ending) If you are talented, do you normally get good grades or bad grades? (good)
- *homework*: Which verb goes with homework? (do, have, get) Do we use it with 'much' or 'many'? (much) Is it countable or uncountable? (uncountable)
- *exams*: What verbs go together with exam? (sit, take, do, pass, fail) What is 'exam' short for? (examination)

2 Ask students to discuss in pairs before sharing ideas as a whole class.

Vocabulary

3 This exercise checks students' understanding of the new vocabulary.

Before students begin, encourage them to use grammar clues to help find the answer. For example, *an* in question 5 means students should be looking for a word beginning with a vowel. Ask students to work alone before comparing with a partner.

ANSWERS
1 curriculum
2 compulsory
3 primary school, secondary school
4 state, private
5 academic, vocational
6 talented
7 pupils, homework
8 exams

4 This exercise provides students with an opportunity to use the language in personal contexts.

Before speaking, encourage students to extend their responses with extra details or their opinion. You could do this by modelling an exchange and follow-up questions yourself. Tell students to discuss in pairs before getting feedback as a whole class.

5 This exercise expands students' range of education vocabulary and prepares them for the pronunciation work in exercise 7.

Tell students to work in pairs. Monitor to check which words students have difficulty understanding. Clarify the meaning of any problematic words as a whole class, such as *literature* (studying written texts like books and poetry) and *geology* (the scientific study of the Earth).

Note: Answers refer to secondary schools in the UK up to age 16. Some countries may have a broader curriculum than UK state schools, so there may be more answers with U/S.

ANSWERS
psychology U   medicine U
geology U   engineering U
chemistry U/S   economics U/S
geography U/S   physics U/S
literature U/S   management U
biology U/S   history U/S

Optional activity
You may like to take this opportunity to encourage students to use a dictionary to look up the meaning of new words. To save time, allocate one word per pair to find in the dictionary. After checking the meanings in the dictionary, divide the class into two groups, with one person from each pair per group. Tell students to share their information with their group.

6 1•1 This exercise prepares students for the pronunciation task by exposing them to the phonetic forms of the target vocabulary.

ANSWERS
1 biology, chemistry, medicine
2 economics, management
3 psychology, history, geography

Audioscript 1•1, 1•2
1 At school, I hated studying sciences, especially **biology** and **chemistry**. However, now I'd like to study **medicine**!
2 I prefer studying vocational subjects connected to my chosen career. I hope to go into business, so **economics** and **management** are particularly important.
3 I enjoy studying **psychology** at university, but at school I didn't like studying in general because most subjects we learnt, like **history** and **geography**, were compulsory.

7 1•2 This exercise raises students' awareness of the variety of word stress patterns in English.

Ask students to copy the table into their notebooks before listening and completing the columns. To help students understand why correct word stress is important, give them an example of a familiar word pronounced with incorrect word stress, for example, try saying com*pu*ter, instead of com*pu*ter. Highlight how much it changes the listener's perception of the word.

ANSWERS

● • • literature, management, chemistry, medicine
• ● • • psychology, geology, geography, biology
● • • physics, history
• • ● • engineering, economics

Teaching tip: Word stress is not as predictable in English as some other languages. Although there are some patterns, students need to check word stress of new vocabulary in their dictionary. Drilling the pronunciation of new words can help students to become more aware of where the stress falls when they hear new words.

Make a habit of marking stress bubbles above new words on the board, and encourage students to copy these into their vocabulary notebooks.

> **Optional activity**
> Show students how stress is shown in the dictionary, and ask them to look up some of the new words from exercise 1 to add them to their table, for example, *compulsory* (column 2), *academic* (column 4), and *primary* (column 1).

VOCABULARY FILE Student's Book page 121
Refer students to exercises 1–5 for more practice of vocabulary related to school and university subjects.

ANSWERS
See page 132 of this book for answers.

8 Students are given the opportunity here to personalize the vocabulary.

You may wish to play recording 1•1 again and draw students' attention to the way the answers are extended, before encouraging them to provide similar details in their discussions.

> **Optional activity**
> You might like to get students to write their answers in full before speaking and do the following:
> a Ask them to draw stress bubbles above the most important words (above the stressed syllable in the word).
> b Get students to practise their pronunciation in pairs by reading their sentences aloud, focusing on their stress.
> c Then tell students to put down their papers and speak from memory.

■ **STUDY SKILLS FILE** Student's Book page 131
Refer students to this page for activities that will help them to improve their vocabulary development.

Grammar

9 1•3 This exercise clarifies the meaning of the sentences and prepares students for the grammar focus.

Check answers as a whole class and clarify any issues students might have with vocabulary or the use of *-ed* for the past.

ANSWERS
1	Past	4	Future
2	Future	5	Present
3	Present	6	Past

Audioscript 1•3, 1•4
1 I **hated studying** sciences.
2 I**'d like to study** medicine.
3 I **prefer studying** vocational subjects.
4 I **hope to go** into business.
5 I **enjoy studying** psychology.
6 I **didn't like studying** in general.

10 1•4 This dictation task draws students' attention to grammar forms used in the model sentences.

You may wish to show students how past, present, and future are signalled: draw three columns on the board for past, present, and future and ask students which phrases should go in each column before writing them in the correct columns. Focus students' attention on the forms which follow the chunks, by highlighting the *-ing* form or infinitive. Drill the chunks and use substitution drills, for example by replacing *sciences* with a different subject each time.

ANSWERS
1	hated studying	4	hope to go
2	'd like to study	5	enjoy studying
3	prefer studying	6	didn't like studying

GRAMMAR FILE Student's Book page 116
Refer students to this page for more explanation and practice of gerunds and infinitives.

ANSWERS
See page 130 of this book for answers.

11 Here the forms used in exercise 10 are presented in a more structured way and students are given an opportunity to personalize the language.

Draw students' attention to the example and the table. Clarify how the colour coding works by asking students if they should say *I'd like going* (wrong) or *I'd like to go* (right). Ask what colour goes with the *-ing* form and what colour goes with the infinitive. Tell students to work alone before comparing with a partner. Monitor and check for errors which you can write on the board and correct as a whole class.

12 Focus students' attention on the speech bubbles with language for showing interest. These responses will not be useful in the exam, but using them in class may encourage other students to extend their responses and so you may find them a useful tool. Demonstrate the activity with a strong

10 **UNIT 1 EDUCATION & LEARNING**

student and encourage students to extend their response. Group students in fours to speak.

Exam skills

13 This exercise introduces students to the importance of extending their responses before they practise an example in Speaking Part 1.

Ask students to discuss in pairs before checking as a whole class.

ANSWER
Candidate 2's response. It shows a greater range of vocabulary and grammar, such as adverbs (*Well, Actually*) and verb forms (present simple, past simple, gerund after *enjoy*).

EXAM TIP 1·5 Before students listen, ask them to suggest possible answers to the question and write these on the board. After they have answered the question, refer students to page 145 for more guidance on how to approach Speaking Part 1.

ANSWER
Try to add some additional information that gives the examiner something more than the basic response. Speak for around 15 seconds each time.

Audioscript 1·5

Speaking Part 1 lasts 4 to 5 minutes and the examiner asks you questions about a range of personal topics, such as your family, hobbies, work or education, and holidays. Listen carefully for the question word – *where, when who, how, how often* – and try to respond in a conversational way. It's important that you understand the question, and give a full response to show that you can use a variety of language. **Try to add some extra information that gives the examiner something more than a basic response.** Each response should be about **15 seconds**.

14 This exercise gives students an opportunity to practise extending their answers in a controlled way to prepare them for the practice Speaking Part 1.

Before speaking, encourage students to reflect on what they have learnt this lesson by telling them to turn back to exercises 1–13. Ask students what they need to remember to do in Speaking Part 1 and write their ideas on the board, for example:

- Use a range of relevant topic vocabulary
- Keep the *Wh-* question words in mind
- Give reasons, make comparisons, talk about their feelings, and explain about how something has changed from the past to now
- Use a variety of tenses and a variety of verbs, e.g. some that require the gerund and some that require the infinitive

After speaking, ask students if they followed their own advice on the board.

Exam practice

15 This exercise gives students a chance to put together everything from this lesson and familiarizes them with the format of Speaking Part 1.

Before students turn to the questions, seat them as if they are in an exam with 'candidates' sitting opposite 'examiners'. Tell students role-playing the examiner to time their partner and to take notes about whether the answers were long enough. Encourage them to give feedback and suggestions on how their partner could extend their answer further.

Optional activity

You may like to encourage students to extend their answers by doing the following:

a Group students in fours, with two teams per group.
b Tell students to time each other's answers to the questions in exercise 3, and allocate a point for every 5 seconds they are able to continue answering the question, to a maximum of four points (i.e. 20 seconds).
c Each person in the group should answer two questions in total before the points are added up. Find out as a whole class who the winning teams are.

If the technology is available, students could record their responses and critique their own performance by listening to themselves. Direct students towards the marking criteria at www.cambridgeenglish.org/exams/ elts so they can assess their own strengths and weaknesses.

STUDY SKILLS FILE Student's Book page 132
Refer students to this page for activities that will help them to improve their speaking development.

LISTENING Completing basic information (page 10)

EXAM FOCUS: SECTION 1

Lesson aims

1 Enable students to transcribe numbers and names accurately.
2 Develop students' ability to predict missing information by considering question words for each gap.
3 Expand students' range of vocabulary related to study and motivation.
4 Encourage students to take responsibility for their learning by setting personal exam objectives.

Key language

Adjective + noun collocations: *private tuition, hard work*

Noun + preposition collocations: *standard of, ambitions for, importance on, under pressure, expectations of*

Nouns: *range, success, effort, value, quality, achievement*

Verbs: *attend, receive*

Adjective: *additional, stressed*

Adverb: *respectively*

Question words: *how much, how long, when, where, who, what*

Optional lead-in

To introduce students to the topic of private tuition, draw attention to the photo and ask:

- *What do you think the relationship is between the two people in the photo?* (It is a student and a teacher.)
- *How is the relationship between the people in the photo different from a normal teacher–student relationship?* (The teacher is giving the student a private lesson.)
- *Why do you think people pay money for this type of class?* (Because students can benefit from the one-to-one attention.)

If necessary, allow students to discuss the third question in pairs.

Background note: How much one-to-one attention do students get at school?
In the UK, for example, there are usually around 30 children in a state school class, so it can be difficult for the teacher to cater to everyone's individual needs.
What is different about the relationship of the people in the photo compared to a normal class?
A private tutor can:
- tailor classes to the student's strengths and weaknesses
- respond to the student's interests and individual learning style
- develop a more personal relationship with the student
- take a more relaxed approach because behaviour is less likely to be a problem.

Why do you think people pay money for this?
Private tuition is often expensive, but many parents feel it is worth it for the one-to-one attention. The student might:
- be struggling or falling behind in a particular subject
- be particularly gifted or talented in one particular area and need to be more challenged
- need help preparing for an exam.

Topic focus

1 This exercise engages students in the topic of private tuition using their personal experiences.

Group students in threes or fours to discuss their responses. Get feedback as a whole class for the second question only, comparing different countries.

2 This exercise develops students' ability to transcribe numbers, and deals with subtle differences in word stress between some numbers.

If necessary, remind students of the work on word stress in the Speaking lesson. Write the words *sixty* and *sixteen* on the board, and say them aloud. Ask students if the stressed syllable is the same or different. Underline the stressed syllable (*six*ty and six*teen*) and focus their attention on the difference in length of the second syllable. Tell students to complete the exercise in pairs. Encourage them to say the words aloud to help them identify the stressed syllable. As you check answers as a class, drill each number by telling students to listen to your pronunciation and then repeating it together.

ANSWERS

With the numbers ending in zero, the stress falls on the first syllable:
sixty, **twen**ty, **se**venty (stress on first syllable)
sixty-**five**, twenty-**one**, seven**teen**, seventy-**one**, six**teen**, twenty-**five**, seventy-**five** (stress on the final syllable)

3 🔊 1·6 This exercise helps students understand numbers in context.

Check the meaning of *ranges* (e.g. ask students what the age range is in their class). Play the recording more than once if necessary, but remind students they will hear it only once in the exam. After listening, tell students to check their answers in pairs. Check answers as a class.

ANSWERS

16, 20, 25, 70, 71, 75
There is only one range: 16–20%

Audioscript 1·6, 1·7

Globally and on average, **25%** of students attend additional courses outside school. More than **75%** of students in Colombia, Latvia, the Slovak Republic, the Philippines, and South Africa have private tuition in mathematics. In Japan and South Korea respectively, the figures are **71%** and **64%**, while in the UK, **20%** of students attend extra courses. In general, the levels of tuition are especially high in East Asian countries, where over **70%** of students receive extra tuition at some point in their school careers. Levels of tuition are lower in European countries, for example in Germany, where recent surveys indicate that around **16–20%** of students receive tuition, usually in mathematics.

4 🔊 1·7 This exercise gives students practice filling gaps with numbers, which is an important skill for Listening Part 1.

Before listening, give students 3 minutes to read sentences a–f. Check the meaning of *attend* (go regularly to a place, e.g. a school), *additional* (extra), *receive* (get), *respectively* (the first number matches the first country, and the second number matches the second country, etc.). After listening, ask students to compare their answers in pairs. Check answers as a class. Clarify that not all the gaps in Listening Section 1 require numbers, but they can expect at least one answer to be a number.

ANSWERS

a 25
b 75
c 71, 64
d 20
e 70
f 16–20

5 Ask students to discuss in pairs before comparing their ideas as a class. Remind students of the importance of justifying their opinions to extend their responses.

Vocabulary

6 This exercise checks students understand the sentences before focusing on the language used. It also raises awareness of different views on education.

Ask students to work alone. As you check answers as a class, clarify any vocabulary problems. Students may have difficulty with *ambitions* (things you really want to do or achieve in the future). Ask students what their ambitions are to clarify the meaning.

7 This exercise expands students' range of vocabulary by encouraging them to use synonyms.

Ask students to work alone before checking in pairs. Check answers as a whole class and clarify the meaning (see below), pronunciation, and part of speech / word class of the new vocabulary (see key language on page 12 of this book for part of speech / word class). You may like to clarify meaning by asking the questions below (note: you might want to expand students' vocabulary knowledge further by focusing on the words in bold in the questions):

- *under pressure*: Have you ever felt under **pressure**? Why? Do you **put yourself** under pressure?
- *effort*: Which subjects at school do / did you **make** the most effort in?
- *value*: Did you place **value** on the same things when you were younger compared to now? What characteristics do you value in your friends? (note: here *value* is used as a verb)
- *expectations of*: What are your **expectations** of this course? Have your expectations been **met**?
- *quality*: If something is **good quality**, is it usually expensive or cheap? In what situations is quality important?
- *achievement*: How is achievement often measured at school? How do you feel if you **achieve** your aims? What do you want to achieve this year? (note: *achieve* is the verb, whereas *achievement* is the noun)

ANSWERS

1 hard work = effort
2 standard = quality
3 ambitions for = expectations of
4 importance = value, success = achievement
5 stressed = under pressure

Teaching tip: Synonymy is a fundamental area of knowledge in all papers of the exam, and it is essential to draw students' attention to synonyms throughout the course and to encourage systematic recording of synonyms. You may wish to do this collectively as a class. Certain websites allow you to record words and definitions together and to play games with them. You could exploit such resources by entering synonyms in place of definitions.

3 This exercise checks students understand the synonyms and helps them learn the vocabulary by personalizing it.

Focus on the example in the speech bubbles. Emphasize that they should not simply repeat the vocabulary used by their partner. Monitor for any interesting opinions to highlight in whole-class feedback.

VOCABULARY FILE Student's Book page 121
Refer students to exercises 6 and 7 for more practice using synonyms.

ANSWERS
See page 132 of this book for answers.

EXAM TIP 1·8 Before students listen, ask them to suggest possible answers to the question and write these on the board. After they have answered the question, refer students to page 146 for more guidance on how to approach Listening Section 1.

ANSWER
Read the instructions and look at the information carefully to find out if names or numbers are required, or both.

Audioscript 1·8

In Listening Section 1, candidates often make mistakes writing down details such as numbers and names. With numbers, think about what would be realistic in each gap because this will help you to understand the number correctly. It's also a good idea to practise listening to longer numbers, like telephone numbers, which are often said quickly. With names, candidates often misspell them because they confuse how each letter is said – particularly the vowels: a, e, i, o, u. **The main thing is to read the instructions and look at the information carefully to find out if names or numbers are required … or both!**

Exam skills

9 1·9 To develop students' ability to transcribe numbers and names, students first hear them in isolation.

Play the recording more than once if necessary, but remind students they will hear it only once in the exam.

ANSWERS

a Pablo Hernandez
b 115
c Irene Allegri
d 8th
e Mohammed Bagabas
f 772289
g 86 kilograms
h 07789 471147

Audioscript 1·9

a Pablo Hernandez – P-a-b-l-o H-e-r-n-a-n-d-e-z
b 115
c Irene Allegri – I-r-e-n-e A-l-l-e-g-r-i
d 8th
e Mohammed Bagabas – M-o-h-a-m-m-e-d B-a-g-a-b-a-s
f 772289
g 86 kilograms
h 07789 471147

UNIT 1 EDUCATION & LEARNING

> **Optional activity**
> Ask students to find out the phone number and email address of their classmates, or any other information you think is appropriate. Tell them they can change key details if they don't want to share them. They should note down the information from their partner but only show it to them once they have finished. Their partner can then correct any mistakes.

10 This is a useful approach to encourage students to predict missing information before listening. This is a vital skill for gap-fill questions in IELTS (in both Listening and Reading), so spend plenty of time preparing students by doing the following:

  a Focus students' attention on the brochure, and ask who might be interested in this type of information (students looking for a college or a course).

  b Explain to students that in Section 1 of the Listening test they will hear a conversation between two speakers in an everyday situation. Ask students who the speakers might be in this situation (receptionist and caller).

  c Explain that there are ten gap-fill questions in Section 1, like there are here.

  d Tell students that in the exam they are given a small amount of time to read the questions. Ask students what they think they should do while they are reading, to elicit that they should think about what type of information is missing.

  e Explain that when they are thinking about what information is missing, it is useful to ask themselves questions which they can keep in mind to stay focused as they listen.

  f Demonstrate how to do this by focusing students' attention on the first gap, and ask them what type of information is missing (a time). Ask which question word it matches from the six options above (*when*). Tell students they should write number 1 next to 'when'.

  g Tell students to complete the exercise alone, and then check in pairs. Check answers as a class, and clarify any vocabulary issues. Students may have difficulty with *length* (the measurement or extent of something from end to end), *content* (the things that are held or included in something), and *location* (a particular place or position).

ANSWERS
1 When?   6 What?
2 What?   7 When?
3 What?   8 Who?
4 How long? 9 Where?
5 How much? 10 What?

Background note: You may wish to share the information below about the exam with the students:

- The questions follow the order of the information in the recording. So if students hear the answer for question 3, but have not yet written an answer for question 2, they should forget question 2 and focus on question 3.
- The answers do not need to be changed in any way from the recording.
- Students' answers will be marked wrong if they write more words than instructed. Before any listening activity, make it routine to ask students *How many words can you write?* so they develop the habit of checking the instructions. The number of words is not always the same.
- Contracted words (e.g. *I'll* or *we've*) are not tested in the exam. Hyphenated words (e.g. *half-time*) count as one word.
- Spelling of common words must be written correctly, as should words that are spelt out, like names. Students should be reminded that they will not be given the mark if their spelling is incorrect. Encourage them to keep a list of their common spelling mistakes and to revise the correctly spelt words regularly.
- While listening, students should write the answers on the question paper. They have 10 minutes at the end of the exam to transfer their answers to the answer paper. They should be given practice doing this at some point during the course to avoid making mistakes when transferring answers and wasting marks as a result.

Exam practice

11 1·10 Students have a chance here to put their prediction skills to the test, and experience an example Listening Section 1.

Focus students' attention on the instructions and ask if they should write names or numbers (both). Ask students how many words they can write (no more than three words or a number). Check the meaning of *no more than* by asking *Can you write four words?* (no) *Can you write three?* (yes) *Can you write two or one?* (yes)

Remind students to think of their question words from exercise 10 as they listen. As students compare their answers after listening, tell them to check together that what they wrote makes sense in response to their question words. Check answers as a class.

ANSWERS
1 10 weeks   6 Culture and business
2 31st May   7 Claire Kuhles
3 communication   8 College Street
4 6.30 p.m.   9 c.kuhles@lastmail.com
5 1,200

Audioscript 1·10
Receptionist: Foxhill House College. Hello?
Caller: Hi, I'm calling about the International Law course. Could you give me some more details?
Receptionist: Certainly, what would you like to know?
Caller: Er, what time do the classes start?
Receptionist: They run from 7 p.m. till 9 every Monday … for **10 weeks**.
Caller: OK. And how much does the course actually cost?

Receptionist: It's £500, but there are discounts available.
Caller: Right. What do we look at in the class?
Receptionist: You look at how international law developed and how it works.
Caller: OK. And where does the course take place?
Receptionist: It's in Nottingham and the next one starts on the … let's have a look … on the **31st of May**.
Caller: Great. Er, what other courses do you have that are international?
Receptionist: Well, there's 'Intercultural **communication**'.
Caller: OK. How long is that?
Receptionist: It's a twelve-week course … and it's earlier, too – from **6.30 p.m.** till 8 p.m.
Caller: And how much does it cost?
Receptionist: Hold on … Ah, here we are. It's £1,200 for the three months.
Caller: OK. What's covered?
Receptionist: In the first month, you study language and culture. In the second month, you look at dealing with cultural change, in other words, cultural training methods … and in the third month, you study **culture and business**.
Caller: OK – sounds useful. Where does it take place? In Nottingham, too?
Receptionist: No, it's in Derby.
Caller: Right. And when does it start?
Receptionist: You can start on the 25th of April or … one moment … on the 2nd of September.
Caller: Great. Er, could you possibly send me information about how to book and register – a full brochure or something?
Receptionist: Of course. What's your name?
Caller: It's **Claire Kuhles**. That's C-l-a-i-r-e .. and family name, K-u-h-l-e-s.
Receptionist: OK … And where do you live?
Caller: 20 **College Street**, Oxford, OX1 5NP.
Receptionist: OK. And what's your email address?
Caller: It's c-dot-kuhles at lastmail dot com.
Receptionist: … at lastmail dot com. OK, I'll put the information in the post to you today.
Caller: Fantastic – thanks a lot!

What do you think?

12 This exercise encourages students to think critically about education, which they may be asked to do in Speaking Part 3 and Writing Task 2.

Group students in threes or fours, and give them four minutes to discuss their views. Remind students of the importance of justifying their opinion. Monitor for interesting opinions to highlight in whole-class feedback.

Study skills

This activity encourages students to take responsibility for their learning by setting exam objectives and reflecting on how to achieve them.

Tell students to answer the questions in their notebook, so they can look back at these aims throughout the course to remain motivated. After students have compared answers in pairs, discuss as a class what students can do outside class to improve their level. Write their ideas on the board. You may like to collect students' notebooks after class to gain a better understanding of their needs.

> ### Optional activity
> If possible, collate students' answers and represent the data visually as pie charts or bar charts on a handout. This shows students how their answers compare to the class as a whole. This information could be used to practise Writing Task 1.

▌ **STUDY SKILLS FILE** Student's Book page 133
▌ Refer students to this page for activities that will help them to improve
▌ their listening development.

WRITING Describing trend data

EXAM FOCUS: TASK 1

Lesson aims
1 Develop students' ability to define and interpret information presented in diagrams.
2 Enable students to describe key trends with appropriate vocabulary and grammar.
3 Improve students' ability to show variety in their use of grammar and vocabulary by transforming sentences.
4 Improve students' ability to write about trends.

Key language
Verbs: *to increase, to rise, to fall, to decline, to drop*
Phrasal verbs: *to level out, to remain stable, to climb up, to slide down*
Nouns: *fall, rise, increase*
Adverbs: *slightly, dramatically, significantly*
Adjectives: *slight, significant, dramatic, marked, moderate, gradual*
Prepositions: *to, in, by, from*

Featured topic vocabulary
Word forms: *globe* (noun), *global* (adjective), *globally* (adverb), *to become global* (verb)

> **Optional lead-in**
> Write *trend* on the board and ask:
> - *What is a trend?*
> - *Can you think of any trends you know about in your country – for example, fashion trends, unemployment trends, spending trends? What do you understand about these trends?*
> - *If something is 'trending' on Twitter or Facebook, what does this mean?*
> - *Do you have any particular ways of keeping up with trends in your countries?*
> - *Are trends part of social behaviour? Why?*

Topic focus

1 This exercise engages students in the topic of the bar chart in exercise 3, to help them better interpret the information.

Tell students to discuss in pairs before comparing ideas as a whole class.

2 This exercise familiarizes students with the variety of diagrams in Writing Task 1 and related terminology.

Focus on the diagrams and ask students to work alone before comparing with a partner. Check as a whole class.

ANSWERS

bar chart B   table E
line graph D   flow chart C
pie chart A

3 The focus here is on interpreting the information given in the bar chart. Ask students to work alone before comparing answers with a partner.

ANSWERS

1 and 3 are true, 2 is false because the number of people attending school increased, and 4 is false because the number is 400 million.

Teaching tip: To help students describe what the data shows and avoid writing meaningless phrases, you may like to:

a write these phrases on the board:
  the bar chart increased
  the line went up
b ask what is wrong with them (they should describe the information and not just the movement)
c ask:
  Who would be interested in this information?
  Why would they want a description of it?
d encourage students to view their role as translators, not between two languages, but translating visual data into words.

Exam skills

4 This is a useful approach to encourage students to rephrase the information in the Writing Task 1 rubrics. This is something they are expected to do in the exam.

Focus students' attention on the example. Highlight that there are usually multiple possibilities by asking them for other ways of saying *the number of people who visited* (e.g. the number of tourists who went to Qatar), and ways of saying *January to December* (over a 12-month period / over the period of a year).

Tell students to work alone. Give them 10 minutes to make as many changes as possible. Monitor and invite students with good answers to write their sentences on the board. Alternatively, write suggested answers on the board yourself (see below).

Alternative for weaker classes: if students have difficulty generating sentences themselves, support them by doing the following:

a Write time phrases from exercise 4 on one side of the board (e.g. *from 2000 to 2012*)
b Write examples of alternative ways to express these on the other side (e.g. *over a period of 12 years*)
c Ask students to work in pairs to match the time phrases
d Look at the possible answers below for examples of other time phrase alternatives.

POSSIBLE ANSWERS

2 The diagram shows the number of hours that people watch television / the amount of television viewed / the amount of time viewers spend watching TV from 9 a.m. to 9 p.m. / over a 12-hour period.

3 The diagram shows the number of days that people went on holiday / how long people took off work to go on holiday / the standard duration of holidays from 2000 to 2012 / over a 12-year period.

4 The diagram shows the number of miles that people travel / how far people travel in miles / the mileage travelled per year / annually from age 18 to 80 / by adults aged between 18 and 80 / by adults between the ages of 18 and 80.

5 The diagram shows the number of females / women / female students who went to university / studied at university / were enrolled at university / attended university / were students at university / were in higher education from 1900 to 2000 / over a hundred-year period / during the 20th century.

Teaching tips: Encourage students to keep a mental checklist of *Wh-* question words (e.g. *who, where, when, what*, and maybe *why* and *how*) and to see how many of these question words they can answer in their sentence. For example, *the diagram shows the number of people (who) who visited (what) Qatar (where) from January to December (when)*.

Explain that a useful way of modifying the rubric can be to consider word families in order to use a different part of speech (e.g. noun, verb, adjective). For example, *television viewing* can be changed to *television viewed* or *viewers*. Ask students what type of word *visitor* is in sentence 1 (a noun), and what type of word *visited* is (a verb in the past simple).

Optional activity

This activity is particularly beneficial for classes where spelling is an issue, as it provides students with repetition of reading and writing the same words. To provide students with extra writing practice, do the following:

a Focus students' attention on sentence 1 in exercise 4. Ask students what the main verb is (*shows*)

b Ask students for other words with the same meaning and write them on the board, for example, *illustrates, highlights, provides information on*, etc.

c Group students in fours or fives, and give each group a piece of paper with one full sentence written along the top (e.g. *The diagram shows the number of people who visited Qatar from January to December*.

d Tell students to pass the paper around the group, and each time they receive the paper they must write a new sentence changing one feature of the previous sentence. For example:
Student 2: *The diagram shows the number of **visitors to Qatar** from January to December.*
Student 3: *The diagram shows the number of visitors to Qatar **in 12 months**.*
Student 4: *The diagram **illustrates** the number of visitors to Qatar in 12 months.*

e The paper is passed around the group until no more changes can be made, or until the time has run out if a time limit had been set. The group with the most correct sentences wins.

EXAM TIP 1·11 Before students listen, ask them to suggest possible answers to the question and write these on the board. After they have answered the question, refer students to page 147 for more guidance on how to approach writing reports about charts or graphs.

ANSWER
You should write a sentence that describes the key trend.

Audioscript 1·11
When you write a report about a chart or a graph, don't focus on the detail straight away. Take a step back and make sure you see the context or 'bigger picture'. Start by defining what the graphic shows. The next thing you should do is to **write a sentence that describes the key trend**. Did the numbers rise or fall? If they didn't rise or fall, you can say that there's no clear trend. Even after you've given the key trend, don't try to describe everything in detail!

5 Focus students' attention on the cartoon and ask what the man is doing and what the problem is.

Many students start describing specific details too early on in their Writing Task 1 answer, and fail to provide an overview of the information.

ANSWER
The man in the cartoon is looking too closely at one aspect of the data and might miss the key trend as a result.

Optional activity

To help students to conceptualize and describe the pattern of an overall trend, ask them to think about the diagrams they see in newspapers and what information they are trying to give us, e.g. employment rates, economic trends, weather patterns, etc.

6 This exercise illustrates the difference between an answer which describes an overall trend, and an answer which launches into specific detail too soon, without giving an overview.

If necessary, ask students what the difference is between descriptions A and B to guide students to the correct answer.

ANSWER
Description A
This is the correct answer because it does not include specific numbers, and uses 'broad strokes' to describe the overall trend.

Vocabulary

7 This exercise provides students with useful vocabulary to describe trends, and promotes accuracy by identifying the different parts of speech.

Before beginning, ask students to copy the table into their notebooks. Highlight that the verbs are in the past simple. Ask students to work alone before comparing with a partner. Draw the table on the board to check answers as a whole class. As you check, you may like to clarify meaning by asking:

- if each verb and noun means 'up' or 'down'
- if each adverb and adjective means 'a lot' or 'a little' (point out that the adjectives and adverbs can refer to an upward or a downward movement)
- how we can recognize an adverb (there is often *-ly* at the end)
- what the base form of the verbs are (highlight that these particular verbs look the same as the nouns to make students aware of the potential for confusion)
- why it is important to know if a word is a noun or a verb (so students can use it correctly in a sentence by making appropriate changes to the word, e.g. changing the tense of a verb or making a noun plural)
- why it is important to know what goes before and after a noun or verb, particularly with regard to whether an adjective or an adverb should be used.

ANSWERS
Verbs: increased, rose, fell
Adverbs: slightly, significantly, dramatically
Nouns: fall, increase, rise
Prepositions: to, in, by, from
Adjectives: slight, significant, dramatic

UNIT 1 EDUCATION & LEARNING   17

VOCABULARY FILE Student's Book page 121

Refer students to exercises 8 and 9 for more practice describing trends.

ANSWERS
See page 132 of this book for answers.

8 This exercise provides students with models of how to use the new vocabulary in sentences.

Focus students' attention on the bar chart in exercise 3 to help them. Highlight that students should also use their knowledge of word class / parts of speech to guide their choice, for example:

- ask students what type of word we normally expect after the indefinite article *a* (a noun beginning with a consonant)
- highlight that there are two gaps after *a* in sentence a, and elicit what the other word could be if one of the words is a noun (an adjective)
- explain that *the number of people* at the start of sentence b forms the subject. Write the phrase on the board, and ask what type of word will follow (a verb)
- ask students what type of word they are likely to need in sentence b for the second gap (an adverb).

ANSWERS
1 significant / dramatic
2 increase / rise
3 from
4 to
5 rose / increased
6 dramatically / significantly
7 increase / rise
8 in
9 by
10 rose / increased
11 slightly

9 This exercise provides students with a model answer, and helps them think about ordering information.

Ask students to work alone before comparing with a partner. Check as a whole class and raise students' awareness of the features of this model by asking:

- *What phrases help to structure the text?* (In general / Looking in more detail / To summarize)
- *Does the text include all the details in the bar chart?* (no)
- *Why do you think the student who wrote this text chose to focus on these pieces of information?* (they are the most striking)

ANSWERS
1 b   2 a   3 c

Optional activity

Write the questions below on the board. Students discuss in pairs and then as a class:

- *Has the number of people attending university increased or decreased in your country? Why?*
- *Do you think this trend will continue? Why / Why not?*
- *If the number of people going to university increases, do you think this is a good thing? Why / Why not?*

Exam skills

10 This exercise demonstrates how students can vary the structures they use, which is another important exam skill.

Ask students to discuss in pairs before sharing ideas as a whole class. You may like to guide students by asking:

- *Is the meaning of the two sentences the same?* (yes)
- *When you change the part of speech, what else do you need to change?* (the word order)

ANSWER
In sentence 1, *rose* is a verb and *dramatically* an adverb; in sentence 2, *rise* is a noun and *dramatic* an adjective.

Teaching tip: Students may need help in understanding the structure of sentences with long noun phrases. Help them by highlighting the subject in exercise 10, sentence 1 (the number of students who attended tertiary education) and then the verb. Ask students to identify the subjects and verbs in all the sentences in question 11 before they attempt the task.

11 This exercise provides an opportunity to practise varying language.

You may like to demonstrate by doing sentence 1 as a whole class. Ask:

- *What parts of speech are 'declined' and 'steadily'?* (verb and adverb)
- *Look back at sentence 2 in exercise 10. What parts of speech can replace verbs and adverbs?* (nouns and adjectives)
- *What is the noun that matches 'declined'* (decline) *and the adjective that matches 'steadily'?* (steady)
- *Is the word order for nouns and adjectives the same as verbs and adverbs?* (no, because the adjective needs to go before the noun)
- *Look back again at sentence 2 in exercise 10. What words do you need to add?* (There was a ...)

Ask students to change the phrases in bold for sentence 1, and write the full sentence on the board. Tell students to work alone to complete sentences 2–4 before comparing with a partner. Check answers as a whole class.

ANSWERS
1 There was a steady decline in the number of female students in Eastern Europe.
2 There was a significant increase in the number of female students in Asia.
3 The number of people studying maths fell slightly.
4 The number of people studying law fell dramatically.

Language note: You may wish to draw students' attention to the different prepositions used to describe trends:

- *It increased **by** 10%*
- *There was an increase **of** 10%*
- *There was an increase **in** foreign students*
- *It increased **to** 100*
- *Unemployment increased **from** 5% **to** 8%.*

12 Ask students to discuss in groups, and then get feedback as a whole class.

POSSIBLE ANSWER
It makes the text more interesting for the reader and demonstrates good control of the language. Students should demonstrate knowledge of a range of structures in the exam.

Exam practice

13 This exercise provides students with an opportunity to put everything from this lesson into practice.

Encourage students to reflect on what they have learnt by referring them back to exercises 4–11. Group students in fours and ask them to brainstorm what steps they should follow when attempting Writing Task 1, such as:
- analysing what the diagram represents
- writing an introductory sentence, which answers the Wh- questions and adapts the rubric
- describing the overall trend before going into more detail
- selecting the key features and trends rather than describing everything
- using a variety of language and structures.

Familiarize students with exam conditions by only allowing them to write for the recommended time (20 minutes). Encourage them to use their copy of the Student's Book as a reference guide by taking useful language from the unit.

Alternative for weaker classes: allow students to work together in pairs to share ideas. Nevertheless, it is important to stick to the time limit, and ensure that both students in the pair write.

MODEL ANSWER
See exercise 2 in the WRITING FILE on page 137 of the Student's Book for a model answer.

WRITING FILE Student's Book page 137
Refer students to exercise 3 on this page for another Task 1 question featuring a bar chart, accompanied by a sample essay.

ANSWERS
See page 136 of this book for answers.

> **STUDY SKILLS FILE Student's Book page 134**
> Refer students to this page for activities that will help them to improve their writing development.

READING Multiple choice page 14

Lesson aims
1 Enable students to identify differences in multiple-choice options to understand which one is correct.
2 Develop students' ability to analyse stems in multiple-choice questions to find the corresponding part of the text quickly.
3 Improve students' understanding and use of the first conditional.

Featured topic vocabulary
Adjectives: essential, motivated, curious, romantic, casual

Topic focus

1 Ask students if they read newspapers and magazines. Ask *How do you choose which articles to read in a newspaper or magazine?* to elicit that they can predict the topic of a text through pictures and title. Check the meaning of *predict* (say or estimate that something will happen in the future). Direct students to the exercise and emphasize that they should not start reading the text itself yet.

2 This exercise develops students' ability to read for *gist* (the overall topic of the text) and highlights the importance of the title, picture, and extra information in understanding the text.

Give students 2 minutes to read. If possible, put a stopwatch in a visible place to encourage students to read quickly. After checking as a whole class, ask students why it is useful to predict what a text is about before reading. (It helps students think about what they already know about a topic. It also helps them engage with the text and stay focused as they are reading.)

Exam skills

3 This exercise prepares students for multiple-choice tasks by introducing the idea of matching sentence meanings and looking at how options differ.

You may like to clarify that this is a simplified version of this style of exam question. Multiple-choice questions will look different in the exam as there will be four options not two, and students will need to find the matching sentence themselves within a text. Here they are given the matching sentence. Tell students to work alone before checking their answers in pairs. Encourage students to justify their choices to each other. Check as a whole class.

ANSWERS
1 b 2 a 3 a 4 a

4 Ask students to compare their ideas with a partner before checking as a whole class. Note that similar lexis appears in both options. To do this task students should instead focus on the relationship between the ideas. To emphasize this, you could write up the first sentences in each question in note form. For example, for sentence 1 you could write up *online learning = important sometimes* and for sentence 2 you could write *internet connections > teachers* and ask students which of the two options has this idea.

ANSWERS
1 more useful than
2 don't use the internet
3 Learning naturally, makes children curious
4 used to learning, rarely do

EXAM TIP 1•12 Before students listen, ask them to suggest possible answers to the question and write these on the board. After they have answered the question, refer students to page 148 for more guidance on how to answer multiple-choice questions.

UNIT 1 EDUCATION & LEARNING 19

ANSWER
They give you an idea of where to look for the information in the passage.

Audioscript 1·12
Multiple-choice questions with four options often feature in the Reading test. As you read the options, underline key words or make a quick note next to any options which you think are possible answers. Of course, you then have to decide which option the passage actually agrees with. The 'stems' are useful because **they give you an idea of where to look for the information in the passage**.

5 This exercise develops students' ability to analyse stems in multiple-choice questions to find the corresponding part of the text quickly.

Stress that students should not underline too much because otherwise the important words will not stand out. Focus their attention on the stems only by telling them not to read the options for now. Ask students to compare their answers with a partner before checking as a whole class. Ask students what the underlined words in 1, 3, and 4 have in common (they are the main topic). Ask students why *Sugata Mitra* in 2 is easy to find (because names have capital letters and so they stand out). Ask how question 5 is different (it asks students to think about the whole text).

ANSWERS
1 reading
2 Sugata Mitra
3 computer games
4 language course, exam
5 main idea

Teaching tip: One of the main issues students face in the Reading exam is completing everything within the time limit. It is vital, therefore, to develop skills to read more efficiently. Skills such as quickly identifying the relevant part of the text, like in exercise 5, help students to avoid wasting time looking repeatedly through the whole text.

Exam practice
6 Remind students of the points they should keep in mind by referring them back to exercises 3 and 4. Ask students to work alone before comparing with a partner. Tell students to justify their answers to each other by referring to the matching part of the text and explaining how it means the same as the option they chose. Ask students to also explain to each other why the other options are incorrect. Check answers as a whole class.

ANSWERS
1 B (*a girl improved her writing so much her angry teacher accused her of copying* – lines 22–24)
A is incorrect because the text says *Studying online may have a similar effect* (lines 26–27).
C is incorrect because the text says *it wasn't important what books they read* (line 13).
D is incorrect because in the case study which was successful the researcher gave students the books (line 18).

2 B (see lines 27–31)
Options A, C, and D are not mentioned in the text, and students should be careful not to presume any of these things based on outside knowledge.

3 A (*watching people play computer games may help more than actually playing them* – lines 43–44)
B is incorrect because the text actually says the opposite (see lines 43–44 above).
C is incorrect because the text does not mention how long. Students again should be careful not to presume this. They may be misled by the statement that using language repeatedly is essential, but this refers to frequency not duration.
D is not mentioned but students may presume D is correct based on the statement that watching people play is better than playing because you have time to listen to or read the language in the games (lines 44–45). Students should be careful not to go too far beyond the text to take such leaps in logic.

4 C (*if you want to take an exam in English, doing a course will be as useful as reading for fun* – lines 52–53)
A is incorrect because the text says *This does not mean that language courses are a waste of time* (lines 50–51).
B is incorrect because it means the opposite of what the text says (see lines 52–53 above).
D is not mentioned but students may be misled by the statement that *doing both is clearly best* (line 54). Students should beware of drawing incorrect conclusions such as presuming that both means 'at the same time'.

5 C (lines 4 to 6, line 13, lines 38–39, and lines 49–50)
A is incorrect because the text states *This does not mean that language courses are a waste of time* (lines 50–51).
B is incorrect because although the examples mentioned are outside the classroom, the focus of the text is not school contrasted with studying alone, but using language for fun contrasted with studying.
D is incorrect because the main idea is that any kind of activity that is enjoyable is useful. Students may be misled by the statement *some kinds of contact may be more useful than others* (lines 40–41), but the words *much more* in option D makes this stronger than the tentative use of *may* in line 41.

Grammar
7 This exercise improves students' understanding and use of the first conditional.

You may like to introduce the first conditional by writing the first sentence from exercise 8 on the board (*If you do something you enjoy using English, …*). Ask students for ideas to finish the sentence and write their ideas on the board. Ask what the key word is which helps them to know this is a conditional sentence (*if*). Then tell students to work alone to find similar sentences in the text. Check the answers by writing the sentences on the board. Highlight the structure by drawing a box around *will learn* and *will be* in one colour and *if* and *have* and *want* in another colour.

> **ANSWERS**
> … children will learn to navigate the web in foreign languages and also teach themselves academic subjects if they have access to the internet.
> Krashen also discovered that if you want to take an exam in English, doing a course will be as useful as reading for fun.

GRAMMAR FILE Student's Book page 117
Refer students to this page for more explanation and practice of first conditionals.

> **ANSWERS**
> See page 131 of this book for answers.

8 Ask students to work alone before comparing sentences with a partner. Write some of the students' examples on the board and highlight the form.

> **POSSIBLE ANSWERS**
> 1 If you do something you enjoy using English, your English will improve quickly.
> 2 If you choose your own reading materials, you will be more motivated to read.
> 3 If you give children access to a computer, they will learn many things by themselves.

What do you think?

9 This exercise encourages students to think critically about the topic of education and learning, and generates ideas they could use in Speaking Part 3 and Writing Task 2. It also consolidates work on the first conditional.

Focus on the example in the speech bubble. Tell students to work in pairs and give them 5 minutes to think of as many reasons as possible.

10 Join pairs into groups of four and appoint a scorer within each pair who is responsible for noting down the points for the other pair. Monitor for good use of the first conditional and write examples of correct sentences on the board, highlighting the form.

> **STUDY SKILLS FILE Student's Book page 135**
> Refer students to this page for activities that will help them to improve their reading development.

EXAM CHALLENGE

> **ANSWERS**

Speaking
1 & 2 Students' own answers

Listening
1 See page 136 of this book for answers and page 141 for the audioscript.
2 Students' own answers

Reading
1 See page 138 of this book for answers.
2 Students' own answers

Writing
1 Students' own answers
2 See page 111–112 of the Student's Book for the model answer.

UNIT 2   Health & medicine

Introduction (page 17)

Featured topic vocabulary
Collocations: *sense of humour, positive attitude, portion of food*
Nouns: *meal, stress*
Adjective: *quiet*

Optional lead-in
Before students look at the infographic on page 17, you might like them to try to guess the answers to the questions below. You could ask them to do this in groups and write their ideas on the board, before they look at the infographic to find the answers.
- How old do you think the world's oldest man and woman are?
- What countries do you think they come from?
- What do you think the world's oldest man and woman say is the secret to a long life?

What do you think?
These questions aim to engage students with the topic, generate ideas, and activate their existing vocabulary knowledge.

Group students in threes to discuss their ideas. In whole-class feedback, write on the board any useful vocabulary that students use in their responses.

Background note: Women live, on average, five years longer than men. It is thought to be partly because the immune system ages less in women. They are also less likely to die in fighting or in accidents.

Optional activity
You can encourage students to engage further with this topic by asking them to discuss one of these questions in groups:
- Would you like to live past 100? Why / Why not?
- How many advantages / disadvantages of being old can you think of?
- Old people sometimes complain they feel useless in society. What can be done to keep them involved?
- How has the role of grandparents changed in your culture over the past century?
- How do you imagine yourself at the age of 80?
- Do you know any old people? What are their secrets for a healthy life?

SPEAKING Extended speaking (page 18)

EXAM FOCUS: PART 2

Lesson aims
1 Prepare students for Speaking Part 2 by analysing prompts and identifying strengths in a model answer.
2 Develop students' ability to use time clauses to give more detailed answers about when something happens.
3 Provide students with a variety of adjectives for evaluating activities and objects.
4 Improve students' use of intonation to communicate more effectively.

Key language
Adjectives: *convenient, demanding, repetitive, effective, dull, expensive, beneficial, ideal, simple*
Adverbs of time: *as soon as, when, every time, whenever, while*

Featured topic vocabulary
Activities: *yoga, Pilates, jogging, go running, go to the gym, go for a walk*
Equipment: *exercise bike*
Verbs: *wear, exercise, cycle, burn (calories), build (muscles), measure (heart rate)*
Adjectives: *active, healthy*
Nouns: *muscle, exercise programme, calories, heart rate*

Topic focus
1 This lead-in encourages students to engage with the topic of sports and think of any related vocabulary they already know. Monitor for useful language, and write any examples of sports or sports equipment on the board.

2 ⓘ 1·13 This exercise introduces students to the topic before listening in more detail for exercise 5. It also provides a series of models for extended speaking, though not yet in an exam context. A common problem students have with Speaking Part 2 is finishing too quickly because of a lack of ideas. This exercise shows students how they can expand descriptions, to help them speak for longer.

Ask students to check their answers in pairs before checking as a class.

ANSWERS
1 C   2 A   3 B   4 D

Audioscript 1·13

1 It was a Swiss doctor called Susanne Klein-Vogelbach who first suggested that **giant plastic balls** could be used for health purposes and 'Swiss balls', as they became known, soon became very popular. Many people believe that sitting on a Swiss ball is an effective way of building your muscles. These days, you'll see them used for general fitness training when you go to a gym. They're also ideal for doing yoga and Pilates.
2 The **Wii Balance Board** arrived with Nintendo's *Wii Fit* in 2007. It's a convenient way of exercising because you can use it whenever you're at home. It's also simple to use because it actually remembers your exercise programmes for you. Obviously, you need a Wii and the *Wii Fit* game to use the Balance Board, which are all quite expensive, but it's worth the money.
3 **Sports watches** measure how far and how fast you walk or run. Most can also measure your heart rate and how many calories you burn. They're really beneficial as they encourage people to be as active as possible. As soon as you turn the watch on, it starts working and can tell you how far you've walked or run. You can wear it wherever you are. For some people, jogging can be a bit dull, but with a sports watch you have something to focus on.
4 **Exercise bikes** are a common sight in gyms everywhere and are used by a wide range of people. Parents can even buy exercise bikes that rock a baby to sleep while they use them. They have a variety of programmes to make the exercise as easy or as demanding as you want and they tell you how far you cycle as well as how many calories you burn. However, some people find doing the same exercise programmes a little repetitive and they prefer to use a normal bike outside.

Vocabulary

3 As ideas run out, students often find themselves repeating language in Speaking Part 2, especially evaluative phrases such as *It's really good*. This exercise enables students to show variety in their speaking by focusing on a range of language for this purpose.

While students are doing the exercise, draw two columns on the board with the headings 'positive' and 'negative'. To check the answers as a class, ask different students to come to the board and write one adjective each in the correct column. As you are checking the answers, drill the pronunciation by modelling it for the class and asking them to repeat together.

ANSWERS
Positive (+): *convenient, effective, beneficial, ideal, simple*
Negative (−): *demanding, repetitive, dull, expensive*

VOCABULARY FILE Student's Book *page 122*
Refer students to exercises 1–2 for extra practice using these adjectives. There are also additional adjectives to help students add variety to their descriptions.

ANSWERS
See page 132 of this book for answers.

Teaching tip: Students should avoid relying on adjectives such as *nice* and *good*, which can make their speaking sound vague and which are very low-level items. Encourage students to use more range and be more specific in their speaking by asking them to replace *nice* and *good*.

4 This exercise clarifies the meaning of vocabulary from exercise 3 and helps students remember the adjectives by working with them in context.

Highlight that students should choose *a* or *an* in questions 1 and 3 depending on whether the adjective they choose begins with a vowel or not. Also point out that sometimes more than one adjective is possible.

Background note: *yoga*: a system of exercises for your body and for controlling your breathing, used by people who want to become fitter or relax
Pilates: a system of exercises, sometimes using special apparatus, designed to improve physical strength, flexibility, and posture, and enhance mental awareness

5 1·14 This exercise provides students with an opportunity to hear the pronunciation of the adjectives, and encourages them to listen in more detail to the example descriptions. It also provides an opportunity to clarify any misunderstandings about the vocabulary.

Only check answers which students are unsure of, as they should be able to hear the correct answers and can copy the spelling from the box, and so do not need to see it on the board.

More than one answer may be possible.

ANSWERS
1 effective (*simple* is also possible)   6 beneficial
2 ideal   7 dull
3 convenient   8 demanding
4 simple (*convenient* is also possible)   9 repetitive
5 expensive

Audioscript 1·14

1 Sitting on a Swiss ball is an **effective** way of building your muscles.
2 They're also **ideal** for doing yoga and Pilates.
3 It's a **convenient** way of exercising because you can use it whenever you're at home.
4 It's also **simple** to use because it actually remembers your exercise programme for you.
5 You need a Wii and the *Wii Fit* game to use the Balance Board, which are all quite **expensive**.
6 They're really **beneficial** as they encourage people to be as active as possible.
7 For some people, jogging can be a bit **dull**.
8 They have a variety of programmes to make the exercise as easy or as **demanding** as you want.
9 Some people find doing the same exercise programmes a little **repetitive**.

6 This exercise encourages students to expand their answers by using adjectives to describe the activities.

Focus students' attention on the example. Suggest that even if their answer is *No*, they could still expand by saying *No, but I imagine it's* … Drill the phrase *Have you ever tried* … by modelling it and then asking students to repeat together. You might like to drill a few examples, like *Have you ever tried yoga / jogging / Wii Fit / a Swiss ball*?

Teaching tip: Don't worry if you feel your students are not familiar with the present perfect structure *Have you ever* … After drilling several examples with different sports, your students will probably accept it as a 'chunk' (like a phrase). If they ask you about the grammar, you can explain that we use this to talk about life experiences. You may not want to go into too much detail at this point to avoid distracting from the aims of the lesson.

Grammar

7 This exercise helps students speak in longer sentences by using time clauses to describe when something happens.

Tell students to work alone before checking as a class. While going through the answers, you may like to check they understand the words in bold by asking:

- *as soon as*: Which one happens first, running or getting up? (getting up) Does the running usually happen a long time after getting up? (no)
- *when*: Does it mean 'before' or 'after' in this sentence? (after)
- *every time*: Does this mean 'always' or 'sometimes'? (always)
- *whenever*: Does this mean 'sometimes' or 'any time'? (any time)
- *while*: Do these activities happen separately or together? (together)

Language note: Highlight that the second half of the sentence is a new clause with a new subject (e.g. *you, they, I*) and a new main verb (e.g. *go, get up, are, have*). The words in bold connect the two clauses, and so these show the examiner the student can use more complex language.

Teaching tip: You can use this exercise again later for revision by asking students to cover a–e on the right and try to remember the ends, or finish the sentences themselves.

ANSWERS
1 b   2 d   3 e   4 a   5 c

8 Ask students to complete this alone before checking with a partner. Help them understand any incorrect answers by using the questions in exercise 7.

ANSWERS
1 while
2 when
3 Whenever
4 as soon as
5 when

Language note: Students may have difficulty choosing between *when* and *whenever*. Highlight that often both are possible, but they have slightly different meanings. In sentence 2, for example, using *when* means 'only if it isn't crowded'; but using *whenever* suggests greater frequency and means 'every time it's less crowded'.

Optional activity

Give students extra practice using time clauses by doing the following:

a Group students in threes or fours. Give each group a pile of strips of paper.
b Students have 10 minutes to create the beginnings of sentences using adverbs of time, like the sentences in 1–5 in exercise 7.
c Students pass their incomplete sentences to the group to their right.
d The other group then has 5 minutes to complete the sentences in a way that makes sense. They then return all completed sentences to the group who sent them.
e Tell students to mark the complete sentences and award points for each correct sentence. Groups can (and will!) then discuss why points were withheld.

9 1·15 This recording demonstrates how intonation can impact on communication by 'shaping' a sentence in a way that highlights important information.

After listening, give students a chance to practise the intonation by saying the sentences from exercise 8 aloud in pairs, copying the pronunciation in the recording.

ANSWERS
The voice of Speaker A has relatively flat intonation; the voice of Speaker B has livelier intonation, rising on interesting or important information and falling at the end of the sentences. Speaker B communicates more effectively because Speaker B uses intonation to keep the listener's attention.

Audioscript 1·15

1 **A** I listen to music while I'm running.
   B I listen to music while I'm running.
2 **A** I go to the gym after 9 a.m. when it's less crowded.
   B I go to the gym after 9 a.m. when it's less crowded.
3 **A** Whenever I can, I try to do yoga.
   B Whenever I can, I try to do yoga.
4 **A** I have a shower as soon as I finish running.
   B I have a shower as soon as I finish running.
5 **A** I don't exercise indoors when it's warm and sunny.
   B I don't exercise indoors when it's warm and sunny.

10 This exercise provides an opportunity for students to personalize the new language, to make sentences they can use in their speaking exam if they are asked about this topic.

Alternative for weaker classes: give students time to prepare what they want to say, as the focus is on accuracy here. However, tell them to turn over their notes before speaking so they are not just reading aloud. Pair students with a new partner to ask and answer the questions again, and encourage them to focus more on their intonation the second time.

GRAMMAR FILE Student's Book page 117
Refer students to this book for more explanation and practice of time clauses.

ANSWERS
See page 131 of this book for answers.

Exam skills

11 This exercise prepares students for Speaking Part 2 by analysing prompts to ensure they speak about everything on the card.

Answer the questions as a whole class. Remind students they will be penalized if they do not cover all the points on the card. Explain that the topic and prompts will not be the same in the exam.

ANSWERS
There are four prompts; the last prompt is less 'factual' than the previous three and requires you to explain your opinions (with reasons).

EXAM TIP 1•16 Before students listen, ask them to suggest possible answers to the question and write these on the board. After they have answered the question, refer students to page 145 for more guidance on how to use the preparation time effectively.

ANSWER
Your first objective could be to speak for 25 seconds about the first prompt on the card.

Audioscript 1•16

In Speaking Part 2, it's difficult to remember everything you want to say but the 1 minute of preparation time can help. Writing notes on the topic during this time is useful or, if you prefer, close your eyes and try to imagine the things you're going to describe. You could also set yourself different objectives for each stage of the extended speaking. **Your first objective could be to speak for 25 seconds about the first prompt on the card.** If you can do this, you should be able to speak for more than 1 minute in total. Then, for the next stages, focus on demonstrating your grammar, vocabulary, and pronunciation in turn.

12 1•17 This exercise prepares students for Speaking Part 2 by identifying strengths in a model answer.

When checking the answers as a class, drill the phrase in question 1, *I'd like to talk about*, to help students speak confidently.

Teaching tip: Encourage students to finish the phrase *I'd like to talk about …* by stating specifically what they are going to talk about, e.g. in the model the student says the name of the friend. Often students just repeat what is written on the card (e.g. *I'd like to talk about a person that I know who is very healthy*) rather than introducing their individual topic.

Note: students should be aware that in the exam they will probably be stopped by the examiner and should therefore not aim to 'finish' their response. The aim is to keep going.

ANSWERS
1 OK, I'd like to talk about …
2 She speaks in an informal style. This can be seen in the frequent use of contractions and more conversational language: *really, actually, going out, too, all sorts of, the good thing about, a lot of, as I said before, things, great, good for, a bit.*
3 Yes, she pauses between prompts on the card. It would be acceptable in the exam to refer to the prompts more clearly, but this isn't mandatory.

Audioscript 1•17

OK, I'd like to talk about a friend of mine called Ann. She's an old friend – she's in her thirties now and has a child, but she's **really** active. **Actually**, she's played sports for as long as I've known her. She always wears a tracksuit and trainers, even when she's shopping or **going out**! Er, her favourite activity is definitely yoga. She goes to the gym to do classes whenever she can and as soon as she gets home she does extra exercises, **too**. I think she probably does it in her dreams! She gets into **all sorts of** strange positions which I could never do. I don't know how she does it. OK. **The good thing about** yoga is that you don't need **a lot of** equipment. Ann uses a long plastic mat – there's always one on the floor of her living room. It's green and looks very soft and comfortable. You have to have loose clothing, too, but she always wears this anyway, **as I said before**. And there are probably **things** you can buy if you want, but nothing important. I think what she does is **great** and I wish I was more like her. She seems very calm and cheerful. But I'm not sure that kind of lifestyle is **good for** everyone. Personally, I think I'd probably find it **a bit** dull and repetitive; I need more variety. I'm quite different from Ann, I think!

Exam practice

13 Students have a chance here to put together all the skills developed in this lesson by doing a practice Speaking Part 2.

In pairs, nominate one student to be the examiner and tell them to think about the points from exercise 12 as they are listening to their partner.

UNIT 2 HEALTH & MEDICINE

Optional activity

You can help students become more familiar with prompts by getting them to make their own Speaking Part 2 cards. Do the following:

a Create an example as a whole class. Write a topic on the board, for example: *Describe a sports match you have watched*.

b Ask students for ideas for prompts. If they have no idea, give them the first words (e.g. *who / where / when*).

c Divide the class into a maximum of five groups and give everyone the same topic, for example: *Describe a piece of sports equipment you have used*.

d Give them 5 minutes to make four prompts before comparing with the other groups.

e Now allocate different topics to each group, for example: *Describe a meal or snack that makes you feel better, describe a person you know who has a healthy lifestyle, describe a PE lesson you remember having, describe a way of staying healthy that is very convenient, describe a traditional sporting activity in your country, describe a good piece of advice you have received*. Tell each group to make four prompts.

f A representative from each group tells the class their topic. The other groups should each guess one prompt and win a point if correct. The team who wrote the card also wins a point for each prompt guessed correctly by the other teams.

g Finally, the team representative should tell the class the rest of their prompts if they are not all guessed correctly by the others.

LISTENING Completing tables (page 20)

EXAM FOCUS: SECTION 2

Lesson aims
1 Develop students' ability to complete tables by predicting the type of information that is missing.
2 Improve students' ability to recognize different forms of the same word family to build their vocabulary and help students listen for the correct word form when completing tables.
3 Improve students' ability to record word knowledge.

Key language
Word formation: *reduction / reduce, strength / strengthen*

Featured topic vocabulary
Activities: *riding a motorbike, playing the drums, scuba-diving, karate, running, swimming, walking the dog, chopping wood, martial arts, aerobics, spinning, Zumba, Boxercise*
Verbs: *strengthen, expose, provide*
Nouns: *joint, tension, impact, thigh, confidence, spray*

Topic focus

1 This lead-in clarifies vocabulary students will hear in exercise 3, and encourages them to engage with the topic.

Draw students' attention to the photos and give an example, if possible, by telling the class about one activity you have done (e.g. *I think photo H is scuba-diving. I did this when I was on holiday in Egypt last year. It was amazing. I saw so many different coloured fish.*).

ANSWERS
A walking the dog   E swimming
B playing the drums   F running
C chopping wood   G riding a motorbike
D doing karate   H scuba-diving

EXAM TIP 1·18 Before students listen, ask them to suggest possible answers to the question and write these on the board. After they have answered the question, refer students to page 146 for more guidance on how to complete a table.

ANSWER
The forms of other words in the same column of the table can help you to decide the type of word or number you need.

Audioscript 1·18

In Listening Section 2, you may have to complete a table with information – numbers or individual words. Candidates often hear the information that's needed but then write it down incorrectly by failing to add articles (*a* or *the*) or the right endings. This will lose you marks in the exam. Make sure you **look carefully at the forms of other words in the same column of the table, as these can help you to decide the type of word or number you need.**

Exam skills

2 This exercise trains students to use the time before listening to predict what type of answer they will need. This increases their chances of hearing the correct answer in the exam by listening in a more focused way.

Ask students what each column contains (activity, benefits, calories per hour) and what direction the questions follow (left to right). Highlight the importance of checking table headings, and the order of the questions. Explain that this is the same order as in the recording. Do number 1 as an example with the whole class. If students need help, draw their attention to the kph after the gap and ask what it means (kilometres per hour). Ask them to work alone to complete the exercise, and then to check their answers with a partner.

Teaching tip: Remember that for students of some language backgrounds, reading the table itself may be a challenge if their script is read in a different direction. They may need extra practice following the order of information in a table to make sure they do not get lost in the exam. Asking them to notice the location of the gap numbers will remind them of the direction in which the table will be read.

26 UNIT 2 HEALTH & MEDICINE

ANSWERS

Gerund	5
Plural / uncountable noun	2, 3, 7, 10
Singular noun	9
Third-person verb	6
Number	1, 4, 8

3 ◉ 1·19 Ask students to check their answers in pairs after the first listening. Play the recording again if necessary. Check answers as a whole class. Encourage students to check if they got the correct type of word, even if they got the wrong answer.

ANSWERS

1 17.5
2 wood
3 stomach muscles
4 704
5 Scuba-diving
6 Releases
7 pets
8 281
9 motorbike
10 knees

Audioscript 1·19

Perhaps you're one of those people who don't actually like taking exercise. Well, the good news is that you don't necessarily need to work too hard to keep fit. Of course, there are some demanding forms of exercise that are good for you. Running, for example, can burn 1,267 calories if you run at **17.5** kilometres per hour. Almost as useful are other forms of physical, outdoor work. Chopping **wood**, for example, can really build **stomach muscles**. If you're worried about injuries, then swimming is an ideal activity because it's a low impact form of exercise but still burns **the same number of calories as martial arts**! **Scuba-diving** is particularly useful because it helps to reduce stress. And there are some things we might not think of as 'proper' exercise but which can still help. Playing the drums, for example, is great for **releasing** tension in the body and just walking the dog or playing with **pets** in the garden can help you to burn calories, about **281** per hour, and also exposes you to fresh air. Even riding a **motorbike** is better than sitting in a car because it can help strengthen **knees** and thighs. So, there you go – no excuses – if you stay active, then you can also keep fit!

4 This exercise helps students generate topic ideas and learn new vocabulary by using it in their speaking.

Ask a strong student their opinion to provide the class with an example. Remind students to justify their answer. Monitor and write any interesting points on the board.

Vocabulary

5 The focus here is on building vocabulary knowledge through word families and using the correct word form. This helps students to predict what type of answers they need in a listening test, by improving their ability to identify word classes / parts of speech.

Do question 1 as an example by asking students if *reduction* is a noun, verb, or adjective (noun). Ask what type of word is needed in the gap (verb). Tell students to complete the exercise alone and then to check in pairs.

Note: in question 5, the noun and verb *increase* is written the same, but pronounced differently. The stress is on the first syllable for the noun, shown here in bold – **in**crease. The stress is on the second syllable for the verb – in**crease**.

Teaching tip: It helps expand students' vocabulary if they record word families rather than just isolated words. Ask if any of them do this already and, if so, get them to show their classmates.

ANSWERS

1 reduce
2 relaxing
3 strengthens
4 motivate
5 increases

> **Optional activity**
>
> Ask students to get out their vocabulary notebooks and record the word families from exercise 5. Then tell them to look at vocabulary they have previously written down, and use a dictionary to find words in the same family.

6 This exercise gives students a chance to practise using the vocabulary, and prepares them for the type of questions they could be asked in the speaking exam.

Encourage students to give as much detail as possible in their answers. As you monitor, check if they are giving very short answers. If so, stop the activity and brainstorm some ideas for answers as a whole class. Then ask them to try again in pairs. As students are speaking, check they are using the correct word forms and write any mistakes on the board for students to correct afterwards.

VOCABULARY FILE Student's Book page 122

Refer students to exercise 3 for more practice of vocabulary with different suffixes.

ANSWERS
See page 132 of this book for answers.

Exam practice

7 ◉ 1·20 This exercise tests students' exam skills developed in exercises 2 and 3.

Ask students what the table shows (a gym timetable) and which direction the questions follow (top to bottom). Tell students to work in pairs to predict what type of answer is needed in each gap (1 duration, 2 time, 3 type of class, 4 name of instructor, 5 type of class, 6 name of instructor). Draw students' attention to the instructions, and remind them that they need to check the number of words carefully in the exam as it may vary.

ANSWERS

1 30 mins
2 9.15 p.m.
3 Beach body workout
4 Gary
5 Advanced yoga
6 Ladies' fitness

Audioscript 1·20

Hi, everyone. Can I just have your attention? Thanks. Well, first of all, welcome to Ab-Solutions Gym. We're going to start this introductory session with a quick look at our timetable. Has everyone got one? Good. As you can see, the group exercise classes are all in the evenings. On weekdays, you can do Spinning with Deborah from 7 o'clock – that's a 45-minute session. After that, we have Abs blast and Core blast – both are pretty hard-core sessions and not ones I'd really recommend for complete beginners! They're a bit demanding so both last for about **half an hour**, but if you want something more relaxing then I do recommend Aerobics at **quarter past nine**. This usually attracts the ladies but if any guys want to have a go, then they're also welcome! At the weekend, things change around. We start with our very popular **Beach body workout** – that's with Paul – before we do Aerobics with Moira. Two great sessions for general fitness. Following that, we have Boxercise, though I'm afraid the timetable is wrong there and, in fact, **Gary** will be leading that session instead of Paul. Don't forget that at the end of the day on Saturday we have **Advanced yoga**, too. Finally, on Sunday it's all change again. We have an energetic session of **Ladies' fitness** with Moira for 45 minutes, then if you haven't tried martial arts before, we have a visiting instructor coming in to take a karate class. It's beginner level, so I'd give it a go. That's then followed by Zumba, and Pilates on Sunday evening.

8 🔊 1·21 In this exercise there is a wider variety of possible answers, and so it provides even more of a challenge for students' prediction skills.

Ask students what information they think might fit in the gaps, and write their ideas on the board. Play the recording more than once if necessary, but remind them they will hear it only once in the exam. Ask students to compare and justify their answers in pairs before checking as a whole class. Help them to correct mistakes in their answers by reading aloud relevant parts of the audioscript as necessary. Ask students to compare the class predictions on the board to the correct answers.

ANSWERS
1 identity card	3 plenty of fluid
2 paper towels	4 pair of headphones

Audioscript 1·21

OK, so if you follow me, I'll show you the main room of the gym. To get in, you have to pass your **identity card** over the scanner here. Look after your card carefully, because you also need it to use the equipment. Anyway, I'll let us all in for now … There we go. OK. Over here, there are several computer screens. I should say these aren't for checking emails! The idea is that you can type in your unique personal code – you get this when you arrive – and then download an exercise programme that matches your level. Now for the equipment itself. OK, first of all, it's very important to leave the equipment clean for the next user, so we expect everyone to wipe down the machines after use with the spray provided and a **paper towel**. When using all machines, please remember to wear clean shoes that haven't been worn outdoors and to wear loose, comfortable clothes. You should also bring **plenty of fluid** so that you don't become dehydrated. All of the exercise machines have an audio socket so you can plug in your own **headphones**, or you can buy **a pair of** them at reception. The machines all allow you to choose from a selection of music and videos so there's no reason to get bored! OK? Great. If you have any questions, please ask a member of staff – there's someone here at the gym all the time and happy to help. So, if you come this way, I'll show you some of the most popular machines …

What do you think?

9 This exercise provides students with an opportunity to put together all the vocabulary studied in the unit so far. It also helps generate ideas for the types of questions they might face in Writing Part 2 or Speaking Part 3.

After students have discussed in pairs, regroup them with another partner to explain the conclusion reached with their original partner. Get feedback from the class by asking who agrees and who disagrees. Ask for opinions to support both sides of the argument.

Study skills

This exercise helps students become better independent learners by improving their use of vocabulary notebooks. Remind students of the work on word families in exercise 5 and ask what else they think might be important to include in a vocabulary notebook. Write any ideas on the board. Direct students to the image of a notebook page, and ask what type of information they can see in this example. Ask them to complete the exercise in the Study skills box alone, and then check in pairs.

ANSWERS
1 from   2 differ   3 differences

> **Optional activity**
>
> Give students practice recording extra information about new vocabulary by doing the following:
>
> a Group students into threes or fours and allocate one word per group from the following list (taken from the Vocabulary file on page 122): *suitable, costly, dreadful, comprehensive, insignificant, trivial, considerate, detailed*.
>
> b Give each group a dictionary. Ask students to work with their group to find as much useful information about the word as possible, following the example in the image of a notebook page. They should note down the part of speech, pronunciation, any other forms in the same word family (e.g. *consider* is the verb in the same word family as *considerate*). Where appropriate, they should also note down the opposite (e.g. *insignificant* and *significant*).
>
> c Then regroup students so they are working with people who researched different words. Tell students to exchange their information.

WRITING Comparing sets of data (page 22)

EXAM FOCUS: TASK 1

Lesson aims
1 Develop students' ability to compare sets of data by identifying and interpreting what is represented.
2 Improve students' analysis of data to help them select key similarities and differences to include in their description.
3 Enable students to use *more / fewer / less than* appropriately and accurately in comparisons of quantity.
4 Increase cohesion in students' writing by using linking words and phrases.

Key language
Comparisons: *more, fewer, less than*
Linking words and phrases: *similarly, in contrast, also, in conclusion, by comparison, in general, likewise, on the other hand, to be specific, whereas*

Featured topic vocabulary
Nouns: *category*
Adjectives: *recommended, annual, male, female, overall*

Topic focus

1 This lead-in encourages students to start interpreting the data by relating it to their own lives.

Make sure students are focused on the pie chart, not the table, to find out how many hours they should sleep (seven hours for adults and eight and a half for teenagers). Work as a whole class to find the answer relevant to the age of your students. Ask a few strong students the question to provide an example for exercise 2.

2 This exercise brings to life the concept of group data by helping students move beyond their own personal experience to think about their age group generally.

Group students in fours to discuss before comparing ideas as a whole class.

Teaching tip: A key issue in Writing Task 1 is identifying what the data represents in order to translate labels, categories, and numbers into meaningful sentences. Encourage students to consider questions like *who* (in this chart, teenagers and adults), *what* (sleep), *when* (per night), and *how many* (measured in hours) to be clear about what they are describing.

Exam skills

3 This exercise helps students identify what is represented in the table and compare the data to the pie chart.

Alternative for weaker classes: you may like to support students by asking:
- *What is the title of the table?* (Amount of sleep for secondary school students)
- *How many different groups of people are there?* (four)
- *In what ways are the groups of people different?* (age and gender)
- *What other type of category is there?* (hours of sleep)
- *What does the arrow before '3 hours' mean?* (less than three hours)
- *Is the arrow before 8.5 hours the same?* (no; it means more than 8.5 hours).

ANSWER
35%

4 This exercise guides students towards an analysis of the data and provides them with model sentences for the grammar section that follows.

Ask students to work alone before checking their answers with a partner. To check the answers as a class, you may like to copy the table onto the board before class so you can highlight the relevant numbers.

Encourage students to underline, circle, and write notes on the data as they are analysing it in the exam. This can help to highlight the most interesting information.

ANSWERS
1 F: 12-year-olds sleep more than 15-year-olds.
2 T
3 F: Many 15-year-olds have less sleep than 12-year-olds.
4 F: Girls have less sleep than boys or a very similar amount of sleep.

Optional activity
Ask students these discussion questions:
- *Why do you think researchers are interested in this type of data?*
- *What do you think are the effects of not sleeping for long enough?*
- *At what age do you think parents should stop being responsible for their children's sleep? Why?*
- *Do you think teenagers should be able to lie in as long as they want at the weekend?*

Grammar

5 This exercise prepares students to use *more / fewer / less* and *than* in their own writing by helping them understand how the structures operate in a sentence.

Encourage students to use two different colours to highlight noun and verb structures. You may like to write the sentences on the board so you can also highlight the structures in whole-class feedback.

Note: although the verb *have* can be seen before *more* in sentences 3 and 4, it does not match the pattern *more than* after a verb, because the structure following the verb is *more* + noun + *than*.

ANSWERS
1 3 and 4   2 1 and 2

GRAMMAR FILE Student's Book page 114

Refer students to this page for a detailed explanation of the language and extra practice. They will also find information about how to form comparative and superlative adjectives.

ANSWERS
See page 130 of this book for answers.

6 Students practise how to use *more* and *than* in comparisons of quantity. The exercise also provides them with more useful model sentences.

You may like to demonstrate by writing sentence 1 on the board. Mark three positions in the sentence, labelling them A–C: these should include the correct position for *more than* and positions where students might place *more than* incorrectly. Ask students to identify which position is correct. Tell them to complete the exercise in pairs. Discussing the language together can help them better remember it. Highlight the *and / or* in the instructions by writing on the board:
- *more*
- *more than* (the words together)
- *more ... than* (separated by other words)

Alternative for weaker classes: you may like to allocate one or two sentences per pair and then regroup students to explain their answers to each other.

ANSWERS
1 The chart confirms that 12-year-olds students sleep **more than** 15-year-old students.
2 Almost 80% of 12-years-olds have more **than** eight hours' sleep, whereas only 65% of 15-year-olds have **more** than eight hours' sleep.
3 There are approximately 12% **more** 15-year-olds who sleep for just six or seven hours **than** 12-year-olds in that category.
4 There are slightly **more** 15-year-olds who sleep for four or five hours **than** 12-year-olds, but overall totals in both groups are very small.
5 It should be noted that male students do not sleep **more than** female students.
6 Although younger students sleep **more than** older students, many students of both ages are not getting the recommended hours of sleep.

7 The focus here is on choosing the correct comparison word depending on whether the word it describes is countable or uncountable, to promote accuracy in students' writing.

Do sentence 1 as a class and guide students to the correct answer by asking:
- *Do 'less' and 'fewer' have the same meaning?* (yes)
- *Can you use both 'less' and 'fewer' in sentence 1?* (no)
- *Is the word 'magazine' countable or uncountable?* (countable)
- *Do we use 'less' or 'fewer' with countable nouns?* (fewer)

Ask students to complete the exercise alone before checking as a whole class. Note that sentences 2 and 5 do not include the word *money* but this is implied by the verbs *spend* (sentence 2) and *earn* (sentence 5).

Language note: Students sometimes have difficulty understanding why *money* is uncountable. Explain that it can help to think of money as referring to the system / currency, rather than individual coins and notes. They also probably know the question *How much is it?* This can help students remember because *much* is used with uncountable nouns and here refers to money.

ANSWERS
1 fewer 2 less 3 less 4 more 5 more

8 Students are given support here to use the target language in their writing by mirroring sentences from the previous exercise.

Highlight that students need to write the opposite of sentences in exercise 7 by asking what words are different here compared to exercise 7 (e.g. sentence 1 uses *fewer* in exercise 7, but *more* in this exercise).

Alternative for weaker classes: ask students to work in pairs to complete the exercise.

ANSWERS
1 People buy more newspapers than magazines.
2 People spend more (money) on holidays than clothes.
3 Swedish employees get more holiday than Italian employees.
4 In Ireland, they have less sunshine than in Spain.
5 Portuguese people earn less than French people do.

> **Optional activity**
> Make personalized sentence stems for your students like in exercise 8. You could use things like your city, country, school, etc. Write the beginnings of sentences on the board and ask students to complete them with their own ideas.
> - *The males in this class sleep ...*
> - *The students on the right of the class talk ...*
> - *People in this class do more ...*

Key phrases

9 This exercise clarifies the different uses of linking words and phrases in order to increase cohesion in students' writing.

Highlight the purpose of learning these words and phrases by asking *What helps us to put different ideas together in a paragraph?* (linking words and phrases) *Why are linking words and phrases important?* (to make it easier for the reader to follow your argument / ideas) Draw the table on the board and, before beginning the exercise, ask students to brainstorm any linking words or phrases they already know for the categories given. Ask them to work in pairs to complete the exercise.

ANSWERS

Describing similar ideas	*Also, Likewise,*
Describing different ideas	*By comparison, On the other hand,*
Describing additional ideas	*Also,*
Describing a whole table or chart	*In general,*
Giving details	*To be specific,*
Giving final comments	*In conclusion,*

10 This text provides students with a model of how to use linking words and phrases in their writing to increase cohesion. It also provides a model Writing Task 1 answer. Refer students back to the sub-headings in the table in exercise 9 to encourage them to think about what type of linking word or phrase they need, e.g. in gap 1, you need a word that describes a whole table or chart. Ask students to work alone first before comparing answers in pairs.

ANSWERS

1 In general,
2 To be specific,
3 In contrast,
4 Similarly,
5 Also,
6 In conclusion,

Exam skills

11 This exercise develops students' analysis of data by encouraging them to notice striking similarities and differences.

Before students answer the question, check they are clear about what the bar chart shows. Remind them that they should not describe everything in the data, but instead need to select key information.

ANSWER

In all countries, women have more sleep problems than men. People in South Africa, Vietnam, and Bangladesh have the most sleep problems. Indonesians and Indians have the fewest sleep problems.

12 This example reminds students of the dangers of using linking words and phrases without considering the meaning of what they are writing and, more importantly, for general statements to refer to the whole data set.

Give students 30 seconds to answer the question in pairs. If no one can find the answer, focus their attention on the phrase *in general* and ask:
- *What does 'in general' mean?*
- *What should a general statement describe?*
- *Is this sentence general?*

There is often a tendency for students to overuse new linking words and phrases after learning them, sometimes resulting in meaningless sentences. Remind them that linking words and phrases will only improve cohesion if used appropriately.

ANSWER

The writer is writing a general statement and they have selected an appropriate phrase (*in general*) to introduce the statement but then referred to one specific country.

EXAM TIP 1·22 Before students listen, ask them to suggest possible answers to the question and write these on the board. After they have answered the question, refer students to page 146 for more guidance on how to write about tables.

ANSWER

You should then compare and contrast these pieces of information.

Audioscript 1·22

In Writing Task 1, when you write about tables (and also bar charts or pie charts), look for key similarities and differences between the categories. **You should then compare and contrast these pieces of information.** Remember that you don't have to write about why the data shows what it does, though you may add some interpretation of the data in your conclusion.

Exam practice

13 This exercise provides an opportunity to put together all the skills developed in the lesson.

Alternative for weaker classes: make a detailed plan as a whole class first and write students' ideas on the board. You may also like to allow them to work in pairs. However, make sure that both people are writing.

Time students and even if you allow them to run over 20 minutes, warn them when 10 and 20 minutes have passed so they develop a sense of how long 20 minutes feels.

MODEL ANSWER

See exercise 2 in the WRITING FILE on page 138 of the Student's Book for a model answer.

WRITING FILE Student's Book page 138

Refer students to exercise 3 on this page for another Task 1 question featuring a bar chart, and accompanied by a sample essay.

ANSWERS

See page 00 of this book for answers.

READING Sentence completion page 24

Lesson aims

1 Develop students' ability to understand difficult words in passages using context and identifying parts of speech.
2 Encourage students to scan for technical / scientific words without becoming concerned about the precise meaning.
3 Improve students' ability to recognize suffixes to help identify the part of speech and predict the meaning of the word.

Featured topic vocabulary

Nouns: *drug, supplement, pill, operation, research, discovery, side-effect, condition, enhancement, retina, implant, sickness, medication, medicine*

Verbs: *enhance, implant, treat, collapse*

Adverbs: *temporarily*

Adjectives: *illegally, powerful, inexpensive, guaranteed, available, robotic, blind, short-term*

Topic focus

1 This lead-in engages students with the topic of the reading passage by encouraging debate of moral dilemmas related to medicine.

UNIT 2 HEALTH & MEDICINE

Check any difficult vocabulary as a whole class, and then ask students to discuss the questions in groups of three or four. In whole-class feedback, encourage debate by taking the opposite point of view if necessary.

If you have any food supplements at home, you may like to show them to the class to clarify the meaning of this word. You may need to check the meanings of:
- *acceptable*: OK
- *illegally*: not allowed by law
- *food supplement*: something added to improve your diet
- *intelligent*: clever; the opposite of stupid
- *operation*: the process of cutting open a part of a person's body in order to remove or repair a damaged part.

2 The focus here is using key words to get a general idea of the main topic of the reading passage.

You could remind students of how to read quickly, by asking:
- *What should you look at first to help you?* (title, any pictures, and any subtitles)
- *Should you read every word?* (no)
- *Which words should you focus on?* (content words like nouns and adjectives, not grammar words)

Give students 1 minute to find the answer, and if possible, time it on a clock they can all see. Count to three, and tell them to shout the number of their choice together after three. Ask someone who picked the correct answer to explain which words helped identify the topic.

ANSWER
3

EXAM TIP 1•23 Before students listen, ask them to suggest possible answers to the question and write these on the board. After they have answered the question, refer students to page 148 for more guidance on how to deal with new or difficult words.

ANSWERS
1 start by deciding what part of speech it is
2 use clues in the surrounding text (the 'context')
3 think of an easier word with the same meaning and see if it makes sense in the sentence

Audioscript 1•23
You won't know the meaning of every word in the passages in the Reading test. If you think a new or difficult word is necessary to answer a question, try to guess its meaning. First, **start by deciding what part of speech it is**: a noun or a verb, for example. Then **use clues in the surrounding text (this is called the 'context')** to help you to guess the meaning. Finally, as a check, **think of an easier word with the same meaning and see if it makes sense in the sentence**.

Exam skills

3 This exercise helps students to understand difficult words by training them to first identify what part of speech / word class it belongs to.

Check students know the terms for different parts of speech by writing *I quickly ate the big cake* on the board. Ask students which word is the noun, verb, adjective, and adverb. Label each one as they tell you the answers.

Tell students to work alone before checking with a partner. Encourage them to use the line numbers in brackets to look at the word within the sentence.

Language note: As you check the answers as a whole class, ask students what helped them to know, for example:
- *side-effects*, *retinas*, and *implants* all have plural *-s* on the end
- *-tion* and *-ment* are common noun endings (on the ends of *condition* and *enhancement*)
- *-ly* is a common adverb ending (on the end of *temporarily*). Words around the difficult word can also help to identify what type of word it is, for example:
- *side-effects* is followed by the verbs *can appear*. *Side-effects* is the subject of the verb *can*
- *condition* comes after the word *treat*. *Condition* is the object of this verb
- *temporarily* comes after the words *went blind*, and so *temporarily* describes in what way she went blind
- *enhancement* comes after the word *promising*. *Enhancement* is the object of this verb
- *retinas* comes after the word *new*, which is an adjective, and so describes a noun. It also comes after the verbs *can implant*, and is the object of these
- *implants* comes after the verb *have*, and you need to have *something*. It also follows *eye*, and as the guards will already have eyes, *implants* seems most likely to be another thing connected with the meaning of *eyes*.

ANSWERS
2 noun   5 noun
3 adverb   6 noun
4 noun

4 This exercise encourages students to use the context of a sentence to help predict the meaning of difficult words. This is an important skill in the exam when students will not have dictionaries and will almost certainly face words they do not know.

Ask students to work alone, and remind them of the line numbers in exercise 3 in order to read the words in context. Ask students to check their answers with a partner and show each other which words helped them to understand. In whole-class feedback, focus on how the context suggests the meaning, for example:

Words that help suggest the meaning:
- *side-effects*: dangerous / the example about the girl who ended up in hospital
- *temporarily*: she only spent a short time in hospital (one night)
- *implant*: to help them see in the dark is not natural / the next example is *extra legs*, which is connected to the eye implants by 'or'

- *retinas*: into the eyes
- *condition*: a medicine used to treat / which stops people …
- *enhancement*: usually you promise something good / powerful is more likely to describe something that improves rather than makes worse / the example in the following sentence is positive.

Teaching tip: Remind students they do not need to know all the words in a text, and indeed, are not expected to. It is a more efficient use of time to practise working out the meaning of a word from a sentence, which is a skill they can apply to any new word, rather than just trying to learn as many new words as possible in the hope that one of them comes up in the exam. Encourage students to routinely predict the meaning of new words first whenever they find themselves reaching for their dictionary.

ANSWERS
1 bad
2 short
3 man-made
4 eye
5 problem
6 improved

5 This exercise trains students in the skill of scanning for specific words or phrases.
Help students understand why this is important by asking:
- *Do you read a story the same way as you read the contacts list in your phone when you are looking for a specific number?* (No. You usually scan a list of phone numbers to find the name you want, but you read a story in more detail for enjoyment.)
- *Why is scanning a useful skill in the exam?* (to match questions with the relevant part of the text, and so answer more quickly)
- *Do you need to know what the words mean in order to scan for them?* (no) *Does this stop you understanding the text?* (no). Remind students that these are technical medical words and even some native speakers might not recognize them.
- *Why might Modafinil and Ritalin be easier to find?* (They start with capital letters so should stand out more.) *Why do they start with capital letters?* (They are proper names.) Remind students to look for capital letters to help them find names more quickly in the exam.

Group students in threes or fours. Nominate one score keeper within the group. This person should keep a note of the number of words won by each person. Before checking the answers as a whole class, ask who the winner is in each group.

ANSWERS
13 Modafinil
11 Ritalin
41 muscle atrophy
12 ADHD
28 TDCS
26 strokes
39 anabolic steroids
14 narcolepsy

6 This exercise encourages students to use the context to focus on the general meaning of a word, rather than getting stuck because they do not know the exact meaning.
Students should be familiar with the idea of context from exercises 3 and 4, but they may not know the term. Clarify by asking *What helped you complete exercise 3 and 4?* (other words in the sentence around the difficult word). Do an example as a whole class first. Tell students to find the word *Ritalin* and look at other words around it. Ask which words help (the word *pills* before it and *medicine* after it, which suggest that Ritalin is a treatment). Ask students to complete the exercise alone before checking with a partner. Some students will use the capitalized proper nouns to infer that some are names of treatments but this is also a valid way of using context to infer meaning.

ANSWERS
T: Modafinil, Ritalin, TDCS, anabolic steroids
P: muscle atrophy, ADHD, strokes, narcolepsy

Vocabulary

7 This exercise helps students understand the meaning of new words by recognizing parts of speech by using suffixes.
Check students understand the term *suffixes* by referring back to exercise 3. Ask *What helped you know that 'condition' and 'enhancement' are nouns?* (-tion and -ment). Focus students' attention on the example.

Alternative for weaker classes: allow students to work with a partner to complete the exercise. When checking the answers as a whole class, ask if they know any other examples of words with the same suffixes.

VOCABULARY FILE Student's Book page 122
Refer students to exercises 4–8 for extra practice using suffixes.

ANSWERS
See page 132 of this book for answers.

8 This exercise trains students in sentence completion questions by narrowing the choice of answers to look for a particular part of speech.
Do question 1 as an example as a whole class. Ask *What type of word is 'students'?* (noun). Ask *What type of word often goes together with a noun?* (adjective). Tell students to predict parts of speech for all the questions before checking in the text. To avoid students rushing to the text, stress that the focus of this exercise is not to find the correct answer but to practise predicting the part of speech. You may therefore want to ask them to cover the text while they do the exercise.

ANSWERS
1 adjective (healthy)
2 adjective (focused)
3 plural noun (periods)
4 adverb (only)
5 noun (advances)

Exam practice

9 This exercise provides students with an opportunity to test the skills developed in exercises 3–8. Remind them to think about these tips as they try to find the answers.

Tell students to work alone. Give them 10 minutes and, if possible, time them on a clock which is visible to everyone. Tell them to check their answers with a partner and discuss which words helped them.

ANSWERS
1. used to treat
2. dangerous
3. memories
4. physical power
5. robotic
6. Wearable

What do you think?

10 This exercise consolidates work from the unit by requiring students to identify what part of speech they need and recognizing the parts of speech of the options.

Do question 1 as an example with the whole class, encouraging students to consider what part of speech they need before making their choice. Ask them to complete the exercise alone before checking with a partner.

ANSWERS
1. healthy
2. enhance
3. medication
4. improve
5. legal

11 This exercise gives students a chance to respond personally to the ideas in the reading text. It also helps generate ideas for the types of questions they might face in other parts of the exam.

Encourage students to explain their ideas in as much detail as possible. Set a 10-minute time limit, but allow them to talk for longer if necessary. Monitor particularly for mistakes using the wrong part of speech. Write any examples on the board to correct as a class afterwards. Also write examples of good language on the board.

EXAM CHALLENGE

ANSWERS

Speaking
1–3 Students' own answers

Reading
1. See page 139 of this book for answers.
2. Students' own answers

Listening
1. See page 138 of this book for answers and page 141 for the audioscript.
2. Students' own answers

Writing
1. Students' own answers
2. See page 112 of the Student's Book for the model answer.

UNIT 3   Society & family

Introduction page 27

Featured topic vocabulary

Nouns: *neighbour, poverty, responsibility, grandchild(ren), population, wealth*

Verbs: *care for, leave (home), raise (e.g. children), own*

Adjectives: *parental, criminal*

Optional preparation

Ask students to investigate:
- the age of criminal responsibility in their country
- their country's rank on an income equality table
- what their fathers and grandparents did for them as babies
- what the international definition of poverty is.

Optional lead-in

To introduce students to the topic of the infographic, you might like to do the following:

a Write the beginnings of sentences on one side of the board, and the ends of sentences on the other side, like this:

1 1 in 5 pre-school children are cared for by …	a their neighbours' names.
2 30 is the average age for Italians to …	b 1% of its wealth.
3 51% of people in the UK don't know …	c raising their grandchildren.
4 1% of the world's population owns …	d their fathers while their mothers go to work.
5 50% of the world's population owns …	e 40% of its wealth.
6 38% of grandmothers say they are …	f leave the parental home.

b Before students open their books, ask them to match the beginnings and ends.

c Ask students to open their books and check their answers by reading the infographic.

ANSWERS
1 d   2 f   3 a   4 e   5 b   6 c

What do you think?

Introduce the topic by asking students to match questions 1–5 with the sentence in the infographic to which they refer:

1 1 in 5 pre-school children in the USA are cared for by their fathers while their mothers go to work; 38% of grandmothers say they are raising their grandchildren.
2 51% of people in the UK don't know their neighbours' names.
3 30 is the average age for Italians to leave the parental home.
4 Age of criminal responsibility: 15 in Denmark and 10 in Thailand.
5 1% of the world's population owns 40% of its wealth. 50% owns 1%.

Focus students' attention on the unit title, and check the pronunciation of *society*. Group them in threes to discuss their responses to the questions. When most students have finished discussing all five questions, write on the board any useful vocabulary related to the topic that they used in their answers.

Teaching tip: Students may ask you to clarify the meaning of *committing* (doing) in question 4. However, they should be able to work out the meaning from the sentence. This is an important skill to develop, so encourage them to guess the meaning first. Guide them by asking what type of word it is: noun, verb, or adjective (verb). Ask what verbs they expect to go together with the word *crime* (e.g. *commit*).

Background note: These poverty statistics were published on a website (www.globalpovertyproject.com), but poverty figures vary and depend on definitions of poverty. You may wish to make students aware of the difference between *relative poverty* (a low standard of living compared to others in a country) and *absolute poverty* (a generally unacceptable standard of living). The number in absolute poverty is lower, and in 2010 the World Bank estimated that 400,000 children were living in 'extreme poverty' (under $1.25 a day).

SPEAKING Expressing opinions

EXAM FOCUS: PART 3

Lesson aims
1 Develop students' ability to give reasons for their opinion by making sentences with the structure *it's* + adjective + infinitive with *to*.
2 Enable students to speak about social issues.
3 Enable students to respond to opinion questions by using phrases to agree or disagree.
4 Improve students' use of word stress to sound interested and enthusiastic by varying their intonation.

Key language
Nouns: *housework, responsibility, well-being, (equal) opportunity, custom, income, immigration, law*
Adjectives: *fair, tolerant, valuable, necessary, wrong*

Featured topic vocabulary
Nouns: *survey, attitude, view, commitment, extent*
Verbs: *restrict, obey*

Note: In Speaking Part 3, students will have to respond to challenging questions about the world around them. These can take a variety of forms, several of which are dealt with specifically in unit 8. However, a common type are questions that ask students to take a stance of agreement or disagreement. This type is particularly important in this course because the lessons often invite students to express opinions on issues, so they need to be equipped to deal with this task.

Topic focus
1 This exercise familiarizes students with the types of statements they might be asked to discuss in Speaking Part 3. It also introduces the phrase *to what extent do you agree*, which is often used by the examiner to frame statements as questions in Speaking Part 3. Before students start reading, you may wish to clarify the meanings of:
- *survey*: a list of questions to ask a group of people
- *attitude*: the way people think and how this affects their behaviour
- *view*: opinion
- *to what extent*: how much.

Draw a scale from 0% to 100% on the board to help students understand the phrase: *to what extent*. Write *agree* under 100% and *disagree* under 0%. Then write: *You should choose your job as young as possible*. Ask a strong student to come to the board and place a mark on the scale to show how much they agree. Invite students with different opinions to the one on the board to place a different mark on the scale. After directing them to the instructions, check they understand that they should not complete the survey yet.

Language note: There are many occurrences of the modal verb *should* in this survey. Students of some language backgrounds often insert *to* after *should*. If you hear students doing this, remind them that we never use *to* after modal verbs, such as *can, could, might, may, would*.

ANSWER
d

Vocabulary
2 This exercise provides students with useful topic-related vocabulary to talk about social issues.

Ask students to work in pairs before checking as a whole class.

Alternative for weaker classes: students may need clarification of some words not in bold in the survey before they can complete this exercise. However, encourage them to try to answer first in pairs before explaining any vocabulary (e.g. *society, equal,* and *respect*):
- *society*: people who are all connected, often by nationality
- *equal*: the same
- *respect (a custom)*: follow.

ANSWERS
1	law	5	well-being
2	immigration	6	equal opportunities
3	customs	7	income
4	responsibilities	8	housework

VOCABULARY FILE Student's Book page 123
Refer students to exercises 4 and 5 for extra practice using words related to society and family.

ANSWERS
See page 133 of this book for answers.

3 This exercise prepares students to give their own opinions in exercise 7 by giving them time to reflect on the questions alone before speaking.

Before students begin, draw their attention back to the scale you drew on the board for exercise 1. Check they understand the instructions by writing numbers 1–5 along the scale and asking what each number represents. Ask students to work alone to complete the survey.

Key phrases
4 1·24 This exercise provides students with models of how to respond to opinion questions.

Play the recording as many times as students need, since the main aim is to learn the phrases. As you check the answers, model and drill the pronunciation of each phrase by asking the class to repeat after you.

ANSWERS
a	not	d	don't
b	depends	e	extent
c	definitely	f	of course

---

36 UNIT 3 SOCIETY & FAMILY

Audioscript 1·24

Interviewer: Right, I'd like you to say whether you agree with these statements. Here's the first one: Men shouldn't do housework. Do you agree?
Respondent: No, absolutely **not**. I think it's important to share housework. If men don't help, women won't be able to go to work.
Interviewer: OK. And here's the next statement: Women should be prepared to stop paid work because of family responsibilities. Do you agree with that?
Respondent: Well, it **depends**. It's right for women to have freedom of choice. Of course, that puts more pressure on the man to earn enough to support the family.
Interviewer: OK, fine. The next statement: People should care for the well-being of everyone in society. Do you agree?
Respondent: Yes, **definitely**. It's necessary to protect everyone in society. If we don't, then some people might lose their homes and possessions and commit crimes.
Interviewer: OK. So here's the next one. Should the government reduce differences in income?
Respondent: No, I **don't** think so. Because it's wrong to take money away from people who have worked hard. If we do, rich people might move to a different country.
Interviewer: OK. Almost there. Should there be more controls on immigration?
Respondent: Yes, to some **extent**. It's necessary to welcome people from all countries nowadays, but for immigrants it's difficult to be part of a society that looks very different from theirs. If we welcome a lot of immigrants, we have to help them to integrate.
Interviewer: OK. Here's the last statement: People should never break the law. Do you agree?
Respondent: Yes, **of course** I do! What kind of society would we have if we allowed people to break the law whenever they wanted to?

5 This exercise clarifies the meaning of the phrases and helps students remember them.

Highlight that students should only use each number once. Ask them to work alone before checking with a partner.

ANSWERS
1 No, absolutely not.
2 No, I don't think so.
3 Well, it depends.
4 Yes, to some extent.
5 Yes, of course I do.
6 Yes, definitely.

6 This exercise develops students' ability to respond to opinion questions using phrases to agree and disagree by removing the pressure of thinking of ideas on the spot.

Refer students to the example in the speech bubbles. Focus their attention on the survey in exercise 1 and remind them that they already decided their opinion in exercise 3.

Alternative for weaker classes: give students 2 minutes before speaking to check which phrases from exercise 4 match their survey responses. They then work in pairs to ask and respond. Encourage them to ask *To what extent do you agree that* … at the start of each question, to help familiarize themselves with this phrase.

Alternative 1

If you have enough space in your class, arrange students in a 'ladder' so they change partners:
a Ask students to stand or sit in two lines, facing each other.
b Give them 2 minutes to ask three questions and respond. They can choose the order of questions.
c Then ask one of the lines of students to move down one space. The person at the bottom of the line should move to the top of the line. The other line stays still. Now students should be paired with the person previously standing to their left / right.
c Students ask each other further questions and respond. Then repeat step c.

With confident students, give students on one side of the ladder the interviewer role and to the other side the interviewee role, and ask the interviewees to close their books during the task. Exchange roles halfway through.

Alternative 2

Give each student one question from the survey and ask them to write the three categories on a piece of paper:
N
?
Y
Students then ask all their classmates their question, and keep a tally of responses next to each category. Collect the results and write them on the board next to question numbers 1–8 as follows:
1 Y 5 N 3
2 Y 3 N 7, etc.
Now get students to 'write up' findings in a report for homework. Assist them with some language.
The majority of students think that …

Exam skills

7 This exercise develops students' ability to give reasons for their opinion by making sentences with the structure *it's* + adjective + infinitive with *to*.

Focus students' attention on the example in the speech bubble. Clarify that there is more than one possible answer by asking them to make another sentence with *it's important to*. Students may need help understanding vocabulary such as:

- *valuable*: very important and useful
- *tolerant*: accepting what other people do or say even if you do not agree
- *obey (the rules)*: do what you are told or expected to do
- *restrict*: limit the size or number of something.

Before students begin, model and drill the pronunciation of words you think they might find difficult to say, such as *valuable* and *equality*. In pairs, ask students to take turns to speak.

UNIT 3 SOCIETY & FAMILY

POSSIBLE ANSWERS
It's **difficult** to obey the rules.
It's **good** to be fair.
It's **necessary** to be tolerant.
It's **right** to have freedom of choice.
It's **useful** to help other people.
It's **valuable** to have equality.
It's **wrong** to restrict immigrant numbers.

GRAMMAR FILE Student's Book page 113
Refer students to this page for more explanation and practice of the structure *it's* + adjective + infinitive with *to*.

ANSWERS
See page 130 of this book for answers.

8 This exercise promotes accuracy by focusing on the form of *it's* + adjective + infinitive with *to*.

Ask students to work alone before checking answers with a partner. Emphasize that there are two errors in each sentence by asking how many errors there are in total (eight).

> **Alternative**
> You may like to replace these sentences with examples of the students' own mistakes. You can collect examples of mistakes by listening to them speaking in exercise 8.
> Make this exercise competitive by putting students into four teams and allocating one sentence per team. Ask a representative from each team to write their corrections on the board. Award a point for every correct answer. If an answer is incorrect, the next team should be given a chance to answer, and awarded points accordingly.

ANSWERS
1 Yes, to some extend̶t because **it** isn't good to change tradition.
2 Well, it'̶s depends because it **is** not normal to do that in some cultures.
3 No, I **do** not think so because for women it's important to work̶i̶n̶g̶, too.
4 Yes, definitely, because **it** is necessary for men to be relax**ed** at home. / Yes, definitely, because **it** is necessary for men to b̶e̶ relax at home.

9 This exercise develops students' ability to expand their responses by justifying their opinion using the structure *it's* + adjective + infinitive with *to*.

This exercise builds on the speaking done in exercise 6, so you may like to pair students with a different partner for variety. Focus on the example in the speech bubbles by asking how the candidate justifies his / her response. Refer students back to the phrases in exercise 4 and highlight that they should now combine these with the phrases in exercise 7.

> **Optional activity**
> Ask students to write their own statements on the topic of society and family like those in the survey. Tell them to ask their partner *To what extent do you agree that …* followed by their statement. Their partner should respond.

10 1·25 This exercise raises students' awareness of the importance of word stress to sound interested and enthusiastic.

After listening, ask students to discuss their answer in pairs before checking as a class.

ANSWER
Student B sounds more interested because student B has a lively voice with strong intonation and stress.

Audioscript 1·25
Interviewer: Do you think the government should reduce differences in income?
A: Well, it depends. It's important to be fair, but I think it's difficult to have complete income equality.
B: Well, it depends. It's important to be fair, but I think it's difficult to have complete income equality.

11 1·26 This exercise improves students' use of word stress to sound interested and enthusiastic by copying a model.

Focus students' attention on the use of word stress by asking which sounds they hear most strongly. Get them to copy the pronunciation as a whole class and then in smaller groups, to check if they are doing it successfully.

Audioscript 1·26
Well, it depends. It's important to be fair, but I think it's difficult to have complete income equality.

Exam practice

EXAM TIP 1·27 Before students listen, ask them to suggest possible answers to the question and write these on the board. After they have answered the question, refer students to page 145 for more guidance on how to sound enthusiastic.

ANSWER
You could try to imagine you're talking with a friend.

Audioscript 1·27
Sounding enthusiastic can help you to get a better mark for pronunciation because your intonation and word stress will be more varied. However, it's not always easy to do this, especially when the examiner is looking down and taking notes. **Try to imagine you're talking with a friend** instead!

12 Students have a chance here to combine all the skills developed in this lesson by responding to some questions of the kind that may be found in Speaking Part 3.

Before students begin, recap what has been studied in this lesson by writing on the board: *What have we learnt to help us speak better in Speaking Part 3?* Encourage students to look back over the lesson in their books. Ask them for their ideas and write these on the board.

LISTENING Understanding agreement page 30

EXAM FOCUS: SECTION 3

Lesson aims

1 Enable students to answer multiple-choice questions by analysing incorrect options.
2 Enable students to answer matching questions by familiarizing students with the instructions.
3 Improve students' ability to recognize agreement and disagreement by focusing on phrases showing varying degrees of agreement.
4 Develop students' ability to manage their study time.

Featured topic vocabulary

Adjectives to describe personality: *sociable, lazy, adventurous, courageous, hard-working, caring, relaxed, fun-loving, responsible, moody, creative, easy-going, funny, generous, clever, shy*
Nouns: *sibling, celebrity*
Verbs: *avoid, compete, admire*

Topic focus

1 This lead-in encourages students to engage with the context of the conversation they will hear in exercise 2. It also provides them with vocabulary to talk about the topic of family.

Before students speak in pairs, you may like to check meanings by asking the questions below as a whole class. You could also drill the pronunciation as you check the meaning of each one. For any words students have difficulty pronouncing, you can mark the stress on the board by drawing a circle above the stressed syllable. The stressed syllable is marked in bold below

- *so**cia**ble*: *Does this person prefer to stay at home alone or go out with friends?* (go out with friends)
- *la**zy***: *Does this person work hard?* (no)
- *ad**ven**turous*: *What type of holidays does an adventurous person go on?* (e.g. climbing mountains)
- *hard-**wor**king*: *What's the opposite?* (lazy)
- *ca**ring***: *Does a caring person think more about others or about themselves?* (others)
- *re**lax**ed*: *Does this type of person get stressed easily?* (no)
- *fun-**lo**ving*: *Does this type of person prefer to read a book or go to the beach with friends?* (go to the beach with friends)
- *res**pon**sible*: *Does this type of person call if they are going to be late?* (yes) *Does this type of person spend lots of money shopping even if they don't have much?* (no) *Can you leave your children with this type of person to look after them?* (yes)
- *moo**dy***: *Does this type of person show few emotions or lots of emotions?* (lots) *Is it a good thing or bad thing?* (bad) *Why?* (Because you never know what to expect)
- *cre**a**tive*: *What kind of things are creative people sometimes good at?* (e.g. painting, design, writing, cooking)
- *easy-**go**ing*: *Is this type of person relaxed or stressed?* (relaxed)
- *fu**nny***: *What effect does this person have on you?* (makes you laugh / smile)
- *ge**ne**rous*: *Does this person share their money or food?* (yes) *Are they happy to share?* (yes)
- *cle**ver***: *What's the opposite?* (unintelligent or stupid)
- *shy*: *Does this person find it easy to talk to strangers at a party?* (no)

VOCABULARY FILE Student's Book page 123
Refer students to exercises 8 and 9 for extra practice using these adjectives.

ANSWERS
See page 133 of this book for answers.

2 🔊 1·28 This exercise aims to improve students' recognition of agreement and disagreement by first checking their general understanding of the conversation before focusing on the specific language (in exercise 3).

Ask students to compare their answers in pairs before checking as a whole class.

ANSWER
They agree on some things but not on others.

Audioscript 1·28, 1·29
A: I think older siblings have more fun.
B: I don't **know** about that. They often have to help look after younger children.
A: That's **true**, so I suppose that makes them a bit more responsible.
B: Definitely!
A: Er, OK. I also think older siblings tend to be brighter – you know, more clever academically.
B: I agree to **some** extent. Apparently, Einstein was the oldest child! But I think younger siblings are probably more creative.
A: Yes, I think so, **too**. And more adventurous, perhaps.
B: Really? I **disagree**. I think older siblings are better at leading and doing more courageous things.
A: Hmm, that's **partly** right, but then I think sometimes parents are usually more relaxed about second children and let them go out more.

Key phrases

3 🔊 1·29 This exercise provides a closer examination of the language used by the speakers to agree and disagree. The aim is to improve students' ability to recognize these different positions in a conversation.

Ask students to predict what might fill the gaps before listening again. If they have already studied the speaking lesson in this unit, they should be able to predict some of the words easily. Play the recording as many times as necessary. Direct students to the audioscript to check their answers. Drill the phrases by modelling them and asking students to repeat as a whole class.

ANSWERS
1 know
2 disagree
3 some
4 partly
5 true
6 Definitely
7 too

4 By using the phrases for agreeing and disagreeing, students have an opportunity here to become more familiar with the language from exercise 3. It also allows them to recycle the vocabulary from exercise 1.

Direct students to the example. Encourage them to use the vocabulary from exercise 1 in their statements, and to use phrases from exercise 3 in their responses. Demonstrate with a strong student by asking him/her to respond to an example statement of your own.

Alternative for weaker classes: ask the two strongest students to demonstrate together.

Exam skills

5 This exercise raises students' awareness of how much information can be understood from the questions before listening. It trains them to focus on piecing together an overall picture of the context, rather than spending too long on individual questions.

If students are unsure of the answer, guide them to the clue (see the answer below) to help.

ANSWER
The conversation will be about a lecture – *next lecture* provides a clue.

EXAM TIP 🔊 1·30 Before students listen, ask them to suggest possible answers to the question and write these on the board. After they have answered the questions, refer students to page 146 for more guidance on how to approach Listening Section 3.

ANSWER
The conversation takes place in an academic environment. The speakers often express different opinions.

Audioscript 1·30

In Listening Section 3, you hear two or three speakers. **The conversation takes place in an academic environment** – for example. a university classroom or lecture hall. But it can also take place anywhere 'on campus' – that means the university grounds – such as in a sports centre or student café. **The speakers often express different opinions** and you may be tested on how well you understand any disagreements.

6 🔊 1·31 This exercise improves students' ability to choose the correct multiple-choice answer by disqualifying incorrect options.

Check students understand they are only going to hear the answer to question 1 at this point. Ask how they chose the correct answer to clarify they did not hear the correct answer, but were able to find it anyway by eliminating incorrect options.

ANSWER
1 A

Audioscript 1·31

Isabella: I thought Professor Greene's lecture today was interesting.
Simon: Yes. I don't think I've ever really thought about why me and my older brothers are different.
Isabella: Hmm. The new research he mentioned into older siblings was really fascinating.
Simon: Yeah, but I'm not sure I understood the idea. I thought that part of the lecture was very difficult. He said that babies who are born first are cleverer, didn't he?
Isabella: I don't think so. They achieve higher scores in intelligence tests than their younger siblings, but only when they're eighteen, **so they seem to become cleverer later**.
Simon: Hmm. So is that because they get all the attention from their parents before their brother or sister is born?
Isabella: No, Professor Greene said that can't be right, because at twelve years of age the younger siblings do better in intelligence tests. So that means that younger siblings …

7 This exercise helps students understand how incorrect answers can seem correct by recognizing the 'trap' of speakers contradicting each other, which is designed to distract.

Ask students to discuss in pairs before checking as a whole class. Ask them to tell you the exact phrase used to contradict, and write it on the board.

Alternative for weaker classes: listen to the recording again to allow students who did not hear the contradiction the first time to try again.

ANSWER
Option B is not correct because the research says that eldest siblings achieve higher scores in intelligence tests *only when they're eighteen, so they seem to become cleverer later*. Also, the research goes on to say that *at twelve years of age, younger siblings do better in intelligence tests*.

Exam practice

8 1·32 This exercise provides students with an opportunity to test the skills developed in exercises 6 and 7.

Play the recording more than once if necessary, but remind students they will hear it only once in the exam. Ask them to compare and justify their answers in pairs before checking as a whole class. Help students to correct mistakes in their answers by reading aloud relevant parts of the audioscript as necessary.

ANSWERS
2 A   3 C   4 A

Audioscript 1·32

Simon: Oh, right. So what was the reason, then?
Isabella: Well, he thinks it's because older children teach their brothers and sisters.
Simon: But I don't get it. Shouldn't the youngest learn more, then?
Isabella: No, because when you teach something, it improves your thinking. It's good for your brain.
Simon: Right. OK. I think I need to go and look at the research! Did Professor Greene say there were copies of the report available in the library?
Isabella: Yes. There's a copy of the research in the social sciences section, I think.
Simon: What, in the main library?
Isabella: No, **in the faculty library**, next door.
Simon: Everyone'll try to borrow that copy!
Isabella: Well, don't forget you can access an electronic copy online. Have you registered with the journals website?
Simon: Yeah. Hope I can remember my password!
Isabella: You have to look in a journal called *Science*.
Simon: OK, I'll make a note of that, but did he say it's available in *Intelligence*, too?
Isabella: Oh, yes. I think so.
Simon: OK. So, are you going to **Wednesday**'s lecture on attachment theory?
Isabella: Definitely, but first there's the lecture tomorrow on infant development. We have to attend that for our research.
Simon: You're right, I forgot. What time's that lecture?
Isabella: Oh, I can't remember. Eleven, perhaps?
Simon: Hold on. I'll check in the timetable. Yeah, you're right … and it finishes at twelve fifteen.

Exam skills

9 This exercise aims to familiarize students with the rubric of matching questions, which can sometimes appear confusing at first.

Check students understand by writing the names *Isabella* and *Simon* on the board. Put a tick under Isabella and a cross under Simon, and ask what letter they should write in the exam (I). Do the same with:
- crosses under both (N)
- ticks under both (B)
- a cross under Isabella and tick under Simon (S).

If students find this technique helpful, suggest they could do this in the exam by writing ticks and crosses as they are listening. Remind them they must then translate the result into the correct letter.

ANSWER
You have to write a letter.

10 1·33 This exercise aims to build students' confidence in their ability to answer matching questions by focusing on only one question first.

Check students understand they are only going to hear the answer to question 5 at this point. If necessary, clarify that this is for practice purposes only. In the exam there will not be a break like this. Play the recording as many times as necessary.

ANSWER
5 I

Audioscript 1·33

Simon: So, Isabella, you're the oldest child in your family. Would you say you're more intelligent than your brother?
Isabella: Well, me and my brother are both students, but … he went to a better university so **I think he's cleverer**.
Simon: Really? I don't think you can say that. Perhaps he's at a better university because he studies harder …

11 This exercise encourages students to verbalize the mental process of disqualifying incorrect options, and so raises their awareness of how to arrive at one choice.

Monitor to listen for a student with the correct answer who is able to explain their choice clearly. Ask this student to share their explanation with the whole class.

POSSIBLE ANSWER
Isabella thinks that her brother is cleverer than her – she says *he went to a better university so I think he's cleverer*.

Exam practice

12 1·34 This exercise provides students with an opportunity to test the skills developed in exercises 9–11.

Remind students of the instructions by asking if they should write *I* and *S* if Isabella and Simon agree (no, they should write *B* for both).

Play the recording more than once if necessary, but remind students they will hear it only once in the exam. Ask them to compare and justify their answers in pairs before checking as a whole class. Help students to correct mistakes in their answers by reading aloud relevant parts of the audioscript as necessary.

ANSWERS
6 B   7 N   8 S   9 N

Audioscript 1·34

Simon: So, Isabella, you're the oldest child in your family. Would you say you're more intelligent than your brother?

Isabella: Well, me and my brother are both students but … he went to a better university so **I think he's cleverer.**

Simon: Really? **I don't think you can say that.** Perhaps he's at a better university because he studies harder.

Isabella: Yes, but **I think you can become more intelligent if you study hard, like the research said.**

Simon: Yes, that's true. Anyway, I think you're probably as clever as him, but you're intelligent in different ways.

Isabella: I don't think so, but I'm definitely better at choosing clothes!

Simon: So why don't you study as hard as him?

Isabella: I think it's because **I'm just not that interested in studying, and my family don't expect me to be successful.**

Simon: I have a different theory. **I think younger children choose to do different things from their siblings** because they don't want to compete with them.

Isabella: Hmm. **Maybe that's true for a few people,** but I know lots of siblings who do similar hobbies. Anyway, I think **there are other things that affect your behaviour a lot more – parents, for example.** I think if your parents go to a good university, you will, too.

Simon: OK. I think **I agree with you there.** Oh, by the way, I meant to ask you about your notes from last week's lecture …

What do you think?

13 This exercise encourages students to reflect on the topic of society and family by expanding on the ideas discussed in the recordings.

Focus students' attention on the example to help them begin. Direct them to the words in the box, and as a whole class, ask if anyone can think of another example. Then ask students to discuss in pairs and remind them to explain the answers as fully as possible.

If necessary, clarify the meaning of *admire* (respect somebody for what they are or for what they have done) by giving an example of a celebrity your students are likely to know, and explaining why you admire them. Check understanding by asking students who they admire and why.

Optional activity

To turn this into a competition, do the following:

a Divide students into teams and provide them with A3 paper to brainstorm ideas for each factor. They only need to write notes on the paper, not full sentences.

b Give the teams 10 minutes to think of as many ideas as possible.

c Ask a representative from each team to explain their ideas to the class. Give each representative 2 minutes to speak.

d Award a point for each idea which no other group has got. Do this by telling the class to listen carefully to each representative as they speak. When they finish, ask if any other group had the same idea, and ask to see their note on the paper to prove it.

Study skills

This exercise aims to improve students' time management by considering different approaches to self-study and encouraging them to share their experiences.

Tell students to read alone, and then group them in threes or fours to discuss.

In whole-class feedback you might like to consider raising the issues below with each statement:

Suggested questions to prompt discussion	POSSIBLE ANSWERS
1 Are there any disadvantages of only focusing on vocabulary?	You need to develop skills as well as just improve vocabulary knowledge. There are many areas which contribute to exam success, such as being familiar with the exam format, and answering within the time limits.
2 Why is it important to study after class?	You can focus on your individual weaknesses. You can consolidate class work by revising and reviewing.
3 What are the disadvantages of leaving it until the last minute to start studying hard?	You put yourself under too much pressure. Improvement takes time.
4 Why is it important to take a break?	It's better to make sure the time you dedicate to studying is quality time by being fresh and alert, rather than tired and bored. Doing a little often can be more effective than working too hard in one session.

You could also ask students for possible solutions to these problems, e.g. making a self-study timetable, keeping a self-study journal, working with a friend, setting achievable goals, using a reward system of 'treats' based on achieving goals.

WRITING Analysing essay questions (page 32)

EXAM FOCUS: TASK 2

Lesson aims
1 Enable students to analyse Task 2 essay questions to identify what type of essay they should write by familiarizing them with different instructions.
2 Develop students' ability to write an effective introduction to an essay by including a background statement and thesis statement.
3 Improve students' understanding of thesis statements.
4 Improve students' use of synonyms and similar phrases in background statements to avoid repeating the essay question.

Featured topic vocabulary
Parts of an essay: *background statement, thesis statement, topic sentences, supporting sentences, conclusion*

Nouns: *consequence, decade, lack (of), unemployment, population, purpose, evidence, progress*

Verbs: *entertain, support, shoot up*

Topic focus

1 This exercise enables students to reflect on their previous experiences of essay writing. It also provides a springboard for discussion about essay writing to show how much they already know.

Students may need clarification of some vocabulary in the question, such as:
- *purpose*: the intention, aim, or function of something
- *entertain*: to interest or amuse someone in order to please them
- *support*: to help to show that something is true
- *evidence*: facts, signs, or objects that make you believe something is true.

ANSWERS
1 F 2 T 3 T

2 This exercise raises students' awareness of the different parts of an essay that make up the overall structure.

Students are unlikely to know all the terms in the box, but there are lots of clues in the definitions.

Alternative for weaker classes: tell students to work in pairs and encourage them to try even if they do not recognize the terms. Explain that doing the exercise will help them understand.

It is important that students follow a clear structure in their essay writing. For some students this may be a new skill they need to develop, depending on their educational background.

ANSWERS
1 supporting sentence(s)
2 topic sentence(s)
3 conclusion
4 background statement
5 thesis statement

3 This exercise helps students understand how the different parts of an essay fit together. It also provides them with a model structure to aim for in their own writing.

Focus students' attention on the diagram and ask how many colours there are (five) to highlight the fact that each colour matches one definition. Ask them to work alone before checking with a partner.

This is a useful diagram for students to refer back to after writing their own essays to check if their structure is clear.

ANSWERS
orange	background statement
green	thesis statement
grey	topic sentence(s)
blue	supporting sentence(s)
pink	conclusion

Exam skills

4 This exercise enables students to analyse essay questions by identifying the purpose of the different parts of the question.

Focus students' attention on numbers 1–3 in the question to highlight that a–c should match 1–3. If necessary, remind them of the meaning of *To what extent do you agree* by referring them back to exercise 1 of the speaking lesson.

ANSWERS
a 3 *To what extent do you agree?*
b 1 women doing jobs that men used to do
c 2 whether women doing jobs that men used to do is beneficial to society

5 This exercise familiarizes students with the types of questions and range of topics they could be asked in Task 2.

Before students read the essay questions, focus on the photos and discuss what they show. Then ask students to complete the exercise alone before checking with a partner.

Note that photo C shows someone looking at job adverts. In many countries, these types of adverts can be found in job centres designed specifically for unemployed people or in the offices of recruitment agencies.

ANSWERS
1 B 2 A 3 D 4 C

6 This exercise provides students with an opportunity to practise the skill developed in exercise 4 of analysing essay questions. It also helps them to isolate the instruction part of the question, in preparation for exercise 7.

Refer students back to exercise 4 to help them identify the different parts. When checking the answers, clarify vocabulary if necessary, such as:

UNIT 3 SOCIETY & FAMILY 43

- *significant*: large or important enough to have an effect or be noticed
- *progress*: the process of improving or developing
- *rapid*: quick
- *unemployment*: not having a job.

ANSWERS

1 topic: increased tourism
issue: whether increased tourism, and its effect on traditional society, has brought progress
instruction: Do you agree? Give reasons for your answer.

2 topic: living alone
issue: the effects of living alone and whether technology has replaced the need for living together
instruction: Discuss

3 topic: population growth in the last 50 years
issue: what governments can do to solve the problem of high unemployment levels due to population growth over the last 50 years
instruction: What can governments do to solve this problem? (implies discussion and suggestion)

4 topic: unemployment
issue: what governments can do to provide jobs and income for everyone
instruction: To what extent do you agree?

7 This exercise focuses students on the variety of question types in Task 2, and encourages them to analyse the instruction part of the question carefully.

Ask students to discuss in pairs before checking ideas as a whole class. As they are discussing, you may like to write the instruction part of each question on the board so you can refer to it more easily. If students have difficulty identifying the differences, ask them guiding questions, such as:
- *Which question asks for both sides of an argument?* (2)
- *Which question asks you to make suggestions?* (3)
- *Which questions ask you to give your own opinion?* (1 and 4)

ANSWERS

Both questions 1 and 4 require students to say whether they agree with the issue. Question 1 specifies that the students must give reasons for their answer, while question 4 asks students to say *to what extent* they agree. Questions 2 and 3 do not ask the student if they agree or not but ask them to write about what other groups of people think. Question 3 does not require students to give a single view or to discuss others' views. It requires them to give several suggestions.

EXAM TIP 1·35 Ask students what the three parts are (topic, issue, and instruction). Before they listen, take a vote on each part. Ask a few students to justify their answer. After they have answered the question, refer students to page 147 for more guidance on the parts of an essay question.

ANSWER

The instruction. If you ignore or misunderstand the instruction, then you won't answer the question properly and you'll get a low mark.

Audioscript 1·35

There are three main parts to an essay question – each of which has a different function. First, the main topic gives the general area to discuss. Second, the issue tells you how you should discuss it, for example, looking at what should be done. Third and probably most important, **the instruction** tells you what type of essay you actually need to write, for example, to show agreement or disagreement. **If you ignore or misunderstand the instruction, then you won't answer the question properly and you'll get a low mark.**

8 This exercise develops students' ability to identify what type of essay the instructions require them to write. It also provides them with more examples of how the question may be worded.

Ask students to work alone before checking their answers with a partner.

Teaching tip: Students often rush into answering the essay question as soon as they recognize the topic. This causes them to write generally about the topic instead of building a structured essay. Explain the importance of answering the question they are given, rather than the question they wish they had been given!

ANSWERS

1 b 2 c 3 a

Optional activity

Ask students to find another essay question example by using their mobile internet devices or an available practice test book. They could also use essay questions they find in the writing lessons from other units in the book. They should then decide which category the question falls into. Note that some questions students find may give more than one instruction and so be possible to put in two categories. They may also find instructions worded differently from the examples given in this lesson, but all questions should fit into the categories.

9 This exercise provides an opportunity for both you and your students to see what they are already capable of writing, and acts as a starting point to improve on.

Before starting to write, refer students back to exercise 2. Ask what they should include in their introduction (background statement and thesis statement). Then refer students to exercise 8 and ask what type of instructions are in question 1 (you must present two opposing sides of an argument). Give them about 5 minutes to write alone. As students are writing, go around and collect examples of good sentences you can share with the class in feedback.

Alternative for weaker classes: allow students to work in pairs. However, both students should still write. If you think this may still be too difficult for your class, work together as a whole class to write an introduction for question 1. Then ask students to write an introduction for question 2 in pairs.

> **POSSIBLE ANSWER**

Economic and technological developments have meant that more and more people have the means to travel – both in terms of the money to do so and access to appropriate transport, such as cheaper flights. Although this has opened up worldwide progress, because people can learn from one another's societies, this progress has sometimes meant that traditional ways of life have been lost or irrevocably altered. In my opinion, the loss of variety and richness of traditional customs and values and so on is not always justified by the progress made.

10 This exercise develops students' ability to write an effective introduction by helping them notice the gaps in their own writing that they need to improve.

When students have finished, group them in threes or fours to compare the types of differences between their introduction and the model.

You may want to point out that just because their introduction is different from the model, it does not necessarily mean their writing is worse.

11 This exercise improves students' ability to write background statements by focusing on the use of synonyms and similar phrases. This helps them avoid repeating the essay question.

Students may need clarification of the word *synonym* (a word that has the same meaning as another, e.g. *difficult* and *hard*). Remind students of the meaning of *background statement* by referring them back to exercises 2 and 3. Highlight that the number of each group of words refers to the same number essay question in exercise 5.

Teaching tip: Explain to students that they will not be given credit for words copied directly from the question. However, words with similar meanings do not always fit into a sentence in the same way because they may not be the same part of speech, e.g. the adjective *increased* (became greater in size, degree, or amount) in question 1 and the noun *rise* (an increase in an amount, a number, or a level). If students ask about this, explain that using synonyms often requires changing the sentence structure, and they will have a chance to practise this in the next exercise.

> **ANSWERS**

1 impact on = *effect on*
  rise = *increase*
2 are concerned = *worry about*
  numerous = *many*
  individuals = *people, others*
  consequences = *effects of*
3 number of people = *population*
  five decades = *50 years*
  shot up = *growth has been rapid*
  past = *last*
4 a number of = *many*
  issues = *problems*
  leads to = *causes*

12 This exercise provides students with practice using synonyms and similar phrases to write background statements by adapting essay questions, rather than copying.

Focus students' attention on the synonyms and similar phrases in exercise 11. Explain that the structure of the sentence may need to be changed in order to use some synonyms, as in sentence 1. Do this as a whole-class example before students complete the exercise in pairs.

> **ANSWERS**

1 rise, impact on
2 Numerous individuals are concerned, consequences
3 number of people, shot up, past five decades
4 leads to a number of issues

> **Optional activity**
>
> Ask one student to come to the front of the class and sit with their back to the board. Write a thesis statement on the board from other sample essays. Take these from the Writing File in the back of the book, or create your own. Tell the other students they have to get their classmate to say the sentence on the board but they must not say the words on the board. Encourage them to use synonyms to paraphrase the words.

13 This exercise provides students with useful models of thesis statements. It also highlights the importance of analysing the question type in order to write a clear thesis statement.

Remind students of the meaning of *thesis statement* by referring them back to exercises 2 and 3. Help them understand how they can choose their thesis statement by referring them back to exercise 7.

> **ANSWERS**

a 2   b 1   c 4   d 3

14 This exercise focuses students on the language they can use in their thesis statement.

Ask students to discuss in pairs before checking as a whole class. Highlight that they need to choose their language carefully in the thesis statement to accurately reflect their essay.

> **ANSWERS**

Thesis statements b and c include the writer's opinion. In b the word that shows this is *argue*, as in *argue that the change is actually progress*, while in c the word that shows this is *suggest*, as in *suggest that it is the responsibility of individuals, not governments*.

Exam practice

15 Students have a chance here to put together all the skills developed in this lesson by applying them to new questions.

Before students start writing, prepare them by guiding them through the skills developed in this lesson. Focus on question 1 and ask:

- *What is the topic, issue, and instruction?* (topic = rise in people living alone, issue = causing negative changes, instruction = to what extent do you agree)

- *What does the instruction mean?* (You must give your opinion and reasons for it.)
- *What synonyms can replace words in the question?* (e.g. rise = increase, alone = on their own / by themselves, negative changes = damaging / impacting negatively)
- *What verb will you use in your thesis statement?* (This essay will argue …)

Ask students to consider the same questions alone in relation to question 2. Give them about 10 minutes to write.

Teaching tip: The two questions here relate respectively to the topics in the reading and listening lessons in this unit. Of course, students do not need to *answer* a question in the introduction and so they do not need to have knowledge of these lessons in order to write either introduction. However, teachers may use the lesson connection to build a sense of cohesion between lessons, either to refer forward to the next lesson or review a previous lesson. If you want students to attempt the whole essay, e.g. as homework, then you may wish to give them the texts in the listening and reading lessons so they can gather some ideas.

MODEL ANSWERS
See exercise 2 in the WRITING FILE on page 141 of the Student's Book for model answers.

WRITING FILE Student's Book page 141
Refer students to exercise 3 on this page for another personal opinion question, accompanied by a sample essay.

READING Short answer questions page 34

Lesson aims
1 Develop students' ability to scan a passage to find information quickly by identifying key words in the questions and recognizing synonyms.
2 Improve students' understanding of expressions with prepositions by raising their awareness of the variety of prepositional phrases in English.

Key language
Expressions with prepositions: *reliant on, dependent on, thanks to, because of, impact on, effect on, resulting in, leading to, satisfied with, happy about, worried about, concerned about*

Featured topic vocabulary
Nouns: *bill, household, rubbish, rate, proportion, widow, consumer*
Verb: *consume*

Topic focus

Optional lead-in
You could introduce the topic by doing the following:
a Ask one student to come to the board. Point to the phrase *getting married* in your book and ask them to draw a picture on the board to represent this.
b Tell the class that the picture is about something to do with becoming an adult. Ask the other students to guess the phrase.
c When students have guessed correctly, ask for another volunteer. Do the same with the phrases *paying your own bills* and *starting work*.

1 This lead-in engages students with the topic of independence, which is the focus of the reading passage which follows.

You may like to check students understand the word *bills* (pieces of paper that show how much you owe somebody for goods or services) by asking them for examples (electricity, water, phone, internet bills, etc.). Check they understand the question by demonstrating with a strong student. Encourage them to give as much detail in their answers as possible. Group students in threes or fours to discuss and then share ideas as a whole class.

Exam skills

2 Underlining the key words helps students identify what words to scan for to find the relevant part of a text. This improves their time management in the exam by making their reading more efficient.

Check that students understand the concept of scanning. Show them an image of a security scanner and write the word *scanner* on the board. Ask them if the security staff hear the alarm when *every* piece of luggage passes it or only when certain things are in the luggage. Tell them the skill of scanning is the same – it involves reading when you already know what you are looking for.

Give students 2 minutes to work alone before checking as a whole class. It is possible some students will prefer to underline more key words than others, but encourage them not to underline too many, or the highlighted words will no longer stand out. Brainstorm similar words or phrases as a whole class and write their ideas on the board. If they cannot think of any, then tell students you will come back to this after reading.

POSSIBLE ANSWERS
1 percentage, alone, Sweden
2 percentage, alone, USA, 2012
3 living with their children, less than, 100 years ago
4 How much rubbish, living alone, each year

EXAM TIP 1·36 Before students listen, ask them to read the first sentence of the tip and see if they can think of daily reading activities when they would scan for information. Write their suggestions on the board. Then focus their attention on the question in the tip and ask for answers. After they have answered the question, refer students to page 148 for more guidance on scanning.

ANSWER
Any question type that requires students to look for specific information such as a word, number, or name. (The multiple-choice and gap-fill question types from the reading lessons in units 1 and 2 are good examples.)

Audioscript 1·36
Scanning is a reading strategy you can use when **looking for specific information such as a word, number, or name**. It's common in real life – think about how you scan a TV guide to see what's on at a certain time, the sports results to look for your favourite team, or a timetable to see when a train or bus is due to leave. It's also useful for questions requiring short answers in the Reading test.

3 This exercise develops students' ability to scan a text to find short answer information quickly.

Before reading alone, clarify students' understanding of scanning as a whole class by asking:
- *Do you need to read every word of the text?* (no)
- *Are you trying to understand the overall meaning of the whole text?* (no)
- *What should you scan for to answer question 1?* (A percentage and Sweden. Remember the capital letter should help it stand out.).

Give students 2 minutes to find the answers, and put them under pressure by timing them. Check answers as a whole class.

ANSWERS
1 47%
2 11%
3 elderly American widows
4 1,600 kilograms

4 This exercise highlights the importance of recognizing synonyms to answer questions

Compare students' predictions of synonyms on the board from exercise 2 to the words in the text. If they were unable to think of any at the beginning, ask them now to look for words with the same meaning as the key words. Remind students of the work on synonyms they did in the writing lesson.

Exam practice
5 This exercise provides students with an opportunity to practise the scanning skills developed in exercises 2–4.

Before turning to the text, remind students of the skills developed in exercise 2 by asking them to underline key words in the questions and to think of other words or phrases that mean the same.

If students ask about the meaning of words in questions they do not recognize, encourage them to try and guess the meaning from the sentence. Remind them that you will not be there to help them in the exam!

ANSWERS
1 40%
2 good jobs
3 luxuries
4 one-person households
5 gas
6 a four-person household

6 This exercise encourages students to reflect on how the skills developed in this lesson can help them find information more quickly.

After discussing in pairs, check students' ideas as a whole class. Highlight the importance of the time constraint in the exam to help them understand the benefit of reading efficiently.

POSSIBLE ANSWERS
1 Students' own answers
2 1 *Sweden has more people living on their own than anywhere in the world, with 47% of households having one person; followed by Norway at 40%.* (paragraph A)
   2 *As far as the younger generation is concerned, many are unable to find good jobs* (paragraph B)
   3 *The explanation is perhaps that they are prepared to do without 'luxuries'* (paragraph B)
   4 *one-person households are the biggest consumers of energy, land, and household goods (e.g. washing machines, TVs, etc.)* (paragraph E)
   5 *61% more gas* (paragraph E)
   6 *in four-person households each person produces 1,000 kilograms of waste annually* (paragraph E)
3 Students' own answers

Vocabulary

7 The focus here is on improving students' understanding of expressions with prepositions.

Do question 1 as a whole-class example before asking students to work alone. Tell them to compare their answers with a partner, and then check as a whole class.

Teaching tip: Choosing the correct preposition can be particularly difficult for speakers of languages like French, Spanish, and Italian because the preposition often translates differently. If your students have difficulty with this, encourage them to start a list of examples of phrases with each preposition.

ANSWERS
1 reliant on
2 thanks to
3 impact on
4 resulting in
5 satisfied with
6 worried about

VOCABULARY FILE Student's Book page 123
Refer students to exercises 1–3, 6, and 7 for extra practice using expressions with prepositions.

ANSWERS
See pages 132–133 of this book for answers.

8 This exercise gives students an opportunity to practise using the prepositional phrases here to help them learn the phrases.

When students have finished, ask them to check their own answers by referring back to the phrases in italics in the text. This gives them extra exposure to the phrases to help remember them.

> **Optional activity**
> Put students in pairs with one student in each pair facing the board and the other looking in the opposite direction. Then write the answers on the board. Ask the student who's looking at the board to read the questions but stop at the gap. They don't continue until the other student has given them the correct preposition.

ANSWERS
1 with 2 on 3 about 4 to 5 to 6 on

What do you think?

9 These questions encourage students to engage with the text to generate ideas on the topic of society and family. They could then use these ideas in their speaking and writing.

When students have finished speaking, pair them with a new partner. Ask them to summarize the main points of their discussions with their previous partner.

EXAM CHALLENGE

ANSWERS

Speaking
1 & 2 Students' own answers

Reading
1 See page 139 of this book for answers.
2 Students' own answers

Listening
1 See page 137 of this book for answers and page 141 for the audioscript.
2 Students' own answers

Writing
1 Students' own answers
2 See page 108 of the Student's Book for the model introduction.

UNIT 4 Population & the environment

Introduction (page 37)

Featured topic vocabulary
Nouns: *temperature, air pollution, public transport, biodiversity, restoration, statistic*
Adjectives: *environmental, green (meaning environmentally friendly)*

Optional lead-in
To prepare, bring pictures into class of your town or city in the past, or encourage students to find images on their mobile devices. First, focus their attention on the before and after images of Seoul and ask them what has happened. Elicit the sentence:
The government has created green spaces.
(Elicit the present perfect by asking if we know when the change took place and if we can see the result now.) Now focus students' attention on the statistics below the main image and ask *What are the results?* Elicit:
Pollution has decreased.
Use of public transport / biodiversity has increased.
Air temperatures have fallen.
Ask students how their town or city has changed over the past 50 years. Encourage them to use the present perfect to express changes and effects. Write their ideas on the board and ask if it is more or less environmentally friendly now.

What do you think?
Put students in pairs or threes to discuss the questions.
Teaching tip: The answers to questions 4 and 5 depend on students' own towns or cities. If you are not familiar with these issues, you may like to find out some information before the class by checking on the internet or asking other teachers in the school.

Optional activity
In a class with students of mixed backgrounds, question 4 could be expanded into a research project. Students could then report their findings to the class. Alternatively, they could use their existing knowledge to write an article about a change that has occurred in their city / town and the effect it has had on the environment.

SPEAKING Describing cause and effect (page 38)

EXAM FOCUS: PART 2

Lesson aims
1 Enable students to describe cause and effect relationships evident in cities they know.
2 Enable students to speak about causes and effects by connecting their ideas using *too much / many* and *there is / are* accurately.
3 Develop students' ability to speak about problems and solutions connected to population growth by learning related noun + noun or adjective + noun phrases.
4 Develop students' knowledge about the effects of population growth to allow them to talk confidently on this topic in Speaking Part 2.
5 Increase students' fluency by encouraging them to insert linking sounds to connect their speech.

Key language
Nouns: *overcrowding, exhaust emission, asthma, cancer, obesity, migration, sanitation, rubbish dump, waste, conservation, development, disposal site, public transport, cycle lane, sewage, planning regulation*

Featured topic vocabulary
Verbs: *destroy, migrate*
Nouns: *litter, traffic jam, settlement, packaging*
Adjectives: *uncontrolled, rural, illegal*

Topic focus

Optional lead-in
a Ask students when they were last in a crowd. Did they enjoy it?
b Write the word *overcrowding* on the board. Ask if they can guess what it means.
c Ask what happens when there are too many people. If they cannot think of any ideas, allow them to open their books to look at the photos, but they should not read the text.
d Write their ideas on the board. Then ask students to read the text in exercise 1 to check if any of their ideas are similar.

UNIT 4 POPULATION & THE ENVIRONMENT 49

1 This exercise develops students' knowledge of issues connected to population growth and introduces key topic vocabulary.

Before reading, focus students' attention on the photos and ask what they can see. Ask how they think the ideas might be connected and write their ideas on the board. Draw their attention to the title of the unit to help them. Tell students to read the text and check their ideas, before completing the exercise alone.

If students ask questions about the vocabulary, tell them you will cover this next.

ANSWERS
B, D, A, C

2 This exercise develops students' ability to speak about the effects of population growth by helping them understand topic-related vocabulary.

Demonstrate by doing question 1 as a whole class. If students are unable to find the answer, focus their attention on the beginning of the sentence before the word *obesity* (the medical term for being very fat, in a way that is not healthy). For example, they should know the words *green spaces* (areas of grass, trees, and other vegetation) and *exercise* (physical activity that you do to stay healthy or become stronger). Remind them to use the context to understand the meanings of new words.

ANSWERS
1 obesity
2 exhaust emissions
3 illegal rubbish dumps
4 uncontrolled migration
5 lack of sanitation
6 overcrowding

3 This exercise helps students generate ideas about population growth and develops their ability to speak more confidently on this topic.

Ask students to brainstorm their ideas in pairs, preferably on a big piece of paper. Make sure they keep this paper to use in exercise 7.

If you used the optional lead-in, tell students to also add their original ideas to their paper.

Vocabulary

4 This exercise develops students' ability to speak about problems and solutions connected to population growth by learning topic-related noun + noun or adjective + noun phrases.

Encourage students to take out their vocabulary notebooks and write notes on the meaning of new words.

Alternative for weaker classes: allocate one sentence per pair. After checking the meanings, each pair could find images representing their words on their mobile devices. Re-group students so they can share their information and pictures. Keep pictures to use as flashcards to revise the vocabulary.

POSSIBLE ANSWERS
Conservation projects: projects designed to preserve the natural environment
Safe disposal sites: places created by local authorities for throwing away waste
Rural development: creation of job opportunities and infrastructure in the countryside
Public transport: buses, trains, etc. made available to the public according to a timetable
Cycle lanes: strips of road marked for use by cyclists
Sewage systems: network of pipes and channels for transporting waste water
Planning regulations: system of laws to control the creation of new buildings

5 This exercise checks students have understood the new vocabulary and helps them use the words by demonstrating how they operate in a sentence. It also provides students with model sentences they can use in their speaking.

If students have difficulty, write the answers on the board in a mixed up order to provide them with a limited choice.

ANSWERS
1 the number of illegal rubbish dumps
2 uncontrolled migration / overcrowding
3 exhaust emissions
4 lack of sanitation
5 overcrowding / the unplanned development of housing

VOCABULARY FILE Student's Book   page 124
Refer students to exercises 1–3 for extra practice using words related to population and the environment.

ANSWERS
See page 133 of this book for answers.

> **Optional activity**
> Ask students to discuss the questions below in pairs:
> - *What causes uncontrolled migration?* (often emergencies like war and famine, and natural disasters like earthquakes or tsunamis)
> - *What can governments do to stop overcrowding?* (provide incentives to move out of the most crowded urban environments and into less populated areas / set up family planning and education programmes to reduce the birth rate / limit immigration)

Grammar

6 This exercise enables students to speak about causes and effects by accurately connecting their ideas using *too much / many* and *there is / are*.

Write the example sentence on the board. Ask students if *packaging* is countable or uncountable (uncountable). Circle *much* and *packaging*, and write the word *uncountable* on the board. Do the same with *household waste*. Do the second sentence as a whole class, and write students' answers on the board. Using a different colour, highlight *many* and *tourists*, and write the word *countable*. Draw

50   UNIT 4   POPULATION & THE ENVIRONMENT

students' attention to the -s to show it is plural. Use the first colour to highlight *is* and *litter*.

Ask students to write full sentences in their notebooks rather than just drawing lines between the ideas in their Student's Books. Writing the sentences will help them remember the language better.

Language note: *Much* is used with uncountable nouns, such as *packaging*.
Many is used with countable nouns, such as *workers*. Uncountable nouns behave like singular nouns. They cannot take a plural -s and they use a singular verb. So uncountable nouns go with *there is*, not *there are*. Uncountable nouns are often used for materials (e.g. paper, wood), substances (e.g. waste, water), masses (e.g. litter, cheese), abstract concepts (e.g. advice), and to denote a group (e.g. furniture, transport, staff).

ANSWERS
Too many tourists visit the city, so there is a lot of litter in the streets.
Too many green spaces are destroyed, so there is a lot of obesity and poor public health.
Too much waste enters rivers, so there is a lot of water pollution.
Too many workers migrate to cities, so there are a lot of illegal settlements.
Too many people use cars, so there are a lot of traffic jams.

7 This exercise provides students with an opportunity to personalize the language from exercise 6 and generate sentences they could use in Speaking Part 2.

Refer students to the list of problems they wrote in exercise 3. Tell them to use their sentences from exercise 6 as models.

GRAMMAR FILE Student's Book pages 113 and 114
Refer students to these pages for more explanation and practice of *there is / are* and *too much / many*.

ANSWERS
See page 130 of this book for answers.

8 1·37 This exercise aims to increase students' fluency by encouraging them to insert linking sounds to connect their speech.

Before listening, get students to try saying the sentences themselves so they can compare their pronunciation to the recording. Write the sentences on the board so you can mark the link between *there* and *is*, and *there* and *are* (like in the example in exercise 9). After listening, drill the sentences by playing the recording again and asking students to repeat together.

ANSWER
an /r/ sound

Audioscript 1·37
There is a lot of household waste.
There are a lot of traffic jams.

9 This exercise provides an opportunity for students to practise connecting their speech, and also helps them learn the language from exercise 6.

Focus students on the example, and drill the words *there are* by modelling and asking them to repeat together after you. In pairs, tell them to take turns to say one sentence each.

Exam skills

10 This exercise helps students develop flexibility in describing causes and effects by using *so* or *because*.

Ask students to work alone before checking answers as a class. To focus on the difference in structure, write the answers on the board and highlight the corresponding parts of both sentences in the same colour (i.e. *shops use too much plastic packaging* should be highlighted in one colour in both sentences, while *there is a lot of household waste* should be highlighted in another colour).

Language note:
Because:
   effect   + because +   cause
There is a lot of household waste + because + shops use too much packaging.
So:
   cause   + so +   effect
Shops use too much packaging + so + there is a lot of household waste.

ANSWERS
1 Shops use too much plastic packaging, so there is a lot of household waste.
2 There is a lot of household waste because shops use too much plastic packaging.

11 This exercise provides students with an opportunity to practise and personalize the structures with *because* and *so* to connect causes and effects.

Ask students to work alone. Monitor and check for correct word order, particularly after *so*. When using *so*, students often mistakenly copy the same structure as *because*, which creates nonsensical sentences, such as *There is a lot of household waste so shops use too much packaging*.

Teaching tip: To achieve a high score, students should not only connect their ideas but also show a range of connecting words. If students rely too heavily on *because*, take time after speaking activities to encourage them to reformulate their sentence using *so*.

12 This exercise trains students to expand their sentences in Speaking Part 2 by encouraging them to explain causes and effects under pressure.

Focus students' attention on the example in speech bubbles. You might like to put them under extra pressure by telling students to give their partner a 10-second time limit to respond.

Teaching tip: In the exam, students need to think 'on their feet' to expand their responses by coming up with new points while they are still in the process of speaking. Although it is important to do exercises with plenty of support for students to develop, it is also important to do activities which replicate the pressure of an exam situation.

EXAM TIP 1·38 Before students listen, ask them to suggest possible answers to the question and write these on the board. After listening to the answer, you might like to follow this up by asking students for possible solutions to the problems raised in exercise 3. Then refer students to page 145 for more guidance on talking about problems.

ANSWER
You'll probably be asked to say what you have done to resolve it (the problem).

Audioscript 1·38
In Speaking Part 2, you may have to talk about a problem you have experienced, and what the causes and effects of this problem are. Also, **you'll probably be asked to say what you have done to resolve it**. For example, when talking about the causes and effects of problems in the environment (such as too much household waste), you might be asked to say what you personally do or could do to help the situation (such as recycle more efficiently).

Exam practice

13 Students have a chance here to put together all the skills developed in this lesson by doing a practice Speaking Part 2 test about causes and effects.

Before beginning, refer students back to unit 2 to remind them of the skills developed in the first lesson about Speaking Part 2. Ask them what they can remember about Speaking Part 2, to try to elicit that:

- they should aim to speak for 2 minutes
- they need to cover all the points on the card and stay on topic
- they have 1 minute to prepare and write notes
- they should introduce their speaking with a phrase like *I'm going to talk about / I'd like to talk about ...*
- they need to speak clearly and loudly
- they should connect their ideas using a range of connecting words.

In pairs, nominate one student to be the examiner to take notes on whether their partner connected their ideas and used a range of connecting words.

LISTENING Completing sentences page 40

EXAM FOCUS: SECTION 4

Lesson aims

1 Train students to analyse questions by identifying key words in sentence completion and multiple-choice questions.
2 Develop students' awareness of the importance of matching key words in the questions with synonyms in the recording.
3 Improve students' ability to understand lectures about environmental problems by recognizing key phrases related to this topic.
4 Encourage students to consider the benefits of studying in a group to ensure their work outside class remains fresh and productive.

Key language

Nouns: *deforestation, impact, loss, risk, habitat, climate change, cure, crops, accident, organism, logging, mining, vegetation*

Verbs: *chop down, construct, burn, access, survive, dominate*

Adjectives: *financial, extinct, suitable, estimated, agricultural*

Topic focus

Optional lead-in

You might like to introduce the topic by focusing on local news stories related to environmental problems specific to your city, region, or country. Show students newspaper articles about the problem and ask what they know about the issue, and what solutions they would suggest.

Alternatively, draw a tree on the board and ask students to brainstorm products that come from trees. They may come up with any of the following:

medicine (like quinine), fruit, nuts, furniture, logs for burning, paper, charcoal, sawdust, cardboard, leaves (for building roofs), oxygen, glue, bark chips (for playgrounds). You may wish to write up each idea against a different branch of the tree.

1 This exercise introduces the topic of environmental problems and engages students by encouraging them to think about what they already know.

Focus students' attention on the picture and write their ideas on the board.

You may wish to try and elicit the word *deforestation* by writing up *forest* on the centre of the board and then some prefixes and suffixes (e.g. *re-, un-, de-, in-, -ity, -ness, -ation, -ition*) around it, before asking students to try and create a word to describe the picture.

> **ANSWER**

Deforestation – the loss of trees not only means that the world is a less beautiful place but we also lose the oxygen that trees make from carbon dioxide (through photosynthesis). This has negative effects on air quality and on the climate. Furthermore, trees provide homes and food for many other species of flora and fauna, so when we destroy their habitat we also destroy these plants and animals, with wide-reaching effects on ecosystems as a whole.

Vocabulary

2 This exercise provides students with useful vocabulary related to environmental problems to prepare them for listening to a lecture on the topic.

Students may need clarification of some words, for example:
- *impact*: powerful effect / result
- *habitat*: a place where a particular type of animal or plant is normally found
- *cure*: a medicine that makes an illness go away.

Ask students to work alone before checking as a whole class.

> **ANSWERS**
> 1 D 2 C 3 A 4 B 5 E

VOCABULARY FILE Student's Book page 124
Refer students to exercises 4 and 5 for extra practice using words related to environmental problems.

> **ANSWERS**
> See page 133 of this book for answers.

3 This exercise provides an opportunity to check that students understand the new vocabulary and help them remember the words by using them. It also develops their knowledge of environmental problems.

Encourage students to write a list in their notebook rather than just numbering the words or pictures. Writing the words will help them remember. Highlight that there is not one correct answer to this question, so they may have different opinions to their partner.

Exam skills

4 This exercise develops students' ability to identify key words to analyse questions before listening.

Remind students of the meaning of key words by asking them what types of words they should underline ('content' words, like nouns and adjectives, rather than 'grammar' words). Monitor and check they are not underlining too many words. When they have finished, ask them to compare their choices with a partner.

> **POSSIBLE ANSWERS**
> 1 Forests, chopped down, financial, reasons
> 2 farmers, clear, space, produce, crops
> 3 Companies, create, roads, reach
> 4 deforestation, accident, fires, burn

EXAM TIP 1·39 Before students listen, ask them to suggest possible answers to the question and write these on the board. After they have answered the question, refer students to page 46 for more guidance on using key words when preparing to listen.

> **ANSWER**

You can also quickly try to think of similar words or synonyms that might be used to describe the same thing.

Audioscript 1·39

When you're preparing to listen, it helps to underline 'key words' in the questions and sentences. Key words are basically the words with the most meaning, so usually nouns and verbs rather than 'small' words like prepositions and articles. **You can also quickly try to think of similar words or synonyms that might be used to describe the same thing.** This can help you to notice when a topic is mentioned in a listening.

5 This exercise raises students' awareness of the importance of matching key words in the questions with synonyms in the recording. It also prepares them for the listening in exercise 6 by checking they understand vocabulary they will hear.

Tell students to work in pairs before checking as a whole class. Afterwards, ask the class why this exercise is important to elicit that they should be prepared to listen out for synonyms in the exam.

> **ANSWERS**
> destroy – burn
> cut down – chop down
> money – financial
> small – little
> area – space
> access – reach
> chance – accident
> purposes – reasons
> plants – crops
> construct – create

6 1·40 This exercise provides students with an example of how synonyms are used to cue the answers in Listening Section 4.

Remind students of the skills developed in unit 2 of predicting missing information. You may like to go through each question as a class and predict what type of word is missing (1 verb, 2 verb, 3 noun, 4 noun). Also remind students to read the instructions carefully to check how many words to write.

> **ANSWERS**
> 1 grow food
> 2 feed their animals
> 3 remote forests
> 4 vegetation

UNIT 4 POPULATION & THE ENVIRONMENT 53

Audioscript 1·40
Part 1

OK, so in today's lecture we're going to look at the causes and effects of deforestation. Well, we all know what deforestation is … but why does it happen? Well, firstly, trees are cut down for a variety of purposes, but generally it's because people need to **earn money** or to **grow food** for their family. Typically, farmers take a small area to produce plants or to **feed their animals**. The number of these small areas combined is what has such a negative impact on the forest itself. The main reason for deforestation, therefore, is the need for agricultural land and not because companies take trees for wood, as is often thought. But this does not mean that logging companies don't play a part. They provide the world's wood and paper products, and cut down large numbers of trees each year. Loggers, some of them acting illegally, also build roads to access **remote forests** – which leads to, well, further deforestation. Not only that but forests are also cut down as a result of expanding towns and cities. I should add, however, that not all deforestation is intentional – it's also caused by chance when fires destroy **vegetation**. I'm sure you've heard about examples of destructive forest fires that happen every summer all round the world …

Exam practice

7 🔊 1·41 This exercise provides students with an opportunity to use the skills developed in exercises 4–6 to improve their analysis of the questions.

Before listening, ask students what they should do first (highlight key words, think of synonyms, and predict the missing information). If necessary, allow them more time to do this than they will have in the exam. It is more important here for them to notice the benefit of going through these steps than to practise under real exam conditions. You may prefer to continue immediately to exercise 8 without checking answers, to provide students with a more authentic exam experience.

ANSWERS
1. 9 million
2. organic waste
3. 190,000
4. plants and animals
5. more suitable temperatures
6. become extinct

Audioscript 1·41
Part 2

Right, before we look at the effects of deforestation on wildlife, let's consider why wildlife is so important to us. So firstly, how many species of wildlife are there on Earth? Well, it's difficult to say exactly. Scientists have already identified nearly 2 million individual species, and even conservative estimates suggest that more than **9 million** remain undiscovered! But the planet's amazing variety of life is more than just something for academics to study; humans depend on it. For example, farmers rely on worms, bacteria, and other organisms to break down **organic waste** and keep soil high in nitrogen levels – processes that are important to agriculture. Pharmaceutical companies use a wide range of different species to create medication … and many more breakthroughs could still be undiscovered in Earth's unknown species. However, a stable food supply and a source for pharmaceuticals are only a couple of the benefits that Earth's biodiversity provides. The next point I'd like to make connects biodiversity to the planet as a whole. It does this by, well, Earth's plant life reduces the effect of global warming by absorbing carbon dioxide, yet 90% of those plants depend on the nearly **190,000** species of insects to keep them alive. Scientists from Cornell University in the US actually calculated the value of the different services that Earth's **plants and animals** provide. They arrived at a grand total of $2.9 trillion – and that was back in 1997. So, what issues does the threat to biodiversity cause? Well, global warming is increasingly forcing species away from their natural environment in search of better, er, **more suitable temperatures**, and scientists fear that not all species will survive climate change. Overhunting, which famously led to the extinction of the dodo, of course, and the passenger pigeon, continues to endanger larger animals like the rhino. Species like kudzu and the brown tree snake, introduced by humans to other environments, can also rapidly force native species to **become extinct**. In the US, invasive species cause between 125 billion and 140 billion dollars in damage every year, and are thought to have played a part in nearly half of all extinctions worldwide since the 1600s. Forests are particularly important to wildlife …

8 🔊 1·42 This exercise provides students with practice identifying key words in a different type of question, as sentence completion questions have been the focus until now. Before listening, remind students of the skills developed in unit 3 of analysing the options. Give them enough time to highlight the key words and think of any synonyms. After listening, check answers and ask students to turn to the audioscript to identify in what way the incorrect answers could be distracting.

ANSWERS
1 A 2 C

Audioscript 1·42
Part 3

So, back to the main theme of the lecture. The greatest threat to Earth's biodiversity is deforestation. While deforestation threatens ecosystems across the globe, it's particularly destructive to tropical rainforests. In terms of Earth's biodiversity, rainforests are hugely important; though **they cover only 7% of the Earth's surface**, they are home to more than half the world's species. Through logging, mining, and farming, humans destroy approximately 2% of the Earth's rainforests every year, often damaging the soil so badly in the process that the forest has a difficult time recovering. OK. As their habitats disappear, plants and animals are forced to compete with one another for the remaining space – those that can't compete become extinct. In recent history, deforestation has led to approximately 36% of all extinctions. So, how can it be stopped? Well, deforestation is particularly difficult to stop because it has so many causes. While it's easy to blame irresponsible logging and mining companies for the destruction, their practices are in some ways a symptom of larger problems. For instance, many rainforests are located in developing countries that don't have enough resources to enforce environmental regulations. **These countries also benefit greatly from the economic activity that the companies produce, making them even less likely to stop deforestation.** Fortunately, hope remains for the Earth's rainforests …

9 Students are encouraged here to reflect on skills developed in this lesson and how well they used these skills to answer the questions.

After students have compared with a partner, discuss ideas for synonyms as a whole class. If they are unable to think of any synonyms, refer them to the audioscript to look for synonyms of words in the questions, for example:
- agricultural businesses – farmers
- need – depend on
- estimated – calculated
- climate change – global warming.

Sometimes it is not one word, but an entire phrase which is changed, for example:
- don't come from a particular area – introduced by humans to other environments.

What do you think?

10 This exercise encourages students to engage with the topic, to expand their knowledge and encourage them to use new vocabulary. This can help generate ideas in speaking and writing, as well as help understand listening questions about the environment.

Encourage students to make a list of their ideas so they can refer back to it in exercise 11. Monitor for useful topic language and write any relevant words on the board to share with other groups.

11 This exercise reinforces work from the speaking lesson about the importance of being able to suggest solutions as well as identify problems.

Remind students of the advice from the exam tip in the speaking lesson to stress the importance of being able to also identify possible solutions.

12 Encourage students to ask each other follow-up questions if possible, in order to help their partner expand their idea.

Study skills

First, you may like to clarify the meaning of *dominate* (take all the time and not let other people say anything). Ask students to work alone, and then compare with a partner. While checking their answers in pairs, ask them to discuss to what extent they agree with these views on group work.

ANSWERS
A: share ideas, learn from people's methods of working, learn from people's experiences, clarify your own thoughts
D: one or two people dominate, easily distracted, progress not obvious, no clear focus

WRITING Brainstorming ideas

EXAM FOCUS: TASK 2

Lesson aims
1 Develop students' ability to analyse questions involving solutions, to determine if they should suggest solutions or respond to one.
2 Raise students' awareness of the importance of brainstorming, and provide them with a technique for generating more ideas.
3 Increase the complexity of students' language by using *could* and *would* in their responses to solution questions.
4 Expand students' range of verbs describing change, to improve the variety of academic vocabulary in their writing.

Key language
Verbs describing change: *decrease, develop, construct, reduce, alter, improve, modify, limit, introduce, adapt*

Featured topic vocabulary
Verbs: *confront, recycle, protect*
Nouns: *destruction, income, western world, ban*
Groups of people: *industry leaders, environmentalists, social workers, the elderly, the disabled*

Topic focus

1 This exercise introduces the concept of solution questions and prepares students to assess the merits of possible solutions.

Focus students' attention on the photo to clarify the meaning of *illegal dumping of waste* (discarding unwanted materials in a way or place which is not legal). Before students read options a–e, ask them for suggestions of solutions and write these on the board. Group them in threes or fours to discuss. Take a vote to find out which solution was most popular.

2 This exercise encourages students to reflect on the process of evaluating solutions, which is an important part of building up an argument in Writing Task 2.

Alternative for weaker classes: you may prefer to discuss as a whole class rather than in groups, to prompt students with questions such as *Why didn't you choose this answer?* Write their answers on the board and try to group them into factors such as consequences, practicalities, effectiveness, dangers, cost, time, etc.

Point out to students that these are the types of factors they could consider when answering solution questions.

Exam skills

3 This exercise develops students' ability to analyse questions involving solutions, to determine if they should suggest solutions or respond to one.

Ask students to work alone before checking in pairs. In whole-class feedback, focus on the parts of the questions which indicate the response required:

- *How can …* indicates students should suggest solutions.
- *To what extent would …* indicates students should evaluate a given solution.

ANSWERS
1 b   2 a   3 c

Grammar

4 This exercise provides students with a model of how to approach a solution question. It also raises their awareness of potential pitfalls.

Insist that students must not shout out the answers in order to give everyone enough time to read and think before discussing. After reading, ask them to compare their ideas in pairs.

Alternative for weaker classes: weaker students may have difficulty identifying which paragraph is more effective. To support them, ask guiding questions such as:

- *Do both paragraphs use the same verb forms?* (No. Paragraph A uses the present simple. Paragraph B uses the present simple but also uses *could* and *would*.)
- *Are IELTS questions about real solutions or imagined solutions?* (imagined solutions)
- *Which one is talking about an imagined solution? How do you know this?* (Paragraph B. It uses *could* and *would*.)

ANSWER
A is answering essay question b.
B is answering essay question a.
Paragraph B is more effective because the writer correctly identifies that the essay requires conditional tenses, which are associated with proposed solutions.
In paragraph A the student's use of the present simple tense is confusing because the student is not writing about real or existing solutions but rather a proposed solution. For proposed solutions any tense that describes things as current is not really appropriate.

5 This exercise increases the complexity of students' language by encouraging them to use *could* and *would* in their responses to solution questions.

Tell students the missing words all come from paragraph B.

Alternative for weaker classes: guide them to the answer by asking:

- *What is the proposed solution?* (ban cars from the city centre) *What verb introduces this idea?* (could)
- *What are the possible effects?* (improve air quality, attract more tourists, more green spaces). *What verb introduces these ideas?* (would)

Language note: *Would* and *could* are examples of modal verbs. Other examples are *should, might, may, can,* and *will*. After modals, the second verb is always used in the base form (also called the infinitive, without *to*). This is the form you find in the dictionary.

ANSWERS
could, would, could

GRAMMAR FILE Student's Book page 118
Refer students to this page for more explanation and practice of *could* and *would*.

ANSWERS
See page 131 of this book for answers.

6 Students are given a chance here to try using *would* and *could* in their writing, to increase the complexity of their language.

Ask students if they remember what the problem is with paragraph A (use of present simple). Focus their attention on the example, and ask what words have changed from paragraph A (*helps* has changed to *could help*). Do not allow students to simply correct the paragraph in the book by crossing words out. Explain that rewriting the whole paragraph on a separate piece of paper will help students to learn the language and improve.

POSSIBLE ANSWER
There are many reasons why a tax on household waste could help the environment. First, it would encourage people to recycle more because they would save money. It would also provide income for the government which they could spend on conservation. Finally, people would see packaging as a cost and they would change their buying habits.

Vocabulary

7 This exercise expands students' range of verbs describing change, to improve the variety of academic vocabulary in their writing.

Write *I want to change my …* on the board and ask students to suggest an ending e.g. hair / IELTS grade / house. Now delete *change* and see if they can complete the gap with other verbs. Then tell them to compare their ideas with the words in the book and complete the exercise alone before checking in pairs.

ANSWERS
Make less: reduce, limit
Make different: alter, modify, adapt
Make better: develop, improve
Create: construct, introduce

8 Before students begin, clarify how to change the parts of speech by reminding them that *-ing* can be added to verbs in a place where nouns would normally be required (the *-ing* noun form of the verb is called the gerund). Tell students to work alone before checking in pairs.

You may need to clarify the meaning of CO_2 emissions (harmful gases from cars and factories).

UNIT 4 POPULATION & THE ENVIRONMENT

ANSWERS
1 Improving / Developing, decrease / reduce
2 altering / modifying / adapting
3 introduce, reduce / decrease
4 improve / develop
5 limit

VOCABULARY FILE Student's Book **page 124**
Refer students to exercise 6 for extra practice using verbs describing change.

ANSWERS
See page 133 of this book for answers.

EXAM TIP 1·43 Before students listen, ask them to suggest possible answers to the question and write these on the board. After they have answered the question, refer students to page 147 for more guidance on brainstorming essay ideas.

ANSWER
five or six

Audioscript 1·43
Always brainstorm ideas or reasons before you start writing an essay. If you don't, you may find you'll repeat the same points or think of extra, better ideas when you have no time left to write them! Of course, you don't have long to brainstorm in the test so you don't need to produce a long list. For example, for a discussion essay, try to think of three reasons for each opposing view. For a personal opinion essay, save time by deciding if you agree or disagree before you start brainstorming! Then, try to brainstorm about **five or six reasons** for your view.

Exam skills
9 This exercise raises students' awareness of the importance of brainstorming by encouraging them to notice how many ideas they are capable of generating.

Give each group a big piece of paper for their ideas. Encourage them to make a spider diagram by writing the essay title in a circle in the middle of the paper. Draw lines out from the circle and show that these should connect to different ideas by writing one example idea on the paper (e.g. reduce air pollution). When students have finished brainstorming in their groups, stick their pieces of paper on the walls around the class. Tell them to look at other groups' ideas and compare them to their own.

10 This exercise provides students with a technique for generating more ideas by considering a variety of viewpoints. Highlight to students that the first letters of each word spell IDEAS, so it can be easily remembered. Ask them to work in pairs before checking as a whole class. You may like to brainstorm groups in society whose viewpoints might be represented by the social worker figure (e.g. parents, teachers, young people, the elderly, religious groups, etc.).

ANSWERS
Industry leaders: B   Artists: E
Doctors: D   Social workers: A
Environmentalists: C

11 This exercise demonstrates why it can be useful to consider a variety of viewpoints by showing the range of ideas that can be generated.

Ask students to work alone before checking in pairs. In whole-class feedback, help students reflect on this technique by asking:
- *Do all these issues affect you personally?* (probably not)
- *Do you agree with all these opinions?* (possibly not)
- *Why is it useful to think about different groups?* (because if these issues are not part of your life, it is difficult to think of them without putting yourself in someone else's shoes)
- *Why is it useful to have a range of ideas at the brainstorming stage?* (because it can help you reach the word count / justify your answers with examples / build a structured argument rather than risk rambling about one issue).

ANSWERS
1 Industry leaders
2 Artists
3 Environmentalists
4 Social workers
5 Doctors

Exam practice
12 This exercise provides students with an opportunity to practise the skills developed in the Exam skills section.

Remind students to use the technique from exercise 10 by asking them what IDEAS stands for

Alternative for weaker classes: allow students to work in groups. Compare ideas as a whole class by asking them for suggestions for each sub-group of the acronym in turn. That is to say, ask students for possible viewpoints of industry leaders, before moving on to doctors, environmentalists, artists, and finally social workers. Write their ideas on the board.

POSSIBLE ANSWERS
We would cut emissions.
We would reduce the spread of disease (plant, animal, and human).
There would be less overcrowding in the summer.
BUT
Tourism has far less impact than other activities (e.g. deforestation).
We would earn less income and have fewer public resources to conserve nature.
Tourism encourages conservation (e.g. national parks and safaris).

13 This exercise demonstrates the importance of brainstorming ideas by showing how multiple ideas can be incorporated into one paragraph.

Refer to students' suggestions on the board from exercise 12, and ask them which viewpoints could be used in this paragraph. Guide students to a logical grouping of ideas.

Alternative for weaker classes: allow students to work in pairs, but stress that both students should write their own copy. To allow them to consider a broader range of viewpoints, you may wish to alter the paragraph topic and simply write *Tourism has many positive effects* or *Tourism has many negative effects* on the board and invite students to brainstorm supporting ideas.

MODEL ANSWER
See exercise 2 in the WRITING FILE on page 142 of the Student's Book for a model answer.

WRITING FILE Student's Book page 142
Refer students to exercise 3 on this page for another discussion essay question, accompanied by a sample essay.

ANSWERS
See page 136 of this book for answers.

READING Matching information page 44

Lesson aims
1 Develop students' ability to recognize different text types, namely problem-solution texts, information texts, and discussion texts.
2 Enable students to predict text organization by text type to increase understanding and reading speed.
3 Increase students' reading efficiency by matching phrases in questions and the text.
4 Improve students' use of key phrases for positively and negatively evaluating solutions to problems.

Key language
Phrases for evaluating solutions: *successfully, no longer possible, ineffective, simply transferred the problem, has done little to solve, might not be able, make sense*

Featured topic vocabulary
Verb: *double*
Nouns: *congestion, suburbs*

Topic focus

Optional lead-in
You may like to introduce the topic by asking students to conduct a survey to find out:
- how many people in the class have a car
- if yes, how often they use it and mostly what for
- if no, why not and if they would like one.

To conduct the survey, ask students to draw a table in their notebooks with the names of everyone in the class in the first column, and the questions above in the following columns. After speaking to everyone in the class, students could write up their results.

1 This exercise engages students with the topic of the text that follows, and encourages them not to overlook information that accompanies texts.

Draw students' attention to the numbers next to the years. Discuss as a whole class.

ANSWER
It has doubled.

Optional activity
You may like to focus on vocabulary similar to *doubled* (e.g. 5 → 10) by writing numbers on the board to check the meaning of *halved* (e.g. 10 → 5), *tripled* (e.g. 5 → 15), and *quadrupled* (e.g. 5 → 20). Note that for higher degrees of change we normally say *increased five- / six-fold*, etc.

2 This exercise engages students with the topic by relating it to their personal situation, and shows what topic vocabulary they already know.

This is a good opportunity to revise the phrase *to what extent … by* reformulating the question in whole-class feedback as: *To what extent do you need a car in your life at the moment / will you need a car?* (depending on your students' situation) and repeating it by asking a number of different students.

Exam skills
3 This exercise develops students' ability to recognize different text types by identifying differences in text organization.

Before attempting the exercise, you may like to focus students on the different text types by writing *problem–solution*, *information*, and *discussion* on the board. Ask students in what way these texts might be different. Write their ideas on the board. Then ask students to complete the exercise independently before checking with a partner. You may need to check they understand that *poor* means 'bad' here, not the opposite of 'rich'.

ANSWERS
a 1 description of problem   2 poor solutions
  3 good solution
b 1 original or past situation   2 current situation
  3 future situation
c 1 advantages   2 disadvantages
  3 your personal opinion

EXAM TIP 1·44 This exercise engages students with exercises 3–6 by raising their awareness of how this skill will benefit them. Before students listen, ask them to suggest possible answers to the question and write these on the board. After they have answered the question, refer students to page 148 for more guidance on different types of reading passage.

ANSWER
You should be able to predict the text's organization.

58 UNIT 4 POPULATION & THE ENVIRONMENT

Audioscript 1·44

In the test, there are many different types of passage. Three common types are problem–solution, information, and discussion, which give an author's opinion. The first paragraph often tells you the type of passage because key words or phrases show that a problem, some information, or a discussion and opinion are going to be described. If you know the type of passage, **you should be able to predict its organization** and, as a result, find information more quickly. For example, if a question about an information passage refers to the future, this information is usually found at the end of the passage – you can then start your search in the final paragraph.

4 This exercise encourages students to try to identify the text type when reading for the first time to get an overall understanding.

Before reading, focus on the title and photo. Ask the class what they think the text is about. Ask what the driving age is in their country to engage them with the text. Focus students' attention on the three options and clarify the meaning of congestion (too much traffic). Remind students they do not need to read every word to get an overall understanding. Ask which words they should focus on more (content words, such as nouns and adjectives). Give students a time limit of 2 minutes, to push them to read quickly. Ask students to compare their answer with a partner.

ANSWER
1 solving the problem of traffic congestion

Teaching tip: If students disagree on their answers for exercise 4, clarify that all three things (solutions, information, opinion) are included in the text, but they need to identify which one shapes the overall structure of the text the most. If students do not agree with their partner, ask them to look at the text in pairs and justify why their answer is correct by showing how it runs throughout the text.

5 This exercise develops students' ability to recognize different text types by identifying the purpose of individual paragraphs.

Focus students on the letters accompanying each paragraph by asking what they should write in the gaps (letters). Tell them to work alone before checking with a partner.

ANSWERS
1 C, D **2** E, F **3** A, B

Teaching tip: You may like to draw students' attention to the importance of the word *however* in paragraphs B and C. This word provides crucial 'signposting' to show that a contrasting point is about to be made. It navigates the reader through the text by indicating a change in direction. It is useful to raise students' awareness of these features of a text to help them follow these so-called signposts and read more efficiently.

6 Focus students' attention on exercise 3 and discuss as a whole class. Remind them why it is important to consider the structure of the text by asking them the question from the Exam tip box again, to consolidate the skill developed here.

7 This exercise introduces the skill of matching phrases in questions with the text by developing students' ability to identify key phrases.

Raise students' awareness of why this is an important skill by asking them why they should underline key words (because it helps them read more efficiently by looking for specific information). Remind them not to highlight too much in the question, or the words will no longer stand out.

ANSWER
solution, not, worked, cities

8 This exercise demonstrates how language in the question matches phrases in the text. It also shows students why it is important to identify text organization, to help limit the choice of which paragraphs could match.

The exercise supports students by narrowing their options to only two paragraphs, so they can focus more closely on the language.

Focus students on paragraphs B and C. Ask them to work alone before checking their answer with a partner.

ANSWER
… has done little to solve congestion in urban areas (paragraph C)

Teaching tip: Remind students that it is crucial to develop this type of reading sub-skill because of the time limit in the exam. If they had unlimited time, they might eventually find the correct answer just by reading over and over again! However, the time pressure means it is vital to read efficiently. Keep students motivated by pointing out this is a useful academic skill which will help them to cope with the huge amount of reading involved at university.

Exam practice

9 Before reading, revise the steps that students should take to match phrases in the question with the text as a class. Give them 10 minutes to complete the exercise. Tell them to work alone before checking their answers in pairs. If students disagree with their partner, they should justify how the paragraph matches.

ANSWERS
1 F (*it surely makes sense to postpone the time that young drivers get their licenses until a little later in life…* lines 44–45)
2 D (*Many older citizens and families also rely on cars…* lines 24–25)
3 E (*Young people make up over 25% of road deaths…* line 33)
4 E (*and therefore cut pollution…* line 40)
5 A (*Car ownership … double each year…* lines 2–3)
6 B (*living costs are growing in many countries…* line 13)

Key phrases

10 This exercise improves students' understanding of phrases from the text for positively and negatively evaluating solutions to problems.

UNIT 4 POPULATION & THE ENVIRONMENT 59

Alternative for weaker classes: ask students to find the phrases in the text and highlight them, because the context of the sentence may help to clarify the meaning. Check the pronunciation of *suc**cess**fully* and *inef**fec**tive* (the stress is marked here in bold), and draw their attention to the double letters in the spelling.

ANSWERS

Positive (+): successfully, makes sense
Negative (−): no longer possible, ineffective, simply transferred the problem, has done little to solve, might not be able

11 This exercise enables students to use phrases for evaluating solutions to problems.

Before students begin, check they know the parts of speech for *successfully* (adverb) and *ineffective* (adjective) because this will help find the right gaps. Clarify the meaning of *suburbs* (areas where people live that are outside the centre of a city).

ANSWERS

1 successfully
2 might not be able
3 no longer possible
4 has done little to solve
5 ineffective, simply transferred the problem
6 makes sense

What do you think?

12 This exercise develops students' knowledge and generates ideas about the topic by encouraging them to respond personally to the text.

If your students are over 25, ask them to think about how it would affect their children or the next generation of drivers in their town or city. You may need to remind them of the meaning of *impact* (effect / result) from the listening lesson. Encourage students to use phrases from the box in exercise 10 as they are talking.

> **Alternative**
>
> Write on the board: *NO to a higher driving age!* Invite groups to make a list of reasons why it would have a negative effect on a sheet of paper. Award points for each idea and give bonus points for each sentence which includes a phrase from the box in exercise 10. The group with the most ideas wins.

EXAM CHALLENGE

ANSWERS

Speaking
1–3 Students' own answers

Reading
1 See page 139 of this book for answers.
2 Students' own answers

Listening
1 See page 137 of this book for answers and page 141 for the audioscript.
2 Students' own answers

Writing
1 Possible answers:
- Exhaust emissions damage health.
- Traffic accidents increase.
- Journey times lengthen, weakening the economy.
- Cities become dirtier and less attractive, discouraging tourism.
- The streets become unsafe, making people reluctant to do exercise or socialize.
- Reduced civic pride may lead to vandalism and antisocial behaviour.

2 Students' own answers
3 Sample answer:
Traffic congestion can have many negative effects. For example, the amount of exhaust emissions could damage people's health. It could also mean the number of traffic accidents increase. Finally, cities would become dirtier and less attractive, which could discourage tourism.

UNIT 5   Culture & entertainment

Introduction <small>page 47</small>

Featured topic vocabulary
Nouns: *museum, theatre, revenue, play, audience, performance, videogame*

Optional lead-in
You may like to introduce the infographic by writing these questions on the board before students open their books:
- *How many hours of TV a week do you think the average American child watches?* (35)
- *Which do you think is the most popular museum in the world?* (The Louvre)
- *What do you think is the most popular theatre show in the world?* (The Phantom of the Opera)

Write students' guesses on the board. Ask them to open their books to the infographic and find out if anyone guessed correctly.

What do you think?
Ask students to discuss questions 1–3 with a partner before sharing feedback as a whole class. Then ask them to discuss questions 4 and 5 in their pairs. When getting feedback, write students' ideas for question 5 on the board to help those who are having difficulty thinking of an answer. Question 5 is particularly useful for generating ideas which could be useful in Speaking Part 3 and Writing Task 2.

Background note: *The Phantom of the Opera* is a musical by Andrew Lloyd Webber based on a French novel which has also been made into films.

SPEAKING Structuring responses <small>page 48</small>

EXAM FOCUS: PARTS 1 & 3

Lesson aims
1. Improve students' ability to extend responses to personal topic-related questions by generalizing, speculating, and giving examples.
2. Familiarize students with the range of question forms in Parts 1 and 3 in order to predict the types of questions they might be asked.
3. Enable students to use adverbs of frequency to speak about how often something happens.
4. Develop students' range of vocabulary to speak about types of books.
5. Improve students' use of sentence stress to highlight the most important part of their speaking.

Key language
Adverbs: *actually, basically, generally, maybe, regularly, often, perhaps, possibly, sometimes, occasionally*

Types of book: *biography, crime novel, romance, historical novel, drama, thriller*

Nouns: *e-book, plot, novel, special occasion*

Topic focus
1 This exercise engages students with the topic of books and prepares them to listen to the model speakers in exercise 2.

2 1•45 This exercise provides students with a model of how to extend their responses.

Ask students what the 'e' in *e-book* stands for (electronic).

ANSWERS
a 3   **b** 1   **c** 2

Audioscript 1•45, 1•46
1 Actually, I have a confession to make. I recently bought an e-reader and I soon realized that nobody can see what I'm reading. So now, **I occasionally read celebrity biographies**! Maybe other people do the same – who knows?

2 **I often buy two or three books a day for my e-reader.** Generally, if I see an advert, read a good review, or a friend recommends a book, I just buy it. Sometimes the books are good; sometimes they're terrible! I know I spend a lot of money, but perhaps because they're only e-books it doesn't feel that bad.

3 Basically, **I'm happy with my e-reader, but I still love my local bookshop.** I regularly spend hours there at the weekend looking at all the covers. Possibly, I'll read for a while, too. But then if I like a book, I don't buy it at the shop – I just go to the shop's café and download a cheap, digital copy.

Grammar
3 1•46 This exercise focuses students on how the model speakers extend and structure their responses using adverbs of frequency.

After listening, ask students to check their answers in pairs. When checking answers as a whole class, drill the pronunciation of each adverb.

ANSWERS
1 actually   6 sometimes
2 occasionally   7 perhaps
3 maybe   8 basically
4 often   9 regularly
5 generally   10 possibly

4 Ask students to work alone before checking with a partner. If they need help, refer them to the audioscript to check how the adverbs are used in context.

ANSWERS
a actually
b basically
c generally, sometimes, often, occasionally, regularly
d perhaps, maybe, possibly
e occasionally, often, regularly

5 This exercise clarifies the varying word order required when using different adverbs of frequency.

Draw students' attention to the comma after adverb 1. Also highlight that the adverb in 2 is positioned between the subject and verb. If students are having difficulty, focus their attention on the meanings of the adverbs in exercise 4 and ask them to predict what the speaker is trying to express here.

Language note: Normally, adverbs are positioned between the subject and main verb. For example, in 2 the adverb comes after *they* (subject) and before *choose* (main verb). The verb *to be* is an exception. The adverb goes after the verb *to be*, for example:
He is often late.
If the sentence includes an auxiliary verb, the adverb is positioned between the auxiliary verb and main verb, for example:
They have actually gone home. (*have* – auxiliary, *gone* – main verb)

ANSWERS
1 a or b   2 c   3 b or d

EXAM TIP 1·47 Before students listen, ask them to suggest possible answers to the questions and write these on the board. After they have answered the question, refer students to page 145 for more guidance on using adverbs correctly.

ANSWERS
Adverbs can help students structure responses in all parts of the exam, but it may be helpful to look for opportunities to use adverbs of frequency when talking about personal habits in Part 1, and adverbs of speculation in Part 3. The adverbs *actually* and *generally* are useful in all parts of the text.

Audioscript 1·47
Using adverbs correctly can really improve your grammar and vocabulary. In **Speaking Part 1**, you can add adverbs like *sometimes* and *usually* to say how often you personally do something. In **Speaking Part 3** – where the ideas discussed are more complicated – you can use adverbs like *maybe* or *perhaps* to show you're not certain about something. In all parts of the Speaking test, you can put adverbs like ***actually*** or ***generally*** at the beginning of sentences to make your ideas seem clearer and more natural.

6 This exercise tests whether students understand both the meaning and the word order of the adverbs of frequency, and demonstrates how answers can be extended.

Students may need clarification of *novel* (story) and *plot* (what happens in the story). Highlight that there is more than one possible answer for each sentence. Ask them to compare their answers in pairs before checking as a whole class.

Alternative
To make it easier to conduct whole-class feedback, you may like to write the sentences on the board and ask students to come and add the adverbs where they think best. If you have an interactive whiteboard, you can write the adverbs on the board and ask students to drag them into position. Alternatively, you could use pieces of paper or Post-It notes.

POSSIBLE ANSWERS
1 Generally, the young people I know only read for their studies.
2 When I read in cars or on buses, I sometimes feel sick.
3 Perhaps I'll read a novel on my next holiday.
4 I like to read regularly. Actually, I can read in three different languages.
5 Basically, I don't like fantasies. Maybe it's because the plots are silly.

7 This exercise provides students with an opportunity to personalize the sentences, to help remember the adverbs. It also enables them to consider how they could use the adverbs in the exam.

Encourage students to try to say their sentences to their partner from memory, rather than reading them.

GRAMMAR FILE Student's Book page 115
Refer students to this page for more explanation and practice of adverbs.

ANSWERS
See page 130 of this book for answers.

Vocabulary

8 This exercise expands students' range of vocabulary to speak about types of books.

Ask students who answered *Yes* to question 1 in exercise 1 if they know what type of book it was that they read. You may need to clarify some words, such as:
- *biography*: a true story about someone's life
- *crime novel*: a story where a crime is solved by the police or an investigator
- *thriller*: an exciting story, especially one about crime or a mystery.

ANSWERS
1 c   2 e   3 d   4 a   5 b   6 f

9 This exercise provides an opportunity for students to practise using the vocabulary related to books.

Encourage students to try to use the adverbs from the previous page. If they say they don't like reading, ask them which book they would choose from the pictures on page 48 if they had to choose one.

POSSIBLE ANSWERS
fantasy, sci-fi, horror story, comedy, mystery, short stories

10 1·48 This exercise raises students' awareness that varying the position of the main stress in a sentence can change the meaning.

You may need to remind students of the meaning of the word *stressed* (pronounced with emphasis). Read them multiple times, and each time change which word you stress, to show students that we can choose where to place the stress in English depending on the meaning we want to communicate.

ANSWERS
Stressed words are shown in bold in the audioscript below.

Audioscript 1·48
1 I often drink **coffee** when I read.
2 I often drink coffee when I **read**.

11 This exercise develops students' understanding of how sentence stress relates to meaning.

Encourage students to first try saying the sentences aloud. Ask them to work in pairs, and then check as a whole class. The focus is for students to show they understand the meaning, rather than to write perfectly formed questions, so a variety of answers can be accepted within reason.

POSSIBLE ANSWERS
1 What do you read on planes?
2 How often do you read magazines (on planes)?
3 Where / When do you read magazines?

12 This exercise improves students' use of sentence stress by encouraging them to focus on using sentence stress to enhance what they want to say.

As you monitor, correct issues with sentence stress, and offer encouragement when the students seem to have understood.

VOCABULARY FILE Student's Book page 125
Refer students to exercises 1 and 2 for extra practice using words related to books.

ANSWERS
See page 133 of this book for answers.

Exam skills

13 This exercise improves students' ability to extend responses to personal topic-related questions by generalizing, speculating, and giving examples.

Students may need clarification of *special occasions* (e.g. birthdays, weddings, romantic holidays, etc.).

Ask students to compare their answers with a partner, and then check as a whole class. Focus on the different ways they can expand their answers by asking which sentences are general (1 and 4), which ones are talking about the future (2, a, d), and which sentence gives an example (b).

ANSWERS
1 b   2 d   3 a   4 c

14 Ask students to complete the sentences individually, then share their sentences with a partner.

Alternative for weaker classes: allow students to work in pairs. Ask them to check with another pair when they finish.

POSSIBLE ANSWERS
1 Generally, I prefer books with pictures. I often read comics and manga.
2 People sometimes read to make themselves look clever. I occasionally do it myself!
3 I regularly read non-fiction, but sometimes I read short stories.
4 I think maybe we won't need 'real' libraries in the future. Possibly, only universities will keep them.

15 This exercise familiarizes students with the range of possible question forms in Parts 1 and 3 in order to predict the types of questions they might be asked.

Ask students which part of the exam features personal questions (Part 1), and which part asks about bigger issues that affect more people than just you (Part 3). When they have finished, check any points that they did not agree on.

ANSWERS
1 P1   2 P1   3 P3   4 P3   5 P1   6 P3

Exam practice

16 Allow 10 minutes' discussion time. Remind students that the Part 1 questions are designed to 'warm you up', but it is important to make a good first impression. Also, highlight the importance of extending answers as long as possible.

> **Optional activity**
>
> Fluency in formulating questions will make students better able to anticipate question forms in the exam. To allow them to practise asking and answering questions more fluently, write up some common stems for Part 1 and Part 3 questions on the board:
>
> Part 1
> *How often do you … Why?*
> *Would you like to …?*
> *When was the last time that you …?*
> *What time of day do you …?*
>
> Part 3
> *Why do you think some people …?*
> *Do you think we will … more in the future?*
> *Is it better to … or …?*
> *Was … more popular in the past?*
>
> Now put students in pairs and call out topics, e.g. books, films, musical instruments, and drawing, and a part of the exam (Part 1 or 3); and have them ask and answer questions accordingly.

LISTENING Labelling plans and maps (page 50)

EXAM FOCUS: SECTIONS 1 & 2

Lesson aims
1 Enable students to complete plans and maps by training them to quickly scan the image and make predictions.
2 Improve students' understanding of listening questions related to entertainment by recognizing words and phrases about entertainment facilities.
3 Raise students' awareness of the difference between concrete and abstract vocabulary, to help them prioritize which words to spend more time learning.

Key language
Entertainment facilities: balcony, VIP box, aisle, ticket office, dance floor, fire exit, screen, cloakroom, snack bar, seating area, main auditorium, main entrance
Events: opera, music festival
Abstract nouns: purpose, opinion, explanation, benefit, trend, cause

Topic focus

Optional lead-in
If you have an interactive whiteboard, display some images taken from the internet. If not, print out some images of arts venues or find some in newspaper arts supplements. Ask students to see how many they can name. Alternatively, ask students to use their mobile devices to find images of arts venues they've been to. Have them show their images and ask others in the class whether they can name them.

1 This exercise introduces the topic of *entertainment venues* and checks the meaning of this phrase.
Focus students on the photo and ask if this is a normal cinema (no, an IMAX cinema shows 3D films). Ask if anyone has been to an IMAX, and if they liked the experience (some people do not enjoy IMAX films because wearing the 3D glasses can cause motion sickness).

ANSWER
IMAX cinema

2 This exercise encourages students to think of topic vocabulary they already know.
When most of the class has finished, ask students if their partner had any ideas different to their own. Write any useful words on the board and ask students to copy them into their notebooks.

POSSIBLE ANSWERS
club, stadium, arena, opera house, theatre, disco

Vocabulary

3 This exercise improves students' understanding of listening questions related to entertainment by recognizing words and phrases about entertainment facilities.
Before students begin, you may like to check the meaning of the vocabulary by asking:

- *balcony:* In an apartment, is the balcony normally inside or outside? (outside) In an entertainment venue, is it normally inside or outside? (inside)
- *VIP boxes:* What type of people go in the VIP boxes? (normally famous people, or rich people. VIP stands for Very Important Person)
- *aisle:* Do you sit or walk in an aisle? (walk) How many aisles can you see in the picture of the theatre at the bottom of the page? (four – two down the middle, and two down the sides of the room)
- *fire exit:* Does exit mean come in or go out? (go out)
- *screen:* What do you have in your house with a screen? (probably a computer and TV)
- *cloakroom:* What do you put in the cloakroom? (bags, jackets, and coats)
- *snack bar:* What can you buy at a snack bar? (food and drink) What type of food can you buy? (e.g. crisps, chocolate, ice cream, hotdogs, but not big meals)

POSSIBLE ANSWERS
balcony – theatre, cinema
VIP boxes – club
aisles – cinema, theatre
ticket office – cinema
dance floor – club
fire exits – cinema, club, theatre
screen – cinema
cloakroom – theatre
snack bar – cinema

4 If students finish talking too soon, encourage them to ask each other questions using the vocabulary in exercise 3, for example: *How many aisles are there?* Motivate students to listen to each other by telling them you will ask questions about what their partner said in whole-class feedback.

VOCABULARY FILE Student's Book (page 125)
Refer students to exercise 3 for extra practice using words related to entertainment facilities.

ANSWERS
See page 133 of this book for answers.

Exam skills

5 This exercise trains students to scan the image and make predictions before listening.
Before students begin, you may like to check the meaning of some words in the box, for example:

- *main entrance:* Do you come in or go out of the entrance? (come in) Is the main entrance normally at the front or back of a venue? (front)

- *stage:* Who stands on the stage? (the performers)
- *auditorium:* Is it normally big or small? (big) What do you find in an auditorium? (normally a stage and seating)

Focus students on the plan of the theatre and tell them to ignore the text for now. Highlight that they should only use their knowledge to try and predict the layout of the theatre. Point out that this is an important step in the exam because it can prevent them getting 'lost' as they listen if they are able to successfully navigate the plan.

EXAM TIP 1·49 Before students listen, ask them to suggest possible answers to the question and write these on the board. After they have answered the question, refer students to page 146 for more guidance on dealing with plans and maps.

ANSWER
Check the instructions to see if you have to write a letter or a word; use your knowledge of similar places to predict the ones on the plan or map.

Audioscript 1·49
On plans and maps, there's a lot to look at and it's sometimes difficult to find all the question numbers. As well as making sure you find the gaps for all the questions, **check the instructions to see if you have to write a letter or a word**. Then, in the 30 seconds you have to prepare, **use your knowledge of similar places to predict the ones on the plan or map**.

6 1·50 This exercise gives students practice at listening for preposition phrases that are essential for following maps and diagrams.

Get students to complete the gaps. They are unlikely to have a similar task in the exam but they are acquiring familiarity with language that will serve them in the exam practice section.

ANSWERS
1 outside
2 To the right
3 on your right
4 in the middle
5 on the left
6 straight on
7 opposite
8 in front of you
9 to your left

Audioscript 1·50
Welcome to the Pitt Lane Theatre. Here we are **outside** the main entrance. **To the right**, you can see the ticket office. As we enter the theatre, **on your right** you'll see a cloakroom and **in the middle** of the foyer there's a snack bar. If you need the toilets, they're **on the left**. When you're ready, go **straight on**, across the foyer and **opposite** you'll see a door into the main auditorium. Through this and **in front of you** there's the stage. Turn **to your left** and you'll see the seating area and on the other side you'll see the fire exit.

7 This exercise raises students' awareness of how much they can predict through their knowledge of the world before they even listen.

Ask students to now read the text and say how many facilities they guessed correctly. Tell them that these are 'free' marks they could get in the exam before they even listen. However, warn them not to simply presume their ideas are correct and 'switch off'. They must listen and check. But it is a good starting point and helps them to focus as they listen.

Optional activity
Ask students to listen again but this time to look only at the map and not at the complete audioscript. They can trace a line on the map with their pencils as the recording 'takes' them through the building. Performing this task in pairs (with one holding the pencil and the other watching / correcting) may help students to support each other and quickly identify errors in understanding.

Exam practice
8 1·51 Ask students what type of map it is (a map of a festival site). You may like to ask students if they have been to a festival like this, to help predict what type of information they might hear. Remind them of the steps they should take by asking what they should do first (find all the gaps and make predictions by looking at the surrounding information). Allow students to listen twice if necessary, but remind them they will only hear it once in the exam. On the first listening they could put away their pens and simply follow the recording by tracing a path through the festival site using their fingers only. After listening, tell students to show their answers to a partner. They should check if the other person's answers make sense. For example, if they have labelled number 3 the John Peel Stage, this is clearly not correct as it is already labelled elsewhere. Check answers as a whole class.

Background note: The map is actually for the UK's most famous music festival, called Glastonbury, which is held over a long weekend in the summer in the south-west of England.

ANSWERS
1 pedestrian gate
2 property locker
3 market area
4 meeting point
5 charging tent
6 medical centre

Audioscript 1·51
OK, so let's look at the map. Er … The Other Stage is at the far side of the festival area. Now we're camping in Spring Field, here, so we're lucky because that's right next to the **pedestrian gate**. You need to go through that and then straight on down the track. OK? On your right, you'll pass a **property locker** if that's useful to you for storing your stuff. There are also a couple of ATMs – erm, here they are. Then eventually you'll come to the **market area** – that's the big square section in the middle of the map, just here. It's really easy to get lost because there are so many stalls and things to look at, but don't worry because there's a **meeting point** just to the right of it. Can you see? OK, so you need to continue to the opposite corner of this area, around the track past the main arena. There you'll find the **charging tent** – useful if your mobile battery dies. Anyway, just behind that you'll see The Other Stage though you'll probably

hear it first! We'll be there all afternoon so come and find us. We usually sit somewhere near the back of the field, sort of here, away from the stage and close to the **medical centre**. Call or text me once you get there! OK?

> **Optional activity**
>
> In pairs, ask students to write directions from the classroom to somewhere else in the school. They should read their directions to another pair without saying where they are heading. The other pair should listen and try to follow the route in their head, and at the end say where they think they have arrived.

What do you think?

9 This exercise provides students with an opportunity to think critically around the topic of entertainment, develop their knowledge, and generate ideas for the writing and speaking parts of the exam.

You may need to clarify the meaning of *opera* (like theatre, but with classical singing instead of speaking). Group students in threes or fours to discuss. Encourage them to expand their responses by justifying their opinions.

> **Optional activity**
>
> You may like to get students to discuss more questions related to this topic, such as:
>
> - *Have you ever been to the theatre / an opera / a music festival? Did you enjoy it? Why / Why not?*
> - *What should theatres do to attract more young people?*
> - *What are the benefits of going to events like music festivals?*
> - *Do you think people will still be going to the theatre in 50 years' time?*

Study skills

This exercise raises students' awareness of the difference between concrete and abstract vocabulary, to help them prioritize which words to spend more time learning.

Ask students to discuss in pairs before checking as a whole class. Write their ideas on the board. You may like to ask them to look back at units 1–4 to find more examples of abstract vocabulary.

ANSWER

Group 1 contains abstract ideas that help organize academic text. They are much more common in academic text and they have more synonyms, too. This means they appear frequently in IELTS questions and it is a better idea to learn this group first. Group 2 contains words that are more concrete than those in group 1 but, because they are all connected specifically to the topic of culture and entertainment, appear less frequently in academic texts and IELTS questions.

WRITING From brainstorm to plan (page 52)

EXAM FOCUS: TASK 2

Lesson aims

1 Improve students' understanding of personal opinion essay questions.

2 Expand students' range of vocabulary by learning eight verbs to describe positive effects.

3 Enable students to plan a personal opinion essay by brainstorming ideas and grouping them into paragraph topics.

Key language

Nouns: *drama, play, attention level, self-respect, confidence, tolerance, investment, benefit, influence, variety, participation, audience, performer*

Adjectives: *tolerant, artistic, social*

Verbs for positive effects: *improve, provide, develop, create, gain, accomplish, enhance, achieve*

Topic focus

> **Optional lead-in**
>
> You may like to introduce the topic by doing the following:
>
> a Before students open their books, write on one side of the board the heading *Activity* and the following:
> *music …*
> *drama …*
> *plays or concerts …*
> *drawing …*
>
> b On the other side of the board write the heading *Benefit* and the following:
> *… memory and grades*
> *… maths and reading skills*
> *… attention level and self-respect*
> *… tolerance of people who are different.*
>
> c Ask students to work in pairs to match the two sides and discuss why they think their sentence is true.
>
> d Tell students to open their books and read exercise 3 to check their answers.

1 This exercise provides students with an opportunity to focus on their existing vocabulary knowledge related to the topic of the lesson.

Focus students' attention on the photos and discuss as a whole class. Write their ideas on the board, including any related vocabulary (e.g. violins).

ANSWERS

A theatre performance
B painting or drawing / art class
C classical music concert

2 This exercise engages students with the topic by drawing on their personal experiences.

Demonstrate by asking a strong student.

Alternative for weaker classes: you may like to write the direct question on the board in a speech bubble and drill it.

3 If necessary, clarify the words *tolerant* (accepting of others), *attention level* (ability to focus), and *self-respect* (having a positive opinion of yourself). Ask students to discuss in pairs. In whole-class feedback, you may like to ask students who answered yes in exercise 2 whether they experienced any of the benefits mentioned here. Encourage students to give longer answers by asking them why they think these activities might have such effects.

Exam skills

4 This exercise improves students' understanding of *to what extent do you agree* essay questions by demonstrating how they can be reworded.

Remind students of the meaning of *to what extent* by drawing a scale from 0% to 100% on the board. If they have difficulty choosing the correct answer, it may be because they do not understand the word *investment* (buying property, shares in a company, etc. in the hope of making a profit). Before clarifying, encourage students to guess the meaning by asking them what the government is normally asked to give more of (money)

Remind students of the importance of using the context to try and guess the meaning of words, given that you will not be there to help them in the exam.

Teaching tip: Encourage students to try to rephrase exam questions in their own words to make sure they are clear about what they are being asked. It will make their answer more focused and help avoid the common trap of just discussing the topic area in general.

ANSWER
c

5 This exercise provides students with a model of how to plan a *to what extent do you agree* essay, and raises their awareness that the answer can be one-sided and should at least express a clear opinion.

Focus students on the brainstorm and remind them of the question in exercise 4. Ask students to read alone before discussing as a whole class. Make sure they understand they can write a one-sided essay by asking:

- *Will this student's essay show both sides of the argument?* (no)
- *Is this OK for this type of question?* (yes)
- *Is it always OK to only write about one side of the argument?* (No, not always. It depends on the type of question.)
- *How do you know what type of answer you can write?* (by reading the instructions carefully)

ANSWER
The instruction in the essay question – 'To what extent do you agree or disagree with the statement? Give reasons for your answer.' – allows students scope to write on one or other side, provided points are justified. In other words, there is no need for the sort of balanced argument of a discursive essay. In the brainstorm the points are in agreement. The decision to agree may be because the writer has thought of more ideas on this side of the argument.

EXAM TIP 1·52 Before students listen, ask them to suggest possible answers to the question and write these on the board. After they have answered the question, refer students to page 147 for more guidance on choosing paragraph topics.

ANSWER
Planning – select the best ideas to help you write the two or three body paragraphs of the essay or combine related ideas in your brainstorm to create larger paragraph topics.

Audioscript 1·52
Before you start writing your essay, **it's important to write a plan with paragraph topics. Choosing good paragraph topics will help you to organize your ideas clearly and avoid repetition.** Each topic you choose must be different from the others, but general enough for you to add examples and explanations in the paragraph. **Look for points in your brainstorm that you could group together in one category** and try to think of labels like 'social', 'economic', or 'cultural' that connect them.

6 This exercise encourages students to organize their ideas into paragraphs by demonstrating how arguments can be grouped into sub-topics.

Check students understand the meaning of the word *paragraph* by asking them how many paragraphs there are in the reading text on page 55. Ask them to discuss in pairs before discussing the options as a whole class.

Teaching tip: Your students may speak languages in which paragraphs are used differently or do not exist at all. If so, you may like to remind them when we use a new paragraph (at the start of a new point), and look back at reading texts in units 1 to 4 to examine when new paragraphs are used.

ANSWER
Paragraph b – a paragraph topic ought to focus on a particular type of benefit and develop it, in this case academic benefits. Paragraph b would also favour a wider readership.

Paragraph a is too broad for a single paragraph, and paragraph c is too specific for the needs of the essay.

7 This exercise improves students' ability to choose paragraph topics and avoid falling into the trap of focusing only on one specific example, rather than a sub-topic.

Tell students to ignore the gaps for now and only look at the two choices for each paragraph topic. Ask them to work alone before checking with a partner. In whole-class feedback, ask students why the other options are not possible, to elicit that they are too specific and should be used as supporting arguments instead.

ANSWERS
Paragraph topic 1: Social benefits of art
Paragraph topic 2: Benefits to individuals
Paragraph topic 3: Effects on community relations

8 This exercise demonstrates to students how they can build their paragraphs by grouping points from their plan.

Draw students' attention to the letters in the brainstorm and clarify that they only need to write letters in the gaps, not the full point. Ask them to work alone before checking with a partner.

POSSIBLE ANSWERS
Paragraph topic 1   D, E
Paragraph topic 2   A, B
Paragraph topic 3   C, F

Exam practice

9 This exercise engages students with the topic by providing an opportunity to respond personally.

You may need to clarify the meaning of *influence* (effect) and *performing arts* (arts such as music, dance, and drama which are performed for an audience). Ask students to discuss in pairs before comparing ideas as a whole class.

MODEL ANSWER
See exercise 2 in the WRITING FILE on page 143 of the Student's Book for a model answer.

> **Alternative**
> You may like to discuss this as a whole class and write students' ideas on the board. This would enable you to return to their ideas after exercise 11 and, as a class, practise grouping the ideas into paragraph topics.

10 This exercise gives students a chance to practise the skills developed in exercises 7 and 8, with more freedom to choose how to organize the ideas.

Demonstrate by asking students for an example of a point which could go under *performers*. Ask students to work with a partner before checking as a whole class. Write the six paragraph topics on the board. Ask for possible matching letters and write their ideas under the topics.

POSSIBLE ANSWERS
performers	A, C, E, F, H
variety in art	A, C, F, G, H
business	C, D, F, H
audiences	B, D, E, G
the internet	B, C, D, G, H
participation in art	B, C, D, H

11 Students now turn the brainstorm into a plan by choosing the most suitable ideas and rejecting others.

Encourage students to consider how their three paragraphs connect. For example, it is logical to consider the benefits for performers followed by benefits for audiences, or vice versa. Tell students they can add their own ideas as well as using the points in exercise 10. When they have finished, ask them to compare their plan with another pair.

WRITING FILE Student's Book page 143
Refer students to exercise 3 on this page for another personal opinion question, accompanied by a sample essay.

ANSWERS
See page 136 of this book for answers.

Vocabulary

12 The eight verbs in this exercise could be used in a Task 2 essay to describe positive effects.

Highlight that the definitions relate to more than one verb by asking students how many definitions there are and how many bold words there are. Tell them that this vocabulary is useful in academic writing to discuss a range of topics, not only art. Ask students to work alone before checking with a partner.

ANSWERS
1 b   2 c   3 b   4 c   5 c   6 a   7 b   8 a

13 As students are discussing, monitor for any misunderstandings to correct, and interesting examples to share in whole-class feedback.

VOCABULARY FILE Student's Book page 125
Refer students to exercises 7–9 for extra practice using words related to verbs for positive effect.

ANSWERS
See pages 133–134 of this book for answers.

READING Matching information and features page 54

> ### Lesson aims
> 1 Improve students' ability to locate information in a passage by identifying key words and scanning for related words in the text.
> 2 Develop students' ability to locate and match opinions in a passage by recognizing verbs such as *believe, consider,* or *think,* and scanning for names.
> 3 Enable students to understand and use phrases that introduce examples, reasons, and effects.

> ### Key language
> **Nouns:** *critic, review, blogger, influence, popularity, standard, status, criticism*
> **Adjectives:** *sophisticated, professional*
> **Phrases to introduce examples:** *illustrates, for instance, such as, for example*
> **Phrases to introduce reasons:** *because, as, since, due to*
> **Phrases to introduce effects:** *so, as a result, consequently, outcome, resulting in*

Topic focus

> **Optional lead-in**
> Look online or in your local newspaper for film reviews (even if they are not in English). Show the reviews to students and ask if they follow the advice of film critics

1 This exercise engages students with the topic of the lesson by reflecting on their personal preferences.

You may need to clarify the meaning of *film critics* (people who write about new films for newspapers and magazines) and *bloggers* (people who write on blogs, which are online journals that can be written by anyone, not only professional writers).

2 Focus students' attention on the example in the speech bubble. Encourage them to expand their answers by explaining why.

Exam skills

3 This exercise improves students' ability to locate information in a passage by identifying key words in the question.

Ask students why it is important to do this, to elicit that it can help them read more efficiently by focusing on the precise information they need.

ANSWER
recent – this should direct students to the last part of the text, which is organized chronologically

EXAM TIP 1·53 Before students listen, ask them to suggest possible answers to the question and write these on the board. After they have answered the question, refer students to page 148 for more guidance on matching questions.

ANSWERS
1 underline all the key words in the questions
2 decide which key word to look for first in the passage

Audioscript 1·53

Some matching questions in the Reading test ask you to look for specific information. To do this, you'll need to scan the passage to identify which paragraph contains the information. Before you actually start looking, **underline all the key words in the questions** and then **decide which key word to look for first in the passage**. Proper nouns, like people's names, and dates are usually easiest to find. Once you've located the word or idea you're looking for, read that part of the passage carefully to make sure that there are synonyms for all the key language in the question.

4 This exercise develops students' scanning skills to find words in the text which match key words in the question.

Allow students only 3 minutes to read, as they should not be reading every word if they are scanning. After reading, ask them to check their ideas in pairs.

ANSWER
E

Exam practice

5 This exercise provides students with an opportunity to practise identifying key words and scanning for matching information.

Ask students to identify the key words in the questions first and check these as a whole class. Discuss as a class what types of words they could be scanning for as a result of the identifying the key words, for example:
- *effects of a change*: a good thing or a bad thing?
- *communicate*: maybe letters / phones / emails?
- *where you can read*: maybe magazines / newspapers / online?

After students read, check answers and ask students what words in the text matched their key words (see answers below).

ANSWERS
1 Paragraph D
   effects – resulting in / outcome
   change – a century after / no longer / now / lower the standards
   communicate – the internet
2 Paragraph E
   where – names of websites (Rotten Tomatoes and IMDb)
   opinions – reviews / insights / view
3 Paragraph B
   1920s – 1928 (dates should be very quick to scan for, but remind students not to be too quick to jump to a conclusion, because 1929 is in paragraph C).
   innovation – the first / was born / key moment
   was not liked – many professional film critics did not like
4 Paragraph A
   change – at first / but at the start of the twentieth century / films started to / soon afterwards
   popularity – popular / low status / higher status
5 Paragraph C
   event – media awards ceremony / The Oscars
   copied – followed with their own
6 Paragraphs A and E
   new way – arrived / started to appear (A)
   evolved / change (E)

Note: Students may ask for clarification of vocabulary such as *innovation* (question 3) and *popularity* (question 4). Encourage students to try and work out the meaning themselves first. For example, if they replace *innovation* with the word *something*, the question still makes sense. Students may know the word *popular* but not recognize *popularity*, so help them to identify what part of speech it is (noun) and what the adjective might be.

> **Optional activity**
> a Put students into pairs and give them a number. Then ask them to turn to the reading text on page 15.
> b Ask each pair to write their number and a paragraph matching question for the text on a slip of paper. You may wish to focus each pair's attention on a different paragraph to make sure they are not working on the same part of the text.
> c Pass each pair's questions onto the next pair. Tell each pair to answer the question they receive but tell them to write their answers on a separate piece of paper, not on the question paper.
> d Repeat until all questions have been answered by each group.
> e Invite each pair in turn to give the correct answer to their question to the class.

Exam skills

6 This exercise raises students' awareness of the importance of scanning for names to read efficiently in opinion matching questions.

Discuss as a whole class. If a student says the correct answer, ask them to justify why. If students have difficulty answering, ask which word is the most specific or unusual in the question.

Teaching tip: Scanning for names is easy in English because capital letters stand out. But some students might not instinctively look for names in this way if capital letters are used differently in their language, or are perhaps not used at all. So you may need to point out that looking for capital letters is a quick way to find names.

ANSWER
The name W.G. Faulkner (since it is easy to locate).

7 This exercise develops students' ability to locate and match opinions in a passage by recognizing verbs which introduce opinions.

The verbs *believe, consider*, and *think* are not used here; the sentence is introduced with the verb *observed*. Highlight to students that they should scan for these types of words around the name of the person when answering opinion matching questions. In this text, the opinion also stands out more clearly because of the speech marks. Remind students to look out for this kind of clue.

ANSWERS
The cinema had now 'become an everyday part of the national life'

8 This exercise provides students with the final step in a three-step approach for matching opinions, namely:
 • scan for the name
 • scan for verbs suggesting an opinion
 • compare the person's opinion to the options, like in this exercise.

If students are having difficulty, focus them on the words *everyday* and *national* to help them match.

Teaching tip: Students may be inclined to read the options first and then try to find a part of the text that matches one of the options. Draw students' attention to the fact that the technique practised in exercises 6–8 involves matching the text to the options, rather than matching the options to the text. Highlight that this technique is preferable as it is usually easier to scan for names first than words in the statements.

ANSWER
1

Exam practice

9 Remind students of the steps in exercises 6–8 by asking what they should do first (find the names) and how (look for the capital letters). To encourage students to follow the technique, you may like to set a time limit for each stage, and allow them to check with a partner after each step, for example:
 • 2 minutes to circle the names (then check with a partner)
 • 5 minutes to underline opinions around those names (then check)
 • 5 minutes to match the opinions with statements in the question (check).

Note: the 'name' in B is harder to find as it is not a proper name and is therefore not capitalized. However, point out to students that the words in the text are identical (i.e. *professional film critics* is exactly what appears in lines 19–20).

ANSWERS
A 2 (*standards in the 'movie' industry in general needed raising…* lines 22–23)
B 5 (*its simplicity…* line 21)
C 1 (*to preserve the neutrality and professionalism…* line 27)
D 4 (*the outcome of this has been to lower the standards…* lines 38–39)
E 3 (*reviews are much clearer now…* line 45)

Vocabulary

10 This exercise raises students' awareness of the importance of recognizing the role of phrases that introduce examples, reasons, and effects, to read more efficiently.

Ask students to discuss in pairs before checking as a whole class. Raise their awareness of understanding the role of these phrases by asking: *How can these phrases help you read more quickly?* (They prepare you for the information that is coming next so you are not reading word by word but instead just reading to confirm what you have already subconsciously predicted you will read. This provides forward momentum, to read more quickly.)

Language note: Students are likely to have most difficulty understanding the structure of *so*. You may like to point out that *so* works in the opposite way to *because* by writing on the board:
 • *Fewer people go to the cinema* **because** *watching films at home is now common.*

70 UNIT 5 CULTURE & ENTERTAINMENT

- *Watching films at home is now common so fewer people go to the cinema.*

Underline the reason in one colour (watching films at home) and the effect in another colour (fewer people go to the cinema).

ANSWERS

1 effect   2 example   3 reason

VOCABULARY FILE Student's Book page 125

Refer students to exercises 4–6 for extra practice using phrases that introduce examples, reasons, and effects.

ANSWERS

See page 133 of this book for answers.

11 This exercise enables students to understand a range of phrases that introduce examples, reasons, and effects.

Encourage students to locate these words and phrases in the text on page 55 to understand the meanings from the context of the sentences:

Phrase	Line number
for instance	28, 47–48
since	3, 45
such as	16, 37
as a result	8
consequently	23
outcome	38
due to	20–21
resulting in	36

Note: *as* and *for example* are not included in the text, but students should be familiar with them.

Analysing the words and phrases in the sentences will also familiarize students with how the structures operate. You may like to help them notice this by asking questions such as:

- *Which phrases are followed by nouns / noun phrases?* (such as, due to, for instance, resulting in)
- *Which word introduces a new clause (a new subject and main verb)?* (since)
- *Which word is used at the beginning of a sentence?* (Consequently)
- *Which words and phrases are followed by commas?* (as a result, consequently)
- *What is the full phrase including the word 'outcome'?* (the outcome of this has been to …)

ANSWERS

Introducing examples – illustrates, for instance, such as, for example
Introducing reasons – because, as, since, due to
Introducing effects – so, as a result, consequently, outcome, resulting in

12 Focus students' attention on the example. Ask them to work alone, or in pairs with weaker classes. After writing, tell students to compare their sentences with a partner / another pair.

Alternative for weaker classes: write the example on the board and highlight which parts of the sentence students can change (i.e. *action films, exciting,* and *society is becoming more violent*).

Alternative

Ask students to write gapped sentences by leaving a space for the phrase from exercise 11. Tell students to pass their sentence to another pair who should guess the missing phrase.

What do you think?

13 This exercise encourages students to use vocabulary from the lesson related to the cinema, and generates ideas which could be particularly useful in Speaking Part 2.

Tell students to ask two follow-up questions based on what their partner says when they have finished speaking. This encourages them to listen more carefully to each other. You may like to get students to discuss more questions on this topic, such as:

- *Do you think people will still go to the cinema in 50 years' time?*
- *Do you think violent films are to blame for an increase in violence?*
- *Do you think it is important to put age restrictions on films? Why / Why not?*
- *Do you think the Hollywood representation of romance gives people unrealistic expectations in life, and puts pressure on relationships?*

Optional activity

For homework, ask students to read a film review online or in a local newspaper or magazine for a film they have seen. In the next class they can then summarize the review and say if they agree with it.

EXAM CHALLENGE

ANSWERS

Speaking
1 & 2 Students' own answers

Listening
1 See page 137 of this book for answers and page 141 for the audioscript.
2 Students' own answers

Reading
1 See page 139 of this book for answers.
2 Students' own answers

Writing
1 Students' own answers
2 See page 108 of the Student's Book for the model answer.

UNIT 6   Careers & success

Introduction page 57

Featured topic vocabulary

Jobs: *architect, carer, author, seller, entertainer, administrator, promoter, helper, advisor, technician, artist, scientist, journalist, inventor, teacher, general*

Nouns: *expert, career, economy, success*

Collocations: *belong to (a group), naturally suited to, earn money*

Optional lead-in

Before students open their books, you may like to do the following:

a Group students in fours and give each group a piece of paper.

b Tell each group to brainstorm as many different jobs as they can think of.

c Stop students after 2 minutes. Tell them to exchange papers with another group.

d Ask students to open their books and look at the infographic. Tell students to give the other group a point for each job they listed that is mentioned in the infographic. The group with the most points wins.

What do you think?

Focus students' attention on the title of the unit and check students understand by asking:

- *Which one is a career: working at a summer kids' camp for two months or teaching?* (Teaching. The other one is temporary. We often talk about 'building a career', because it has a sense of progression with possibilities for promotion and development.)

- *What would a footballer consider to be success in his career?* (playing for a top team / many goals / winning)

Before students discuss, you may need to clarify words such as:

- *expert*: a person with specialist knowledge, skill, or training in something

- *economy*: the financial situation of a country as a whole

- *suited to*: right or appropriate for

- *earn*: get money by doing a job.

Group students in threes. Ask them to discuss questions 1–3 in their groups first. Get feedback as a whole class before moving onto the next question. Ask students to discuss questions 4 and 5 next. Then get feedback.

Background note: The information in the infographic is based on the famous Myers Briggs Type Indicator (MBTI) test, which is still commonly used by careers counsellors. It is based on the assumption that we all have preferences in the way we experience the world. The test was originally developed by Katharine Cook Briggs and her daughter, Isabel Briggs Myers, to help women who were entering the industrial workforce for the first time to identify the sort of wartime jobs that would be 'most comfortable and effective' for them. It was first published in 1962. The career descriptions were later mapped onto the sixteen categories by David Keirsey in the Keirsey Temperament Sorter questionnaire. The statistics given show in which proportions the MBTI tends to categorize test takers in the USA. The data is published at www.myersbriggs.org.

SPEAKING Varying language page 58

EXAM FOCUS: PART 2

Lesson aims

1 Develop students' ability to vary their language by using different parts of speech and avoid repeating the same type of structures.

2 Enable students to use the second conditional to speak about hypothetical situations in order to show the examiner they can construct complicated sentences.

3 Expand students' range of character adjectives and nouns to describe people and personalities.

4 Improve students' pronunciation by using contractions to sound more natural.

Key language

Character adjectives: *inspiring, intelligent, fair, determined, imaginative, passionate, ambitious, courageous, forward-looking, competent, honest, supportive*

Character nouns: *inspiration, intelligence, fairness, determination, imagination, passion, ambition, courage, competence, honesty, support*

Featured topic vocabulary

Nouns: *leader, skill, encouragement, characteristic, hero, role model*

Adjectives: *brave, enthusiastic, successful*

Adverb: *equally*

Verbs: *treat, look up to*

Topic focus

Optional lead-in
You may like to take photos into class of famous leaders your students are likely to know (e.g. Barack Obama) or find some images online. Display them for the students and ask:
- *Who are these people?*
- *What do they have in common?* (They are all famous leaders.)
- *What makes them good leaders?*

Discuss as a whole class and write students' ideas on the board.

1 This exercise introduces students to the topic of characteristics and encourages them to think about vocabulary they already know to describe people.

Students may need clarification of vocabulary such as:
- *leader*: a person who leads a group of people, especially the head of a country, an organization, etc.
- *skill*: the ability to do something well
- *encouragement*: giving someone support to do something
- *treat*: behave in a particular way towards someone
- *brave*: willing to do something difficult, dangerous, or painful
- *enthusiastic*: feeling or showing lots of excitement and interest about something
- *successful*: achieving your aims or what was intended.

Ask students to discuss in pairs before taking a vote as a whole class. As students are speaking, take a note of any topic-related vocabulary they use and write it on the board.

Optional activity
If your students are reluctant to speak, you may like to do the following to encourage communication:
a Write statements a–j on a piece of paper and make one photocopy per group of four students.
b Cut up the paper so the statements are on separate pieces. Tell each group to order their papers from most to least important.
c If they do not agree, they should try to justify their opinion.

The papers can also be used again in exercise 2.

Vocabulary

2 This exercise expands students' range of character adjectives to describe people and personalities.

Alternative for weaker classes: ask students to work in pairs. Write the words from the box on the board. Check answers as a whole class by asking students for adjectives they are most sure about first, and write the correct letters next to the adjectives on the board. After each correct answer, drill the pronunciation and mark the stress on the word.

Optional activity
If you have cut up the statements in exercise 1 on separate papers, then you can do the same here with the adjectives. Students can then physically match the vocabulary papers and definitions papers before doing the exercise in the book. Keep the papers for vocabulary revision, using games like snap. To play snap:
a Students turn up one adjective and then turn over the definitions until they see the one that matches.
b The first person to put their hand on the matching paper and say 'snap' wins a point.
c Put the definition back into the pile. Turn over a new adjective and start again, turning over the definitions until the matching paper appears.

ANSWERS
a competent   f passionate
b supportive   g forward-looking
c fair   h inspiring
d courageous   i imaginative
e determined   j ambitious

(*intelligent* and *honest* are not defined in exercise 1)

3 If students involved themselves in discussion in exercise 1, then you may wish to skip this task. If you choose to do it, encourage them to justify their opinions. Give students 5 minutes to discuss before taking a vote. Read out each adjective and tell them to put their hands up if it is in their top five. Reading out the words revises the pronunciation. Write the number of votes next to the adjectives on the board.

4 Ask students to discuss with a partner before getting whole-class feedback.

5 This exercise encourages students to vary their language by learning word families rather than just individual words.

Ensure students all have access to a dictionary (one per pair or group is sufficient). Demonstrate by asking them to find *inspiring* and *inspiration* in the dictionary. Draw their attention to the letters at the end of each word in the dictionary which indicate what part of speech they are. Ask students to work in pairs before checking answers as a whole class.

You may like to draw students' attention to the endings of the nouns (called *suffixes*) to improve their ability to identify parts of speech. Ask them which nouns have the same ending (*intelligence* and *competence* / *determination* and *imagination*).

ANSWERS

intelligent	intelligence
courageous	courage
fair	fairness
forward-looking	–
determined	determination
imaginative	imagination
competent	competence
passionate	passion
honest	honesty
supportive	support

6 This exercise provides students with an opportunity to personalize the language to help them remember new words.

Students may need clarification of the word *characteristics* (typical features or qualities that someone has) and *admire* (respect someone for what they are or for what they have done). Encourage students to use both the adjectives and nouns in their speaking. After speaking, regroup them into fours. Tell students to summarize their partner's answers to the other pair. Their original partner should listen and check if the information is correct.

VOCABULARY FILE Student's Book **page 126**
Refer students to exercises 1 and 2 for more practice using character adjectives and nouns.

ANSWERS
See page 134 of this book for answers.

Exam skills

7 This exercise raises students' awareness of the positive effect of varying their language compared to the negative effect of being repetitive.

Focus students' attention on the photo and ask: *Why do you think some people admire him?* Ask them to discuss their opinion in pairs before checking as a whole class. Students may need clarification of the word *skilful* (good at doing something, especially something that needs a particular ability or special training). Refer them back to the word *skill* in exercise 1 sentence a and ask what part of speech *skilful* is (adjective).

Alternative for weaker classes: you may like to write sentence 2 on the board so you can highlight the parts that are better than sentence 1.

ANSWERS
Sentence 2 is better because the grammar and vocabulary are more varied. It uses different tenses, different sentence lengths, and changes words to avoid repetition, e.g. *really – so*. Word forms also vary more.

EXAM TIP 1·54 Before students listen, ask them to suggest possible answers to the questions and write these on the board. After they have answered the questions, refer students to page 145 for more guidance on varying your language in the Speaking test.

ANSWER
Part 2, because there aren't as many questions.

Audioscript 1·54
Varying your language helps you to get a higher mark for vocabulary and grammar. In Speaking Parts 1 and 3, the different questions you're asked usually give you the chance to demonstrate different language. However, **during the 2 minutes of Part 2 it's less easy to keep your language varied because there aren't as many questions.** Try to show variety by using different parts of speech or grammar structures, like a passive or conditional sentence.

8 This exercise provides practice at varying language. Focus students on the example and ask:
- *How has this student changed the word 'supportive'?* (adjective changed to noun)
- *What else do you need to change?* (the verb)
- *What verb do we often use with character adjectives?* (to be – here 'is')

Focus students on sentence 2 in exercise 7 and ask:
- *What verb do we often use with character nouns?* (have / have got)
- *If we use the character noun at the beginning of the sentence as the subject, what verb do we need, for example if we say 'his ambition'?* (verb *to be*)

Refer students back to the vocabulary table in exercise 5 to find the nouns for the adjectives *passionate*, *determined*, and *ambitious* to help them. Ask them to work alone before comparing answers with a partner. Check as a whole class.

POSSIBLE ANSWERS
2 He has a lot of passion for his job.
3 She is really fair.
4 I admire my friend's determination.
5 My brother's ambition means he's going to succeed.

Teaching tip: Weaker classes may require a lot of support to manipulate language in this way, because it requires control of the language that they may not have. Support students by guiding them through the sentence one word at a time, for example:
a Write the original sentence on the board. So for sentence 2, write: *My cousin is passionate about his job*.
b Highlight the changes that have already been made in the book by drawing a box around *my cousin*, and underneath writing *He*. Then draw a box around *is*, and ask students how this has changed in the book (*has*).
c Direct students to the first word they need to change by drawing a box around *passionate*. Ask students what type of word they should use with *has* – an adjective or noun? (noun)
d Direct students to exercise 5 to find the noun.
e Draw a box around *about* and ask students if they can change the preposition. Write *for his job* on the board under *about his job*.

9 This exercise provides students with an opportunity to practise the language from exercise 8 more naturally.

Focus students on the example in the speech bubble, and ask how this candidate has varied her language (uses noun, *determination*). Give students 2 minutes to prepare their ideas. Stress that students must use both adjective and noun structures. Monitor for good examples and write these on the board to share with the class.

Grammar

10 Focus students on the example and ask which comes first in this sentence, the *if* clause or result clause (*if* clause). Ask which verb form is used in the *if* clause (past). Ask which sentence puts the result clause first (4), and so what goes in the first gap in sentence 4 (*would be*). Tell students to work alone before checking with a partner.

Ranked 8th most powerful businesswoman by *Fortune Magazine* in 2013, Marissa Mayer became president and CEO of Yahoo! in 2012. Before that she worked for Google as an executive and key spokesperson.

ANSWERS

2 If I had to describe my hero in one word, it would be *courageous*.
3 If I could meet any famous person, it would be a world leader.
4 I think many actors would be successful if they were models, too.
5 If a young woman wanted to look up to a strong female role model, I would suggest Marissa Mayer for her ambition.

GRAMMAR FILE Student's Book page 118
Refer students to this page for more explanation and practice of the second conditional.

ANSWERS
See page 131 of this book for answers.

11 This exercise provides students with an opportunity to personalize the language to help remember it, and create model sentences they can use in the exam.

Do an example with a strong student by asking what famous person they would like to meet, and writing an adapted version of sentence 3 on the board. Tell students to take turns with a partner to say a sentence.

Alternative for weaker classes: get students to write the sentences in their notebooks first before speaking.

12 This exercise raises students' awareness of how they can use contractions to sound more natural.

Ask students to compare their answer with a partner before checking as a whole class. On the board, write:
it + would = it'd
I + had = I'd

You can also use your fingers to show the contraction by putting up one finger for *it*, another for *would* and then pushing your fingers together. Drill the pronunciation by modelling it and telling students to copy.

Teaching tip: Raising students' awareness of the use of contractions in English is also important to develop their listening skills. Students sometimes complain that people 'eat their words' in English, and contractions contribute to the problem. Helping them to produce the contracted form will improve their receptive ability to decode contractions when they hear them.

ANSWER
They use contracted forms (*it'd, I'd*).

13 This exercise aims to ensure students use contractions appropriately.

Discuss as a whole class. If students are unsure, ask questions such as:
- *Do you think we use them more in speaking or writing?* (speaking)
- *Is it OK to use them in writing?* (yes, but not for more formal writing, like academic writing)
- *Why do you think we use them in speaking?* (because the words join naturally when you are speaking quickly, so it's easier to say).

ANSWER
Contractions are normally used in spoken English or informal written English.

14 This exercise improves students' pronunciation by using contractions to sound more natural. Ask students to practise in pairs. Monitor and correct where necessary.

Exam practice

15 This exercise provides students with an opportunity to incorporate everything from the lesson into their speaking, and reflect on how this improves their performance in Part 2.

Tell students to work in pairs, make notes of any language used from this lesson as they are listening to their partner. Get feedback as a whole class by asking if anyone's partner used contractions / the second conditional / adjectives and nouns for character.

Alternative for weaker classes: you may like to provide more support by doing the following before they speak.

a Demonstrate how students can incorporate everything from the lesson in this lesson. Ask them to listen to you answering the question and tell them to make a note of anything they hear from the lesson. In your answer, make sure you include examples of varied language with nouns and adjectives, and the second conditional with contractions.

b Then ask students to choose one famous person as a whole class and brainstorm ideas together first. Encourage them to think about the language they studied in this lesson. Write their ideas on the board.

c Tell students to practise speaking in pairs using the ideas you prepared as a class. You may like to get them to do it again with a new partner.

d Then ask students to think of a different famous person and prepare their own answer. Tell them to listen to each other and make a note of any language from the lesson that their partner uses.

LISTENING Completing notes page 60

EXAM FOCUS: SECTION 3

Lesson aims
1 Improve students' ability to complete notes from a recording by identifying matching information that is similar but not identical to that given.
2 Expand students' range of vocabulary to recognize words and phrases related to working conditions, to improve students' ability to listen to talks on this topic.
3 Develop students' techniques for recording and learning vocabulary by reflecting on their current method and considering alternatives.

Key language
Working conditions: *salary, full time, company car, company pension, overtime, promotion, flexitime, bonus, training opportunities, attractive location, pay rise, holiday*
Nouns: *applicant, position, commission, placement*
Adjective: *generous*

Topic focus

1 This exercise engages students with the topic of working conditions and develops their knowledge by reflecting on satisfaction levels in relation to salary.

After discussing in pairs, take a class vote to find out which is more popular.

2 Ask students to discuss in pairs before comparing ideas as a whole class. Encourage them to explain why they think people in the study chose number 1.

Vocabulary

3 This exercise develops knowledge of words and phrases related to working conditions, to improve students' ability to listen to talks on this topic.

Ask students to try the exercise first before clarifying meaning, as it means you can then focus on the words they found most difficult. Group them into fours to check their answers. Write the three headings on the board and ask a representative from each group to come to the board and take turns to write one word in each column. Allocate a point for each correct answer. You may like to check the meaning of each word as it is written on the board by asking:

- *company pension:* At what age do you normally get a pension? (around 65 in most countries)
- *overtime:* If you work overtime, do you work more or fewer hours than normal? (more)
- *promotion:* If you are a teacher, what job do you think you would get with a promotion? (e.g. head of department or head teacher)
- *flexitime:* Why do parents often want to work flexitime? (because they can choose when they start and finish work so they can arrange it around their child's schedule)

- *bonus:* When and why do people get bonuses? (Usually at the end of the year or when you hit your target. It's extra money on top of your salary, to reward you for good work.)
- *training opportunities:* Why do young people often want this with their job? (because it gives them extra qualifications and experience, to help them get a better job next time)
- *attractive location:* What makes a location attractive? (if it's in a beautiful and safe area, and is easy to get to by car or public transport, with good cafés and facilities nearby)
- *pay rise:* When do you usually get a pay rise? (When you get promoted or get more qualifications. Most companies used to give regular pay rises, for example at the end of each year, but it is less common to automatically get a pay rise every year nowadays.)
- *holiday:* How many days' holiday do people normally get a year in your country? (In the UK, employees are entitled to a legal minimum of 28 paid annual leave days per year, but the average is 34 days a year.)

ANSWERS
Financial: company pension, bonus, pay rise
Working hours: overtime, flexitime
Other benefits: promotion, training opportunities, attractive location, holiday

4 This exercise prepares students to listen and develops their prediction skills, which are crucial in the listening exam.

Ask students for suggestions as a whole class, and write their ideas next to the words on the board. If students disagree, write the same number next to more than one word. Check that they understand the £ symbol, which means *pounds* (the currency used in the UK).

ANSWERS
1 full time
2 overtime
3 salary / bonus / pay rise
4 salary / bonus / pay rise
5 bonus / pay rise
6 holiday
7 flexitime
8 salary / bonus / pay rise

5 🔊 1·55 Ask students to compare their answers with a partner and play the recording again if necessary. Check answers as a whole class by ticking the correct predictions already on the board and deleting any wrong answers.

Optional activity
To consolidate the vocabulary further, you may like to ask students to turn to the audioscript on page 168 of their books and highlight the vocabulary from exercise 3. Encourage them to notice the verb (*get*) before each item, or any adjectives (*good salary*). This will encourage them to notice collocation and help them remember the vocabulary.

ANSWERS
1 full time (hours a week)
2 overtime
3 salary
4 not mentioned
5 pay rise
6 holiday
7 no flexitime
8 bonus

76 UNIT 6 CAREERS & SUCCESS

Audioscript 1·55
Anna: Sam, hi. How's it going?
Sam: Good. Anna, guess what! I've been offered that job!
Anna: Congratulations! Great news!
Sam: I know, I know. But I haven't accepted it yet.
Anna: Oh. Why not?
Sam: Well, actually … I just wanted to ask what you think about conditions.
Anna: OK. So what are they offering?
Sam: Well, it's a **full-time** position – working 40 hours a week – but they say I'll be expected to do a couple of hours' **overtime** most days, which isn't paid.
Anna: Mmm, that doesn't sound so good.
Sam: I know, but the **salary** is quite good. I get £25,000 a year and there's a profit-related **bonus** of up to £5,000. After one year, I'll get a 10% **pay rise**, too.
Anna: That is good. What about the other conditions? How much responsibility will you have?
Sam: Well, at first I won't be in charge of anyone. But if things go well and I get a promotion, I'll be responsible for a team of six people.
Anna: Wow! Great!
Sam: Yes, but some of the other benefits don't seem so great. I only get 20 days' **holiday** and there are **no flexitime** arrangements – we have to be in the office from 9.00 to 5.00 every day. I'd like to be able to finish early some days, say at 3.00.
Anna: Hmm. OK.
Sam: So, do you think I should take it?
Anna: Well, it's a difficult one. I think it depends on whether time or money is more important to you at the moment. You know, if I were you …

6 This exercise helps students remember the vocabulary by personalizing it.

Before speaking, you may like to remind students of the work on second conditionals from the speaking lesson and encourage them to use it at least once in their answer, e.g. *If I had a boring job, I think a bonus would be important because I would want more financial benefits if I only did the job for the money.* Give students a minute to think about their answer before speaking, to be able to expand their points.

VOCABULARY FILE Student's Book page 126
Refer students to exercise 3 for more practice of words related to working conditions.

ANSWERS
See page 134 of this book for answers.

Exam skills

7 1·56 This exercise improves students' ability to complete notes from a recording by identifying matching information that is similar but not identical to that given.

Before listening, encourage students to predict the type of words they think might fill the gap, particularly what parts of speech:

1 noun, because of *a*.
2 verb, because of the subject *courses*; verb, because of the semi-modal *have to*.
3 probably two nouns connected with *and*, because of *both* and *a*, and *access to*, which requires an object.

After listening, tell students to turn to the audioscript on page 169 to check their answers. Then ask them to underline words in the audioscript which match words in sentences 1–3. Tell them to discuss with a partner how the words were changed and how the word order was changed. Check as a whole class:

- *Forms* is at the end in sentence 1 but at the beginning of the recording. Sentence 1 is active (with the subject *students*), but the sentence in the recording is passive, so it uses the past participle form (*filled in*).
- *Earning money* is the gerund form used as the subject of the sentence in the recording; but the base form of the verb, *earn money*, is used at the end of sentence 2.
- In sentence 3, the noun used is *access*, but in the recording this is changed to *free use of*. The recording is also complicated by the addition of adjectives for each noun, which are not included in sentence 3 and separate the nouns from each other in the recording, making them harder to identify.

ANSWERS
1 form
2 finish, earn money
3 gym and a restaurant

Audioscript 1·56
1 **Forms** have to be filled in.
2 **Earning money** is a priority for most students when their courses **finish**.
3 The hard-working employees have free use of a lovely **gym** and a subsidized **restaurant**.

EXAM TIP 1·57 Before students listen, ask them to suggest possible answers to the question and write these on the board. After they have answered the question, refer students to page 146 for more guidance on completing notes.

ANSWER
Think about possible answers and possible types of words that could fill each gap.

Audioscript 1·57
When you complete notes from a recording, make sure you read the notes before you listen. While you read them, **think about possible answers and possible types of words that could fill each gap**. It's very important that you do this before the recording starts, because it's hard to read, listen, and write at the same time! The sentences that you hear will be different from the sentences that you read, so don't listen for the exact sentences on your paper.

8 This exercise raises students' awareness of how much information they can predict before listening.

After checking the answers, you might like to help students understand why this exercise is useful by asking them to predict the words for the gaps.

ANSWERS
a 7 & 8   b 1   c 6   d 2   e 9   f 3   g 5   h 4

9 1·58 Focus students on the instruction by asking how many words they can write (two words or a number). After listening, ask them to check their answers with a partner and play the recording again if necessary. Remind students they will only hear it once in the exam. As in exercise 7, get them to check their own answers by looking at the audioscript and identifying in what ways the language in the notes is different to the recording.

Guide students to an understanding of the importance of predicting the type of information they expect to hear by asking them how exercise 8 helped them to fill the gaps correctly.

ANSWERS
1 65%
2 graduate course
3 applications
4 full-time
5 study
6 bonus
7 20 / twenty
8 gym
9 time management

Audioscript 1·58
Student: Hi. I'm interested in graduate places at Sterne Consulting. Can I ask you some questions?
Representative: Sure. Are you graduating this year?
Student: That's right. I'm graduating in business and management.
Representative: OK – excellent. What grade do you think you'll get?
Student: Well, what grade do I need to apply to your company?
Representative: You need at least **65%** when you come to do your final exams.
Student: OK, that should be fine. I hope I'm going to get a first-class honours, which is over 70%. Is there anything else that can help my application?
Representative: It's always an advantage to do a part-time **graduate course**. It helps if you've already booked or started one before you apply.
Student: OK, I'll look into that. How many positions do you have?
Representative: Quite a lot. We have twenty-five positions available, but we actually get over 500 **applications**.
Student: I know it's a trainee position, but could I ask some questions about basic conditions?
Representative: Of course.
Student: Do trainees work full-time or do we go to college as well?
Representative: It's **full-time**, so you have to work quite hard. Any extra **study** is done in your own time.
Student: Can I ask about conditions now? What's the starting pay like?

Representative: The basic salary is quite high at £30,000, but we don't pay a **bonus** or commission at first. You may not be interested in this yet, but there's also a good company pension scheme.
Student: How many days off do employees get?
Representative: Usually **twenty** days' holiday a year.
Student: And what other benefits do you provide?
Representative: Well, it depends on the office you work in. There's a staff restaurant in all our office locations and an onsite **gym** that you pay nothing for.
Student: Great. What training do you provide?
Representative: Well, for graduate places there's an extensive training programme in your first year. We train you to use a range of computer software and we teach you a range of skills from **time management** to negotiating.
Student: OK, great. So what should I do next?
Representative: Well, the best thing is to leave us your email and I'll send you a link to our online application …

Exam practice

10 1·59 Give students 2 minutes before listening to work with a partner to predict what could fill the gaps. If they checked their own answers in exercise 9 using the audioscript, you may like to vary the technique here by allocating one answer per pair or group (depending on your class size). Ask each pair or group to find their allocated answer in the audioscript and to identify if the language or word order is different in the notes. Ask for a representative from each pair or group to share their answer with the class.

ANSWERS
1 classrooms
2 two to six
3 reflect on
4 essays
5 control the children
6 weeks of holiday / weeks' holiday
7 pension

Audioscript 1·59
Representative: So you're thinking of becoming a teacher?
Student: Yes, but I'd like to find out a bit more about the training course and the long-term job prospects first.
Representative: OK. So what would you like to know?
Student: Well, firstly, what happens on the training course?
Representative: It's a mixture of learning theory at college, but for a lot of the time you'll have to go out of college and teach in real **classrooms**. In fact, you'll work in four during the year.
Student: How long do you work in each classroom?
Representative: It varies, but generally it's between **two and six weeks**.
Student: What happens afterwards?
Representative: You go back to college, **reflect on** the experience, and continue your theory work.
Student: How are we assessed during the course?
Representative: Some of the grades come from watching you teach and the other half are based on **essays** you write.
Student: What do people find the hardest?
Representative: It's different for everyone, but for most people it's **controlling the children**. They can be quite unkind to new teachers.

Student: What are the benefits like?
Representative: The salary isn't high compared to other postgraduate positions but you do get twelve weeks' holiday every year, including six weeks in the summer, and a good pension when you finish.
Student: OK, thank you. Could I take a brochure?
Representative: Of course. Please do.

What do you think?

11 This exercise encourages students to think critically about the topic and generates ideas they could use in Writing Task 2 or Speaking Part 3.

Tell students to work alone, and to think about why they feel this way as they make their choice.

12 Before students discuss, you may like to encourage them to use language from this lesson by revising exercise 3 first. Write the three headings on the board and ask them what words they can remember for each column. Write their ideas on the board. Get them to check which ones they have forgotten by referring back to exercise 3.

> **Optional activity**
>
> You may like to ask students to use the internet to research working conditions in their country. For example, they could find out:
> - what the minimum legal paid annual leave allowance is
> - what the rules are around maternity and paternity leave
> - how common flexitime / bonuses / company cars are in their country
> - if there is a state pension and how much it is.

Study skills

This exercise develops students' techniques for recording and learning vocabulary by reflecting on their current method and considering alternatives.

Discuss the first question as a whole class and write students' ideas on the board. Focus students' attention on the next part and after discussing in pairs, take a class vote on how many people already use each technique. For each idea, ask a student who says yes why they like doing this. Finally, ask if they have any other suggestions.

ANSWER
Other things students might need to know when they learn new words include: word formation, collocations, register, different meanings.

WRITING From plan to topic sentences page 62

EXAM FOCUS: TASK 2

> **Lesson aims**
> 1 Enable students to write topic sentences from plans
> 2 Improve the way students connect paragraphs to other paragraphs by using linkers *is / is that* in topic sentences.
> 3 Expand students' range of vocabulary to express academic ideas in topic sentences.

> **Key language**
> **Academic ideas:** *explanation, drawback, advantage, consequence, justification*

> **Featured topic vocabulary**
> **Rewards:** *friendship, fame, job satisfaction, medal, trophy, comfortable lifestyle, respect*
> **Verbs:** *motivate, predict, impact*
> **Nouns:** *income, public sector employee, job security, risk*

Topic focus

1 This exercise engages students with the lesson topic and encourages students to think critically about motivation in the workplace.

Before students begin, you may like to check their understanding of some of the vocabulary, for example:
- *reward*: *What reward do the police offer for information about a criminal?* (money) *Do you need to do something in return for a reward?* (yes)
- *motivate*: *If you are motivated, do you work a little or a lot?* (a lot) *How can you motivate a child to be good?* (offer a treat like sweets or chocolate)
- *medal*: *What colours are the medals in the Olympics?* (bronze, silver, gold) *Where do you usually wear a medal?* (around your neck)
- *trophy*: *What shape is a trophy usually?* (like a cup with two handles) *What do footballers often do when they win a trophy?* (hold it in the air)

2 Encourage students to expand their answers as much as possible. Monitor to check if they need any extra help understanding the vocabulary.

Exam skills

3 This exercise prepares students to analyse an essay plan and provides an opportunity to revise the skills developed so far in answering Task 2.

Students may ask for clarification of *relatively* (to a fairly large degree, especially in comparison to others). Encourage them to try to guess the meaning from the context before helping.

UNIT 6 CAREERS & SUCCESS

Refer students back to unit 3, page 32, to remind them of the different parts within the question itself (the instruction, the topic, and the issue). Ask students what identifies the different parts in the question. Ask them to look at exercise 8 on page 33 of unit 3, and check which description matches the question they have here (you must give your opinion and reasons for it).

> **Optional activity**
> You may like to develop students' ability to generate ideas by brainstorming a plan together as a class. If students have difficulty thinking of arguments, give them individual words from the reasons part of the plan in exercise 4, for example, write on the board: *experience, training, choice, money, other rewards*. Ask students to construct arguments from these words. Then tell them to compare their ideas with the reasons in exercise 4.

4 This exercise illustrates how topic sentences might be structured to create cohesion between paragraphs.

Before beginning, remind students of the concept of topic sentences by referring them back to unit 3 to look at the structure of a Task 2 essay in the diagram on page 32. Ask them where they find the topic sentence in the diagram (at the beginning of each paragraph).

Ask how sentences 1–3 differ from a–c. (1–3 is just a list of ideas as might appear in a plan, but a–c is organized so each sentences follows on logically from the one before, and connects back to the thesis statement.)

ANSWERS
1 b   2 a   3 c

EXAM TIP 1·60 Before students listen, ask them to suggest possible answers to the question and write these on the board. After they have answered the question, refer students to page 147 for more guidance on topic sentences.

ANSWER
If you give your opinion in the thesis statement, each topic sentence should give a reason for this opinion OR if you say you are going to discuss an argument, each topic sentence should introduce one side of the argument OR if you say you are going to explain causes or effects, each topic sentence should state a cause or effect.

Audioscript 1·60
The first sentence in each paragraph of an essay is often a topic sentence. It contains the main idea of the paragraph and should connect to your thesis statement. For example, **if you give your opinion in the thesis statement, each topic sentence should give a reason for this opinion. Or, if you say you're going to discuss an argument, each topic sentence should introduce one side of the argument. If you say you're going to explain causes or effects, each topic sentence should state a cause or effect.** Note that each point in your plan should become a topic sentence.

5 This exercise develops students' ability to construct topic sentences by identifying how they are formed.

Ask students to compare their answer with a partner before checking as a whole class.

ANSWERS
a 2   b 3   c 1

6 This exercise provides students with more models of topic sentences and examples of useful phrases for connecting paragraphs.

As students are completing the exercise, you may like to write the sentences on the board to make it easier to check answers afterwards. Ask them to compare their answers with a partner. Check as a whole class by asking for volunteers to come and divide each sentence on the board.

ANSWERS
1 The second reason for my position in this debate is that / public sector employees / have more job security.
2 The final explanation for salary differences is that / companies / are free to decide how much they pay.
3 One negative effect of giving a lot of bonuses is that / the people who want them / may take risks in their work.

Vocabulary

7 This exercise expands students' range of vocabulary to express academic ideas in topic sentences.

Students may have difficulty with the word *drawback* (disadvantage or problem). If so, encourage them to leave this until last, and then focus them on *back* by asking if it is usually a positive or negative movement (negative). As students are completing the exercise, write the words in column A on the board. Ask them to compare their answers with a partner before checking as a whole class by writing the definitions in brackets to the left of the word on the board.

ANSWERS
result 4   method 6
positive effect 3   cause 1
negative effect 2   reason / excuse 5

8 This exercise enables students to use the vocabulary accurately by demonstrating how these words operate at sentence level.

Focus students on column B first, and ask them to work with a partner to decide which preposition matches which word in column A. Check as a whole class by writing these next to the words already on the board from exercise 7. At the bottom of the board, write:

for / of +
to +

Ask students which one is followed by the *-ing* verb form (*for / of*) and which one is followed by the infinitive with *to*. Ask which one can be followed by a noun (*for / of*). Write the answers on the board. Then ask students to open their notebooks and complete the exercise alone before comparing with a partner.

ANSWERS
1 An explanation for low motivation is a lack of support from managers.
2 A drawback of working from home is that you can't attend meetings.
3 An advantage of employing younger people is that they are easier to train.
4 A consequence of modern communications is that more people work from home.
5 A justification for raising university fees is that it will improve standards of education.
6 A way to motivate staff is to increase pay.

9 This exercise provides students with an opportunity to check they have understood the meanings of the words correctly and practise using them accurately. It also helps them generate ideas on the type of topics they might face in Task 2.

You may like to give students the options of working alone or with a partner, depending how confident they feel. Monitor and check they are writing answers that make logical sense, to ensure they understand the meaning of the new words.

POSSIBLE ANSWERS
2 a drawback of factory work
3 a consequence of bad management
4 an explanation for unemployment
5 a way of improving equality
6 a justification for paying bonuses

VOCABULARY FILE Student's Book page 126
Refer students to exercise 4 for more practice using vocabulary to express academic ideas.

ANSWERS
See page 134 of this book for answers.

Grammar

10 This exercise guides students to an understanding how the linkers *is / is that* are used within a sentence.

Before students begin, check they understand the meaning of *is followed by* by asking *Do you need to look before or after the linker?* You may also like to check the meaning of *infinitive* and *subject* by asking for examples. Ask students to work alone before checking as a whole class.

ANSWERS
a is   b is that

11 Encourage students to use exercise 10 to help them here, by asking how they can know which linker to choose. Do sentence 1 as an example as a whole class. Ask students to work alone before comparing with a partner. Check answers as a whole class.

Alternative for weaker classes: provide more support when doing the example by writing sentence 1 on the board with a gap after *pay* where the linker should be. Draw a box around *workers* and a box around *are*. Ask students what type of word each one is (subject and verb), and write the answer on the board. Refer students to exercise 10 to decide which linker they should use.

ANSWERS
1 A consequence of low pay is that workers are less motivated.
2 A way to get job satisfaction is to do something you are good at.
3 An advantage of paying people the same is that they will work better with others.
4 A drawback of fame is lack of privacy.

GRAMMAR FILE Student's Book page 116
Refer students to this page for more explanation and practice of *that / is that*.

ANSWERS
See page 131 of this book for answers.

12 This exercise provides support to enable students to write their own topic sentences and generate ideas on a different Task 2 style question.

Group students in threes to work together to brainstorm ideas as well as the language. Remind them of what word should come next in their sentence by referring them to column B in exercise 8 (a preposition). Encourage them to vary their language by thinking of synonyms for *going to university* (e.g. studying at university, studying for a degree, continuing to higher education, university studies, degree-level studies).

POSSIBLE ANSWERS
1 The first advantage of going to university is the chance to earn more money.
2 Another consequence is that you can meet many different people.
3 A final justification is that you can get a variety of skills and more employment options.

Exam practice

13 Students have the chance here to put all the skills developed in this lesson together. It also provides them with revision material by creating model plans on the type of topics they may face in the exam.

Remind students of what they are aiming to produce by referring them back to the model in exercise 4. Before they begin, encourage them to use the skills developed in this lesson by asking:

* *How should you start the topic sentences?* (with a phrase connecting the paragraph to the other paragraphs)
* *How many different examples of these phrases can you find in exercises 4 and 6?* (Exercise 4: The first reason for my position is that …, Secondly, I would argue that …, The final reason for my view is that …. Exercise 6: The second reason for my position is that …, The final explanation for X is that …, One negative effect of X is that …)
* *Which other exercise helps you vary the way you start a topic sentence?* (the words in column A in exercise 8)
* *How many parts should there be in your topic sentence? What are they?* (three: phrase connecting to the other paragraphs, main subject, and claim about the subject)

- *How can you link the first and second parts? (is / is that) How can you know which one to choose? (see exercise 10)*

Divide the class into three groups and allocate a different essay question per third of the class, to expose students to a range of ideas in exercise 14. Ask them to work alone.

Alternative for weaker classes: tell students to work in pairs or groups of three.

> POSSIBLE ANSWERS

1 Nowadays, too many people young people want to become famous. Do you agree or disagree?
I agree:

Introduction:
The concept of celebrity has widened the concept of fame. When once famous people were quite rare, nowadays anyone who acts in a reality show can become a celebrity and acquire some measure of fame. Access to technology has meant young people are more and more aware of fame and may see it as a goal. On the whole, I see this as potentially damaging for youngsters.

Body:
- *Fame is difficult to deal with*
- *Not everyone can be famous*
- *We need people to do less glamorous jobs*

The first drawback of fame is that it is not easy for young people to deal with their success.
A second negative effect is that so few people can achieve fame.
A final point is that if everyone were famous, we'd have nobody left to do the less glamorous work.

Conclusion:
Despite the trappings of fame, its elusive nature means many young people do not focus on their studies and realities in the pursuit of a false dream.

2 What can bosses do to motivate their staff?
Work is a fact of life and this means there is a need for employers to employ employees. Bosses want to get the most out of their staff and members of staff want to enjoy their work and succeed in it.
- *Offer bonuses*
- *Provide flexible hours*
- *Make the office environment attractive*

The first way to motivate staff could be to offer higher bonuses.

A second solution is giving workers more flexibility about when and where they work.
Finally, companies should make their working environment more attractive.
If bosses look after their employees, the employees work hard and businesses thrive. It is a symbiotic relationship, and when it works, it works well.

3 Success at work brings happiness. Do you agree?
I disagree:
Since humans have arranged their lives such that they spend a great deal of time at work, it is important that they enjoy their jobs and are appreciated for what they do. Whether workers have to be successful to be happy is a different matter. It largely depends on what is meant by 'success' – if success in work means achieving and moving forward, then I would argue that there is more happiness in this than in stagnating. However, I would not say that the pursuit of success makes people happy, the earning of it might.
- *You work harder to maintain success*
- *Family life suffers*
- *Success makes people jealous*

The first drawback to success at work is that it often makes you work still harder to maintain it.

The second consequence is that family life may suffer when you have many responsibilities at work.
A final problem is that success can make friends and other people jealous of you.
The concept of success and how it relates to one's working life is subjective; but in the end, the people you love, and doing something you enjoy doing with your time, are more likely to bring happiness than success for its own sake.

14 Within each third of the class, give students a number. Tell students to find people with the same number and sit together, so each group of three students should include an example of each essay question. After the class, you may like to photocopy the best student's plan for each question to provide the class with good examples to keep as models.

> MODEL ANSWER

See exercise 2 in the WRITING FILE on page 144 of the Student's Book for a model answer to essay question 2.

WRITING FILE Student's Book `page 144`
Refer students to exercise 3 on this page for another explanation essay question, accompanied by a sample answer.

> ANSWERS

See page 136 of this book for answers.

READING Matching headings

Lesson aims

1 Enable students to match headings with paragraphs by identifying topic sentences.

2 Expand students' vocabulary about factors for success to improve their ability to understand texts on this topic.

3 Develop students' knowledge about the topic of success to generate ideas to use in the Speaking and Writing exams.

Key language

Nouns: *tip, reputation, appearance, luck, integrity, wealth, capacity*

Verbs: *surround (yourself)*

Collocations: *make an impression, high achiever*

Factors for success: *looks, height, dress, intelligence, motivation, drive, curiosity, family background, educational background*

Topic focus

1 This exercise introduces students to the lesson topic of success, and prepares them to read a longer text by focusing on just short passages here.

Focus students' attention on the title, and ask them to predict what the three passages are about. Ask students for their ideas about how to be successful in life and write any ideas on the board. Focus on the photo and ask if anyone knows who this is (Richard Branson). If not, ask them to look at passage A to find his name. Before answering the question, ask students who each passage is about and what their jobs are. After reading, ask them to summarize the tip for each passage in one or two words only, for example:

- *enjoy it / enjoyment / enjoyable*
- *determination / dedication / work hard*
- *other people / parents / top professionals*

Then discuss as a whole class and take a vote to find out which tip is the most popular in the class.

2 This exercise engages students with the topic by drawing on their own personal experience.

Conduct whole-class feedback by asking students for any particularly good tips they received from their partner.

Exam skills

3 This exercise enables students to understand the main idea of a paragraph by identifying topic sentences.

Encourage students to find the part of the topic sentence that contains the main idea. They need to identify the point the writer is making about the topic, rather than simply the topic itself, which means being selective. The skill lies in being able to *disregard* information that is not essential to understand the main idea.

Ask students to compare with a partner before checking as a whole class.

ANSWERS

More than any other element, fun is the secret of Virgin's success.
But ex-paralympic athlete Linda Mastandrea believes that the key to success is really determination.
She believes it's the people around her that have made the difference to her life.

EXAM TIP 1·61 Before students listen, ask them to suggest possible answers to the question and write these on the board.

After they have answered the question, refer students to page 148 for more guidance on finding topic sentences.

ANSWER

Topic sentences are usually located near the beginning of each paragraph; they can help you to understand the main ideas of the passage and the information that each paragraph contains.

Audioscript 1·61

Finding topic sentences is a very important skill. They're usually located near the beginning of each paragraph. If you just read the topic sentences, you'll be able to understand the main ideas of the passage and, more importantly, the information that each paragraph contains.

4 This exercise raises students' awareness of why it is useful to identify topic sentences to help match paragraphs with headings.

Focus students' attention on the title of the lesson and ask what the purpose of a heading is (it summarizes the main idea of the paragraph). Explain that matching headings with paragraphs is an important skill for the exam. Ask students how it can also help them in their academic lives (to quickly identify whether a paragraph is relevant). Ask why it is important to find the topic sentence (because it encapsulates the main idea of the paragraph).

ANSWERS

A 2 & 5 **B** 1 & 3 **C** 4 & 6

5 This exercise raises students' awareness that the topic sentence is usually at the start of the paragraph. It also improves their ability to match topic sentences with paragraphs by developing their ability to eliminate choices.

Focus students on the first part of the exercise, and make sure they find the topic sentences before answering the second part of the exercise.

ANSWERS

The topic sentence is the first sentence in all but paragraphs A and G.

A In short, what's on the inside is key.
B Few could deny that intelligence is essential to success in early life.
C In fact, it seems that during working life, educational background has much less impact than it once did.
D Admittedly, the capacity for hard work is probably important, too.
E Indeed, new research suggests that a wide variety of external factors also assist high achievers.
F Self-presentation and the way we dress may also play a role.
G Perhaps teaching the art of making an impression on others may be as valuable to today's generation as a traditional schooling.

According to the author, hard work may result in success and appearance certainly contributes to it.

6 This exercise raises students' awareness that there are extra headings they do not need.

Help students understand that they need to identify which ideas are not included, as well as those that are, in order to eliminate headings. Warn students that sometimes vocabulary might match, but they need to be sure that the idea matches, not just isolated words. To demonstrate, refer them back to exercise 5. Intelligence is mentioned in paragraph B, but in relation to early life, not career.

ANSWER
No

Exam practice

7 Focus on the topic sentences students identified already in exercise 5, to remind themselves of the main idea of each paragraph. Then focus on the headings and remind students of the danger of just matching words rather than ideas. Tell them to work alone before comparing their answers with a partner. Check as a whole class and help students understand how the headings which are not necessary could be confusing:

- In i, the word *voice* matches paragraph E, but this is not only about the voice
- In v, the word *now* could be confusing because paragraph C talks about the past compared to now, but sentence v is too general to summarize the meaning of C
- In viii, *successful people* could refer to the people in paragraph A, but paragraph A is not one of the five options

ANSWERS
1 Paragraph B: vii
2 Paragraph C: iii
3 Paragraph D: iv
4 Paragraph E: ii
5 Paragraph F: vi

Vocabulary

8 This exercise expands students' range of vocabulary about factors for success, to improve their ability to understand texts related to this topic.

Write the three headings on the board and elicit an example for each column by asking students as a whole class for suggestions. Focus on the clarification of *external*, *internal*, and *situational* underneath each heading.

ANSWERS
External: looks, height, dress
Internal: intelligence, motivation, drive, curiosity
Situational: family background, educational background

VOCABULARY FILE Student's Book page 126
Refer students to exercises 5 and 6 for more practice using vocabulary related to factors for success.

ANSWERS
See page 134 of this book for answers.

9 This exercise requires students to understand the author's opinion by considering the main idea of the text.
Students can complete the pie chart individually before checking in pairs.

ANSWERS
A Situational   B Internal   C External

10 This exercise encourages students to engage with the text and think critically about the opinions they read.
Focus students' attention on the example in the speech bubble. Direct them to the text and encourage them to skim it again if they cannot think of anything to say.
Alternative for weaker classes: you may like to support them by discussing as a whole class and prompting students with questions like *What do you think about paragraph F?*

What do you think?

11 This exercise develops students' knowledge of factors for success to generate ideas to use in the Speaking and Writing exams.
Ask students to work alone. Encourage them to think about reasons for their opinions as they make their choices, but stress that they do not need to speak yet.

12 Focus students on the example in the speech bubble. Before they begin, encourage them to respond to their partner's opinion by brainstorming phrases such as *Really? / I totally agree. / That's interesting. / I'm not sure I agree.* Get feedback as a whole class on the points they did not agree with their partner about.

EXAM CHALLENGE page 66

ANSWERS

Speaking
1 & 2 Students' own answers

Listening
1 See page 136 of this book for answers and page 141 for the audioscript.
2 Students' own answers

Writing
1 Students' own answers
2 See page 108 of the Student's Book for the model introduction.

Reading
1 Students' own answers
2 See pages 138–139 of this book for answers.

UNIT 7 Nature & biology

Introduction (page 67)

Featured topic vocabulary
Collocations: *natural wonder, protect the environment, conserve the environment*
Nouns: *rainforest, fjord, reef, crater, canyon, island, falls*

Optional lead-in
Before students look at the infographic, you may like to introduce the topic by doing the following:
- Group students in threes or fours and give each group a large piece of paper.
- Tell students they have to organize a tour around the world. They need to choose ten natural wonders to visit. You may like to clarify the meaning of *natural wonder* (a naturally occurring spectacle that fills you with surprise and admiration) by giving an example of a *natural wonder* from your students' country / countries
- Give students 10 minutes to brainstorm a list on their paper as a group. Then tell them to open their books and check how many are the same as the natural wonders in the infographic. Find out which group has the most.

What do you think?
Focus on the photos and ask if they have been to any of these places. Use the photos to clarify the meaning of *rainforest, fjord, reef, crater, canyon, island,* and *falls*. Group students in fours to discuss questions 1–5 before getting feedback as a whole class.

Optional activity
Ask students to choose one natural wonder to research. Tell them to look on the internet for information such as:
- why it is special
- how many visitors go there every year
- whether it's under threat from tourism or climate change.

Group students in threes to present their research. Tell the students who are listening to make notes on the most important information, and check if they heard correctly afterwards.

SPEAKING Adding detail to descriptions (page 68)

EXAM FOCUS: PARTS 1 & 2

Lesson aims
1 Improve students' ability to extend their answers using techniques to remember details about places.
2 Enable students to use 'empty' subjects (*it* and *there*) accurately.
3 Add impact to students' descriptions using adverbs of degree.
4 Expand students' vocabulary for describing weather.

Key language
Adjectives: *mountainous, seasonal, attractive, extreme, icy, varied*
Nouns: *region, climate, shower, thunder, mist, hurricane, temperature, umbrella*
Weather adjectives: *changeable, pleasant, chilly, overcast, wet, stormy, mild, humid, sunny, cool, dry, windy, rainy*

Featured topic vocabulary
Adjectives to describe details: *thrilled, pretty, noisy, sweet, colourful, impressed, disgusting, peaceful*

Topic focus

Optional lead-in
Before students open their books, you may like to introduce the topic by demonstrating a model Part 2 without showing them the prompt card. Answer the Part 2 topic in exercise 16 on page 69, and be sure to mention something for each point. Get students to guess what is written on the prompt card. Tell them to listen to your model answer and make notes about what could be written on the prompt card. Then tell them to look at the card on page 69 to check.

1 Students are encouraged here to consider a common Part 2 topic.
   Group students in threes to discuss before getting feedback as a whole class.

2 You may like to check students understand *best time of year* by explaining about the best time of year to visit a country you know well. For example, in the UK the best time of year to visit is the summer (June to August) because it's cold and rainy in the winter.

Tell students to discuss in their same groups as exercise 1 before getting feedback as a whole class.

Vocabulary

3 1·62 This exercise provides students with models of how to add detail to descriptions of places, and sets a context to help them understand the new vocabulary.

It also develops students' knowledge of different climates around the globe.

Before listening, ask students what type of weather they would expect in the places in a–c. Write their ideas on the board. After listening, ask them to compare answers in pairs, and listen again if necessary. Check answers as a whole class, but continue to exercise 4 before discussing what vocabulary helped them find the answers.

ANSWERS
1 c 2 a 3 b

Audioscript 1·62, 1·63

1 The weather in my part of the world is quite varied. It's **humid** and **wet** by the sea but as you move away from the coast it becomes very **dry** and **chilly** in the winter. It also changes a lot during the year. In the summer months it's really wet but then it won't rain again for the rest of the year.

2 Where I'm from, the weather is less extreme than in many parts of the world. Winters are not very cold, quite **mild** in fact, and summers can be relatively **cool**. The weather can be **changeable**, too – **overcast** and cloudy one day, with sunshine the next. It's best to be prepared. Carry an umbrella in the summer and watch out for icy roads in the winter!

3 Generally speaking, the weather where I'm from is **pleasant** and it's **sunny** all year round. There's a rainy season, but rainfall varies depending which side of the island you're on. The most dangerous time is the hurricane season when it gets **stormy** and extremely **windy** in some areas.

---

4 1·63 This exercise focuses on the range of vocabulary used in the models, to help students vary the way they speak about the weather.

After listening, ask students to turn to the audioscript to check their answers and highlight the adjectives. Tell them to highlight any other useful weather words in the audioscript which helped them find the answers to exercise 3 (for example: *varied, extreme, umbrella, icy*, and *hurricane*). Clarify the meaning of any new vocabulary if necessary. Here are some that might cause difficulty:

- *pleasant*: a comfortable temperature – not too hot, not too cold
- *chilly*: too cold to be comfortable
- *overcast*: lots of clouds / grey sky
- *mild*: not as cold as you would expect
- *humid*: warm and damp.

ANSWERS
1 humid, wet, dry, chilly
2 mild, cool, changeable, overcast
3 pleasant, sunny, stormy, windy

5 Ask students to compare with a partner, before checking as a whole class. You may like to clarify the meaning of *temperature* (the measurement of how hot or cold a thing is).

ANSWERS
pleasant, chilly, mild, cool

6 This exercise consolidates vocabulary from exercise 4 and provides students with some more weather words.

You may like to clarify the meaning of the word *associate* (connect / think of) in questions 2 and 3. Give students a minute to discuss each question and check each one as a whole class before they move on to the next.

ANSWERS
1 a *mild* describes winter weather that is warmer than usual; *cool* describes summer weather that is colder than usual
  b It is *overcast* when there is heavy cloud. When it is *stormy*, there is also strong wind and rain.
2 a wet
  b stormy
  c cool
3 a changeable, chilly, stormy, cool
  b wet, stormy, humid
  c mild, humid, cool, changeable

VOCABULARY FILE Student's Book page 127
Refer students to exercises 1–3 for more practice using weather adjectives and nouns.

ANSWERS
See page 134 of this book for answers.

Grammar

7 This exercise enables students to vary their descriptive language by using sentences with the 'empty' subject *it*.

Write a sentence about the climate in your country, but leave out *it*. For example:

In (name of country), _____ is (hot / cold) in January.

Ask students what word should go in the gap (it) and write *it* on the board. Ask if the word has any meaning in this sentence (not really, but we use it because we need a subject). Ask students if they know where Ecuador is, and what the climate might be like. Focus on the exercise and ask them to work alone before comparing with a partner. Check as a whole class.

ANSWERS
In Ecuador the temperature varies by region. By the coast, to the west of Ecuador, **it** is usually warm – about 25°C on average. However, the capital, Quito, is in the mountains and so its climate is fairly cool. During the day, **it** is just 18.9°C and 10°C at night. There are seasonal changes, too. Between January and April **it** is particularly hot and it rains a lot because **it** is the middle of the wet season.

86 UNIT 7 NATURE & BIOLOGY

8 This exercise raises students' awareness of the difference in usage between the empty subjects *it* and *there*.

As you check the answers, write each sentence on the board. Draw a box around *snows, wind, mist,* and *sunny*. Ask students if each word is a noun, verb, or adjective and label them on the board. Ask *Do you need it or there with* …

- *a verb?* (it)
- *a noun?* (there)
- *an adjective?* (it)

ANSWERS
1 It **2** There **3** There **4** It

GRAMMAR FILE Student's Book page 113
Refer students to this page for more explanation and practice of *it* and *there*.

ANSWERS
See page 130 of this book for answers.

Exam practice

9 These are similar to the type of questions students might be asked in Part 1. The examiner will ask questions covering a range of grammatical structures, like the questions here. For example, question 2 is formed with present simple, but the present perfect is used in Student A's question 3, and the past simple in Student B's question 3.

You may like to raise students' awareness of this before they speak, if your students usually have issues with accuracy rather than fluency. If they have difficulty with fluency, you may instead prefer to discuss their grammatical accuracy after they have spoken.

EXAM TIP 1•64 Before students listen, ask them to suggest possible answers to the question and write these on the board. After they have answered the question, refer students to page 145 for more guidance on Speaking Part 2.

ANSWER
The four Ss: sights, sounds, smells, and sensations.

Audioscript 1•64

In Speaking Part 2, you'll be asked to describe something, for example a place, for 2 minutes. When you're feeling nervous or under pressure, it can be difficult to think of details to talk about. Use the preparation time to try to remember things that could extend your talk. One way you could do this is to use 'The four Ss': sights, sounds, smells, and sensations. These four categories should help you to think of some interesting details.

Exam skills

10 This exercise improves students' ability to keep talking for 2 minutes in Part 2 by suggesting a technique that will help them to remember to add sensory details to descriptions. The symbols are a useful visual aid to help them remember to consider each one.

Focus on the symbols and ask what they represent (sight, sound, smell, and sensation). Students may need clarification of vocabulary such as:

- *thrilled*: very excited and pleased
- *pretty*: attractive without being very beautiful
- *impressed*: you want to say 'wow!'
- *disgusting*: extremely unpleasant; with food, it means it tastes bad.

ANSWERS
eye   pretty, colourful
ear   noisy, thrilled
nose   sweet, disgusting
hand   impressed, peaceful

11 1•65 This exercise provides students with a model of a Part 2 speaking style answer, and demonstrates how to vary a description by giving details for each sense.

Remind students of the meanings of *sight, sound, smell,* and *sensation* by referring back to the symbols for each. Play the recording as many times as necessary. Ask students to compare their answers with a partner, before checking as a whole class.

ANSWERS
Any one of the following answers:
Sights: rocky bays / old, burnt cars / makes the sky look colourful / It's amazing to see
Sounds: noisy tour buses / children shouting
Smells: disgusting smell of sulphur
Sensations: a really peaceful place / warm clothing / fairly chilly and cloudy near the top / worried faces / feel quite scared

Audioscript 1•65, 1•66

I'm going to tell you about Mount Etna in Sicily near my home town of Caltagirone. A lot of tourists go there in the summer so it can be a little chaotic then. There are always a lot of **noisy tour buses** taking visitors to and from the main attractions and families with **children shouting**, but it's **a really peaceful place** at other times of the year. The easiest place for tourists to travel from is one of the popular towns on the coast such as Taormina, which is an absolutely lovely resort with lots of scenic beaches and **rocky bays**. It takes about an hour to get to Etna from there. Anyway, when you get to the volcano, you can go right to the top if you have a guide. I recommend taking **warm clothing** even in the summer because it's often **fairly chilly and cloudy near the top**. In fact, it can be a bit disappointing if you can't see the views because of the mist, so it's worth taking a lot of photos as you walk up. You can take a cable car when you're near the top, which children love, although you see a few **worried faces** when the passengers go over some **old, burnt cars**. The volcano is still active and there can be a **disgusting smell of sulphur**, but it's still worth going up. It sometimes erupts, too. You obviously can't climb it when that happens but it **makes the sky look colourful**. It's amazing to see, especially at night, and even at a distance it makes you **feel quite scared** at the power of nature.

Grammar

12 ♪ 1·66 This exercise raises students' awareness of how detail is added to a model description using adverbs of degree.

Focus on the box but avoid clarifying meaning at this point, as the context of the recording and exercise 13 will help students understand.

ANSWERS
absolutely
a little
fairly
a bit
quite
really

13 You may like to get students to copy the scale into their notebooks to keep as a reference. Draw the scale on the board to check answers as a whole class. Students are likely to be most unfamiliar with: *fairly / quite / pretty* (more than normal, but not as much as *very*).

ANSWERS
a little   a bit   fairly / quite   pretty   really
completely / absolutely / extremely

14 This exercise develops students' ability to use adverbs of degree by clarifying how they operate within a sentence.

Draw three columns on the board with the headings from 1–3. Ask students if they know any more examples of each type of adjective, such as:
- strong adjectives: *freezing, boiling, terrified, starving*
- non-gradable adjectives: *dead, alive*
- adjectives with negative meaning: *dirty, polluted.*

ANSWERS
1 absolutely
2 completely
3 a little, a bit

GRAMMAR FILE Student's Book page 116
Refer students to this page for more practice using adverbs of degree.

ANSWERS
See page 130 of this book for answers.

15 This exercise checks students understand the way the adverbs are used and their meaning.

Focus on the photo and ask if students can guess where it is. Ask them to read the first part to check their guesses. Tell students to work alone before comparing answers with a partner. Check as a whole class.

ANSWERS
1 absolutely   6 really
2 completely   7 pretty
3 really   8 quite
4 pretty   9 a bit
5 A fairly

Exam practice

16 Remind students of how they can add more detail by asking what they can remember about:
- adjectives for weather
- whether they should use nouns, verbs, or adjectives after *it* and *there*
- the four senses to remember to add detail
- adverbs of degree.

Get students to practise under exam conditions first, and tell their partner to listen and make notes about sights, sounds, smells, and sensations they hear described. Then give them 5 minutes to discuss their partner's notes and plan how to add more detail to their description. Then give them the chance to do it again.

LISTENING Labelling diagrams

EXAM FOCUS: SECTION 4

Lesson aims
1 Enable students to use visual clues to predict the content of a lecture.
2 Develop students' ability to recognize and transcribe compound nouns.
3 Improve students' ability to recognize key phrases for direction and location, to navigate a diagram.
4 Raise awareness of techniques to prepare for the exam independently.

Key language
Describing location: *in the top right corner, on the left, in the centre, on the right*
Describing direction: *to the left, below, downwards, to the right*
Compound nouns: *seabed, rainfall, coastline, rock pool, ice cap, waterfall, sea level, air pressure, hillside, cliff edge, ice storm, windbreak, pothole, sea eagle, filter zone, water plant, pool bottom*

Featured topic vocabulary
Nouns: *flipper, galaxy, shell, hammer, beak, lobster, claw, silver, copper, pump, filter*

Topic focus
1 This exercise engages students with the topic of using nature to solve problems and introduces the concept of making predictions from visual clues.

Focus on the photos and discuss as a whole class. Rather than give an example, try giving students a clue by asking if there is anything in nature with feet like these (for picture A).

POSSIBLE ANSWERS
A duck feet
B shell, galaxy
C bird's beak

Exam skills

2   This exercise enables students to use visual clues to predict the content of a lecture connected to a diagram.

The options are deliberately close in meaning, to encourage students to carefully analyse the pictures and the diagram on page 71. Take a vote for each option and write the score for each one on the board.

3   2•1 After checking the correct answer, explain to students that this is an example of the type of diagram they might have to label in Listening Section 4. Raise students' awareness of the importance of predicting content by asking why it helps (it makes their analysis of the diagram more focused, and encourages them to think about how the different parts are connected, rather than just identifying each feature of the diagram in isolation).

ANSWER
Option 4 – the lecture is about using nature to solve problems.
In the three pictures the problems represented are: increasing speed (picture A), saving space (picture B), improving strength and grip (picture C). In the diagram, plants are being used to create a more attractive and cleaner swimming environment.

Audioscript 2•1
Part 1

Good morning. Good morning and welcome to this lecture on applied biology. Ever since the industrial revolution, people have turned away from nature in an effort to make progress. We have learnt how to burn and destroy things in nature to create energy or to engineer new materials like concrete, asphalt, and glass, with which we've covered the natural landscape. But with this violence towards nature, have we perhaps overlooked the benefits of **working with nature to solve our problems**? Today we'll be looking at ways in which humans are increasingly turning towards nature for a range of solutions to our everyday problems …

Key phrases

4   This exercise improves students' ability to recognize key prepositional phrases for location, and encourages them to predict what they might hear in connection with different locations. Under the pressure of the exam, it is easy to become 'lost' when following the description of a diagram. It is vital that students stay one step ahead of the recording by anticipating what is coming next.

Focus on the diagram and tell students to discuss their ideas in pairs. Check answers as a whole class.

ANSWERS

in the top right corner	UV filter and pump
on the left	silver or copper beads
in the centre	swimming area
on the right	pump

5   The focus here is phrases for direction. This raises students' awareness of the importance of predicting what language they might hear and what order the phrases might come in.

Students may need clarification of the difference between *up / down* and *upwards / downwards* (the *-wards* suffix means *in the direction of*. *Up / down* can have the same meaning but usually suggest a quicker movement or a fixed location, e.g. *put your hand up / your hand is up*). Focus on the diagram and tell students to discuss their ideas in pairs. Check answers as a whole class.

6   2•2 Ask students to compare their answers with a partner before checking answers as a whole class. Raise their awareness of the value of this exam skill by asking how exercises 4 and 5 helped them follow the recording as they listened.

ANSWERS
1 to the left   3 to the right
2 downwards   4 below

Audioscript 2•2, 2•4
Part 2

OK, so I want to start by showing a good example of how we can use natural processes to replace processes that we once used chemicals for. The slide shows a diagram of a natural pool. In the centre, you can see the main swimming area. **To the left** of this, we have the filter zone, which is separated from the swimming area by a dividing wall. In the filter zone, the water is naturally cleaned and impurities are removed. It consists of silver or copper beads and rocks, with water plants above them on the surface. A pump, seen on the right of the diagram, draws water in a circular motion around the pool. It first flows to the left, then **downwards** through the filter zone, and then back **to the right below** the pool bottom. It is then pumped into a UV filter, seen in the top right corner of the diagram, which kills harmful bacteria. The water then flows out over a waterfall, which adds oxygen to it, and into the swimming area once again. Meanwhile, surface leaves and debris are removed by a machine called a skimmer, which is on the left of the diagram. This basically clears the unwanted material by sucking it out. And there you have it – the natural swimming pool. I'm sure you'll agree, it sounds a lot more pleasant than swimming pools you're used to. Of course, the idea of using nature to purify and clean is nothing new, but natural pools are only now becoming popular …

> **Optional activity**
> You may like to give students further practice by doing the following:
> a Draw an object on the board, for example a tree, **but use only vertical and horizontal lines**. Represent any curves with a series of shorter lines. You may remember doing or seeing similar drawings made with an 'etch-a-sketch' toy. Ask students to guess what you have drawn.
> b Tell students they are going to get their partner to draw an object using vertical and horizontal lines only.
> c Write the following objects on the board and ask them to choose one: *key, umbrella, dog, flower, spade, scissors, fish, robot, mobile phone, saucepan*.
> d Students then guide their partner's drawing hand using instructions such as *start at the bottom, in the middle. Move to the right. Stop, now move upwards* … Their partner should say when they think they know what the object is.

Vocabulary

7 This exercise raises students' awareness of the importance of listening out for compound nouns when labelling diagrams. Labelling normally requires the use of nouns, and in technical diagrams compounds are particularly prevalent. In the exam, students are sometimes asked to choose labels from a list rather than transcribe them, but learning to recognize compounds is nevertheless useful.

Clarify the meaning of *compound noun* by eliciting some examples students will be more familiar with (e.g. *computer screen, bank account, taxi driver*) and some that are so common they are now written together, such as *handbag, classroom, website*. You could draw attention to objects on your person, like car keys, mobile phone, ID card, and a bank note. Elicit the words and write them on the board. Highlight that both words are nouns. Explain that compound nouns are often used in Section 4 to label a diagram. Then refer students to the exercise. Ask them to work alone before comparing answers with a partner. Check as a whole class.

ANSWERS

1 seabed
2 rainfall
3 coastline
4 rock pool
5 ice cap
6 waterfall
7 sea level
8 air pressure

VOCABULARY FILE Student's Book **page 127**
Refer students to exercise 4 for more practice using compound nouns.

ANSWERS
See page 134 of this book for answers.

Exam skills

8 2·3 This exercise develops students' ability to recognize and transcribe compound nouns by focusing on the impact of connected speech at word boundaries.

After listening, ask students to compare answers with a partner. Check as a whole class. If they are unsure why the compound nouns are difficult to hear, demonstrate by repeating the words *coast* and *line* separately and clearly. Then repeat them quickly together so the *t* is dropped. You may like to refer students back to exercise 7 and ask them to predict how the sounds in those compound nouns might be affected by connected speech, for example:

- *rainfall / coastline / rock pool* – the consonant sound at the end of the first noun is hardly heard or is deleted in order to make way for the next consonant sound
- *seabed / sea level / ice cap* – because the sound at the end of the first noun is not 'closed off' in any way, it is difficult to hear where the word boundary falls.

You may like to ask students to listen to recording 2·3 again, and make a note of the features of connected speech they can hear (see below). More practice of transcribing connected speech is given on page 90 of the Student's Book.

ANSWERS
1 hillside
2 cliff edge (the /f/ at the end of *cliff* connects to the beginning of *edge*)
3 ice storm (the letter 'c' at the end of *ice* is pronounced /s/ and so joins with the /s/ at the beginning of *storm*)
4 windbreak (the /d/ at the end of *wind* almost sounds like an /m/ because it combines with the /b/ sound at the beginning of *break*)
5 pothole (the /t/ at the end of *pot* is normally difficult to hear or is dropped totally)
6 sea eagle (the vowel sound at the end of *sea* is the same as the vowel at the beginning of *eagle*, so the two sounds merge together)

It is sometimes difficult to hear them because when the two words are spoken together in connected speech, the sounds of the words may change slightly.

Audioscript 2·3
hillside
cliff edge
ice storm
windbreak
pothole
sea eagle

9 2·4 After listening, ask students to compare with a partner. Check answers as a whole class. Ask them how many of the individual words they know (e.g. do they know *water* and *fall*, even if they don't know *waterfall*?) to help them understand the advice from the Exam tip.

ANSWERS
1 filter zone
2 water plants
3 pool bottom
4 waterfall
5 skimmer

EXAM TIP 2.5 Before students listen, ask them to suggest possible answers to the question and write these on the board. After they have answered the question, refer students to page 146 for more guidance on labelling diagrams.

ANSWER
Try to recognize smaller, individual words, using the context to help you to guess.

Audioscript 2.5
In Listening Section 4, you have to label diagrams and you'll hear a lot of technical words. Quite often you'll hear words that you haven't heard before. If this happens, don't panic! Many of the words will be compound nouns – words made from two (or more) other words. Even if you don't understand the meaning of a particular compound noun, you should know the individual words that make it up. Listen carefully to the whole word and **try to recognize smaller, individual words, using the context to help you to guess.** The words in less common compound nouns are usually written separately.

Exam practice
10 2.6 Students have a chance here to test the skills developed in exercises 2–9. After listening, ask them to compare answers with a partner. Check as a whole class.

ANSWERS
1 wind pressure   2 nest   3 gardens   4 cellar   5 central

Audioscript 2.6
Part 3
Something new and exciting is now happening in biotechnology – and this is the idea of taking ideas from nature and copying them, a process called biomimicry. So, why copy nature? Surely we've advanced beyond what nature can do? Well, let's consider this for a moment. Nature has existed for millions and millions of years, and over this time it's evolved and adapted to survive and be successful in extreme environments. In short, we have around us millions of solutions to survival problems. One good example is the termite mound. You can see a diagram on this slide here. Termites – these tiny creatures – have learnt to create a comfortable home in some of the world's toughest climates. Outside, in the African savannah, the temperatures vary from forty degrees in the day to one degree at night. Yet, inside the mound, the temperature stays constant. How? Well, let's have a closer look. To the left of the diagram, the arrows represent wind pressure that forces air into the mound and makes currents of air flow around the radial channel. Meanwhile, at various points of the mound, there are small vents through which water evaporates, cooling the structure. Let's look at the middle section now, and we'll see a large space, which is the nest. Inside, at the top of this area, the termites look after their fungus gardens, which are their main food source. Below the nest area, and connected to the radial channels, is the cellar. Interestingly, the termites carry nothing out of their nest so they have found a way of recycling or removing all the waste that must be produced here. Above the nest is a long structure, a central chimney through which warm air currents rise up and leave the nest. Throughout the whole mound you can see a network of lateral tunnels that give the mound a strong structure and also channel air. The termites constantly work to open and close off these tunnels and modify the airflow and keep the temperature of the nest constant. Already architects have tried to copy the structures identified in the mound to create tall buildings that require no additional energy to heat or cool. Perhaps one day all buildings will have a similar structure …

11 2.7 This exercise encourages students to apply their skills to a different type of Section 4 question.

Focus on A–F and remind them of the importance of highlighting key words. Tell students not to worry about whether they understand the words in 1–4; the important thing is to recognize the words, so they should predict the pronunciation to prepare for the sounds they will hear, even if they do not know the word.

After listening, ask students to compare answers with a partner. Check as a whole class.

ANSWERS
1 D   2 B   3 E   4 C

Audioscript 2.7
Part 4
But of course there are millions of other species that we could learn from, too. Water will be one of the biggest challenges in the future. There are organisms that pull water out of the air such as **the Namibian beetle, which manages to extract water from fog.** Wouldn't it be amazing if we could create artificial beetles with the same properties? Research is currently under way to do just that. While we're on the subject, another fascinating insect is the locust. There can be 80 million of them in a single square kilometre, but they don't crash into each other. We have a similar number of cars in the whole world yet we have 3.6 million car collisions a year **Scientists are trying to copy the neurons that help the locusts to navigate.** Copying shapes is interesting, too. Scientists have noticed that **whales have small bumps on their fins. By putting similar bumps on the wings of airplanes, they've been able to increase efficiency** by about 32%, which saves a lot of fuel. **There are also bumps on the underside of lotus leaves that help keep them clean.** Paint manufacturers have already invented a paint that uses this design to help keep walls clean every time it rains. The list is endless and there's almost limitless potential. I hope you're beginning to appreciate what an exciting area applied biology can be …

What do you think?
12 This exercise develops students' knowledge and promotes critical thinking around the topic of the lesson, to generate ideas for Writing Task 2 and Speaking Part 2.

Group students in threes. You may like to allocate one topic per group so students can regroup afterwards and give a summary of their discussion to two people who discussed different topics.

Study skills

This exercise encourages students to be more autonomous by raising awareness of techniques to prepare for the exam independently.

Ask students to compare their answer to the first question with a partner before checking as a whole class. For the second part, give students 5 minutes to think of as many ideas as possible. In whole-class feedback, write their ideas on the board and make your own suggestions if necessary (see the possible answers below).

▶ POSSIBLE ANSWERS

The reading and listening papers can be prepared for most easily because the answers are right or wrong and not as open to interpretation as the speaking and writing. For the latter papers you usually rely on teacher feedback.
Speaking activities that might be useful:
- Recording your voice and then playing it back can help you to check things such as your pronunciation of words, intonation, stress, and speed
- Look at some sample answers, which can act as models of both good and bad candidates
- Record yourself doing a speaking exam – this allows you to see yourself as the examiner will see you, encouraging you to remain communicative
- Remember it's important to always listen carefully to the actual questions in the exam.

Writing activities that might be useful:
- Analyse your own writing against model answers to assess possible strengths and weaknesses in your response, e.g. structure, register, grammatical accuracy. Good model answers also provide examples of good writing practice
- Look at some samples of poor writing so you can consider other weaknesses you need to avoid
- Read a lot – good reading samples usually provide good writing samples
- Write essay plans to get you used to generating and organizing ideas.

WRITING From topic sentence to paragraph page 72

EXAM FOCUS: TASK 2

Lesson aims

1. Develop students' ability to structure paragraphs by writing sentences which connect logically and support the topic sentence.
2. Improve students' ability to describe causes and effects using the zero conditional.
3. Expand students' range of vocabulary to write about natural threats and their effects.

Key language

Natural threats: *flood, food shortage, volcano, asteroid, drought, earthquake, disease, predator, erosion, climate change*
Nouns: *malaria, wildlife, farmland, dam, intervention, resources*
Verbs: *harvest, threaten, poison, spray, multiply, collapse, damage, emerge*

Topic focus

1. This exercise prepares students for exercise 2 by providing them with necessary vocabulary.

▶ ANSWERS
A rat **B** cat **C** mosquito **D** gecko

2. This true story presents an example of the problems humans face in managing ecosystems, and introduces the lesson topic: controlling nature.

The events in this true story are complex, and you may find it useful to do prediction work before students do the task. If so, write the four animals on the board. Then ask *Which animals do cats eat?* Elicit *gecko* and *rat* and draw two arrows connecting the cat to them both. Then ask *Which animals do geckos eat?* and draw a further line connecting the gecko and the mosquito. Now write up *poison*, elicit the meaning, and ask *What would happen if the mosquitoes ate poison?* Elicit the idea that all the animals in the chain would be affected by putting a large X through first the mosquito, the gecko, then the cat (leaving the rat).

Now focus on the picture and ask students to discuss in pairs why the cats are being dropped. Before reading the text, ask students for their ideas.

▶ ANSWER
They are being parachuted into a jungle (to control the rat population).

3. After completing the exercise alone, ask students to compare their answers with a partner. Check as a whole class. Note that passive structures are prominent in this lesson, so you may wish to ask students if they can identify them. If they are not familiar at all with the passive, they may have difficulty understanding the diagram. You may therefore wish to concept check by writing up *cats were poisoned* and then writing two definitions:
   A *Cats ate poison.*
   B *Cats gave poison to someone.*
   Check students can match the sentence with the correct definition (A). The passive will be dealt with explicitly in unit 10.

▶ ANSWERS
1 mosquitoes **2** geckos **3** cats **4** rats

92 UNIT 7 NATURE & BIOLOGY

Vocabulary

4 In this exercise, students learn vocabulary for describing natural threats.

The meaning of some of these words can be best clarified using actions and drawings on the board. However, you may need to verbally explain:

- *food shortage*: a situation where there is not enough food
- *asteroid*: a rock from space
- *drought*: a long period of time when there is little or no rain
- *predator*: an animal that kills and eats other animals
- *erosion*: when the land becomes damaged by the weather.

Discuss as a whole class and write students' ideas on the board.

POSSIBLE ANSWERS

food shortage	people, animals
volcano	people, buildings, wildlife
asteroid	potentially everything
drought	people, animals, ecosystems
earthquake	buildings, infrastructure, people, animals
disease	ecosystems, people, animals, plants
predator	prey
erosion	ecosystems, landscapes
climate change	potentially everything

5 This exercise consolidates the vocabulary and encourages students to include examples in their writing. It may also highlight difficulties students may have forming the zero conditional, but be aware that this structure is dealt with later in the lesson so at this stage focus on ideas.

POSSIBLE ANSWERS
When there is a food shortage, people can change their diet.
When a volcano erupts, people can change the flow of the lava.
When an asteroid is close to Earth, people can monitor space to see if it is a risk with a view to taking precautions.
When there is drought, people can try to save water.
When there is an earthquake, people can avoid high buildings or move to a safer area.
When there is a disease, people can improve hygiene and try to find a cure.
When there is a predator, people can hunt it down.
When there is erosion, people can build houses in safer areas.
When climate change is a problem, people can reduce emissions, travel less, recycle more, and do other things to limit man's impact on nature.

VOCABULARY FILE Student's Book page 127
Refer students to exercises 5 and 6 for more practice using nouns related to the topic of natural threats.

ANSWERS
See page 134 of this book for answers.

Exam skills

6 This exercise prepares students for exercise 7 by clarifying vocabulary and encouraging them to engage with the topic. Discuss as a whole class.

Alternative for weaker classes: you may like to ask guiding questions such as *What's the problem? What are the people doing in A? Why? What have people built in B? Why?*

ANSWERS
In A, the people are harvesting water plants that are taking over the lake, so as to protect the lake's existing ecosystem. In B, a dam is being used to control water flow.

EXAM TIP 2·8 Before students listen, ask them to suggest possible answers to the question and write these on the board. After they have answered the question, refer students to page 147 for more guidance on paragraph structure.

ANSWER
Sentences are all connected logically, and everything is directly related to the topic sentence.

Audioscript 2·8
Make sure your paragraphs are well structured. What this means is that **the sentences are all connected logically**. A main idea is given first in the topic sentence, and then other sentences in the paragraph support the idea of the topic sentence, providing explanation or examples. Your examples might include causes and effects, depending on the essay question. **Make sure everything is directly related to the topic sentence** and doesn't go too far from the main point of the paragraph.

7 This exercise develops students' understanding of how to structure paragraphs with sentences which support the topic sentence.

Focus on the numbers in the text. Ask students to work alone before comparing answers with a partner. Check as a whole class.

ANSWERS
1 d 2 b 3 c 4 a

8 This exercise improves students' ability to structure paragraphs by ensuring their sentences follow one another logically.

Ask students to work alone before checking as a whole class. Focus on the language which signals the role of each sentence (a *For example*, b *causes / affecting*, c *it can be*, d *if this happens*). Students may need clarification of *species* (different types of animals).

ANSWERS
c a b d

Grammar

9 This exercise provides students with the vocabulary and ideas to produce zero conditional sentences in exercise 10. It also expands their range of vocabulary related to nature.

Students may need clarification of *hurricane* (a violent storm with very strong winds), *collapse* (fall down suddenly), and *damaged* (harmed or spoiled, for example, broken windows or a hole in the roof).

ANSWERS
1 b 2 c 3 d 4 a

UNIT 7 NATURE & BIOLOGY

10 Describing causes and effects can be a useful way to support the topic sentence in a paragraph. This exercise improves students' ability to describe causes and effects using the zero conditional.

Write the example on the board and draw a box around *if there is a flood* and a separate box around *buildings are often damaged*. Ask students which one is the cause and which one is the effect. Draw boxes around the verbs *is* and *are*, and ask *Do we use past, present, or future to talk about causes and effects?* (present) *Do we use present simple or continuous?* (present simple) Tell students to use the example as a model to complete the exercise alone. Ask them to compare with a partner before checking as a whole class.

Alternative for weaker classes: you may like to give extra support by doing an example as a class. Encourage students to use the example as a model by asking:
- *What is the first word you need to write?* (if)
- *What three words come before the first noun in the example?* (there is a)
- *What punctuation comes after the noun?* (a comma)
- *What verbs can you see in a–d?* (fall, are, collapse, need)
- *What are the subjects of the verbs in a–d?* (trees, buildings, buildings, people)
- *Why don't we use 'will' before the verb?* (because we use the present simple to talk about things that are true in general)
- *Why don't we need -s after the verb?* (because they are plural nouns)

Ask students to complete 3 and 4 alone before comparing with a partner. Check as a whole class.

ANSWERS
2 If there is an earthquake, buildings may collapse.
3 If there is disease, people usually need medication.
4 If there is a hurricane, trees often fall over.

GRAMMAR FILE Student's Book **page 117**
Refer students to this page for more explanation and practice of the zero conditional.

ANSWERS
See page 131 of this book for answers.

Exam practice

11 Students may need clarification of *intervention* (involvement in something you would not normally be involved with in order to improve or help it), *emerge* (gradually be seen), *resources* (a supply of something that costs money, for example scientific research). Check the answer as a whole class.

ANSWER
The writer disagrees with the statement in the question: the topic sentences suggest that natural processes are difficult and expensive to control.

12 This exercise provides students with an opportunity to use the skills developed in this lesson. It also enables them to focus on the structure of their paragraph by supporting them with a pre-prepared topic sentence.

Remind students of exercises 7 and 8 by asking *What are the three other types of sentences that come after a topic sentence? What order should they come in?* (example, explanation, and result). Ask them to work alone.

Alternative for weaker classes: you may like to allow students to work in pairs to share ideas, but ensure that both students in the pair write the answer.

POSSIBLE ANSWERS
Human interventions often cause more problems than they solve.
Many solutions deal with short-term problems and do not take into account long-term consequences. For example, biofuels help to reduce pollution, but they cause problems with food shortage. Farmers grow crops for fuel instead of food because they can make more money this way, and so, as a consequence, food shortages may occur.

Not all natural threats can be controlled.
Many of the most devastating natural threats, such as earthquakes, volcanoes, and hurricanes, cannot be controlled. If these events happen, there are many places that can do little to protect themselves against the effects. Major disasters, such as the destruction of a nuclear power station, could occur as the consequence of a natural threat, against which man-made precautions cannot prevail.

New natural threats continue to emerge.
For example, new bacteria and viruses are constantly evolving. It takes time to understand these viruses and to develop anti-viral drugs. Then, no sooner is an anti-viral drug developed, than the virus adapts to survive the drug and the battle continues. If a deadly virus emerges, it can cause many deaths around the world before anything can be done to combat it.

Some natural disasters are difficult to predict.
Although we now know where many natural disasters are likely to occur, we cannot predict when they will occur. If we cannot predict when an event will happen, then it can be dangerous for people in the area. Furthermore, there are many natural disasters that are unpredictable, particularly those involving the weather and those coming from outer space, such as asteroids.

It takes money and resources to control nature, which few governments have.
Governments have limited financial resources and have to decide what to spend it on. If a flood affects an area, the government must decide how many people are in danger and how much it will cost. If the cost is too high for the numbers at risk, the government will not spend the money.

13 Get feedback by asking how many people guessed correctly. You may like to ask students to compare their answer to the suggested model answers (see above). Focus on the structure by asking them to label each answer like in exercise 7, and ask them to highlight examples of the zero conditional.

READING True / False / Not Given page 74

Lesson aims
1 Enable students to answer *True / False / Not Given* questions by identifying information that contradicts a statement, to be able to select *False*.
2 Enable students to answer *True / False / Not Given* questions by identifying information that is related but irrelevant, to be able to select *Not Given*.
3 Develop students' reading efficiency by improving their ability to identify pronoun referents in a passage.

Featured topic vocabulary
Nouns: crab, butterfly, penguin, species, antennae, magnetic field, compass, pesticide, cell
Verbs: navigate, breed

Topic focus
1 This exercise prepares students for the reading passage by clarifying vocabulary.

Focus on the pictures. Write students' ideas on the board. Focus on the title and picture accompanying the text on page 75 to help them understand what the pictures might have in common. Give students 2 minutes to skim the text to check if their ideas are correct.

ANSWERS
A crab   B butterfly   C bird   D elephant   E fish

Exam skills
2 In this exercise, students learn the difference between *True / False / Not Given* options in two stages. In this exercise, they are simply being asked to understand the difference between *true* and *false*. This idea should be familiar to students, so little introduction should be needed.

Ask students to highlight key words in the questions that they should scan for (e.g. 1 *elephants / hotel* 2 *butterfly / north / temperatures* 3 *crab / travels / eggs* 4 *Arctic* (it has a capital letter, so is easier to scan for) / *travels / straight*).

ANSWERS
1 True
2 False (not *north* – in line 16, the text says *south*)
3 True
4 False (not *in a straight line* – in line 46, the text says *in an 'S' shape*)

EXAM TIP 2•9 Before students listen, ask them to suggest possible answers to the question. After they have answered the questions, refer students to page 148 for more guidance on *True / False / Not Given* questions.

ANSWER
Not Given, because it means that a statement could be *True* or *False*. Also, *Not Given* doesn't always mean that the information is not mentioned.

Audioscript 2•9
In *True / False / Not Given* questions, you have to compare several statements with information in the reading passage. The *Not Given* option can make this type of question confusing. This is because **Not Given** doesn't mean *Not True* – instead, it means that a statement could be *True* or *False*. Also, *Not Given* doesn't always mean that the information is not mentioned. Information related to *Not Given* options may sometimes be in the passage but it won't be similar enough to decide if the answer is *True* or *False*.

3 Now students practise understanding the difference between *False* and *Not Given* options. You may wish to illustrate the concept by doing the following. First, write on the board: *I am very happy today. I had a great breakfast and this is my favourite class.*

Now write below:
The teacher had a banana.
The teacher hasn't eaten.

Now, ask students which sentence is false and which is not given.

Now ask students to highlight key words in the questions that they should scan for (1 *elephant migration / dangerous* 2 *crabs / move* 3 *butterflies / die / before completing* 4 *moon / when / migrate* 5 *number / butterflies / rising*).

After reading, ask students to compare their answers with a partner and explain in what way the *Not Given* answers are related to the text.

ANSWERS
1 Not Given   4 Not Given
2 Not Given   5 False
3 False

4 This exercise aims to increase students' confidence by realizing they are not alone in finding *Not Given* options more difficult.

Alternative for weaker classes: you may like to draw a scale on the board to help them answer question 1. Write *very confident* at one end and *not very confident* at the other end, and write numbers 1–5 along the scale. Reassure students that *Not Given* options often cause the most doubts. Encourage them to be aware of keeping a close eye on the time, to not spend too long checking the passage repeatedly at the expense of other questions.

Exam practice
5 This exercise provides students with an opportunity to combine the skills developed in exercises 2–4.

Focus on the reminder of what each option implies in the instructions, and encourage students to highlight the words *agrees*, *contradicts*, and *no information*.

After completing the exercise alone, ask students to compare answers with a partner and justify *False* and *Not Given* choices. Check as a whole class, and if students chose the wrong options, ensure they understand how they made the mistake (see below).

UNIT 7 NATURE & BIOLOGY

ANSWERS

1 True
2 False (Line 28: … *migrate each year from the island's high central rainforest to the sea to lay their eggs*. Students may be confused by the term *located in the Indian Ocean* (line 27), which refers to the island's location, not the crabs.)
3 Not Given (There is no reference to tourists. Students need to be careful not to assume something is true based on their knowledge of the world. This may be true in real life, but the passage does not say this, so it must be marked *Not Given*.)
4 Not Given (Warn students of the danger of making assumptions or inferring meaning based on the text. For example, it follows logically that if the terns try to save energy, then they probably face many challenges. However, the text does not explicitly say this.)
5 False

6 This exercise develops students' scanning skills and their ability to identify synonyms and matching phrases.
Remind students of the importance of highlighting key words in 1–7, to find matching phrases quickly. If students ask for clarification of vocabulary (e.g. *altered* and *navigate*), encourage them to try to work out the meaning from the context, and from their knowledge of the passage.

ANSWERS

A 5, 7   B 1   C 2, 3   D 4   E 6

Grammar

7 This exercise develops students' reading efficiency by improving their ability to identify what each pronoun in a passage refers to.
Focus on the example and ask students to look at line 4 to find *their*. You may like to raise their awareness of the difficulties of identifying pronoun referents by asking the questions below:
- *How many lines back do you need to read to find what 'their' refers to?* (*elephants* is in line 1)
- *How many nouns are there between 'elephants' and 'their'?* (four – Zambia, fruit, group of mango trees, luxury hotel Mfuwe Lodge)
- *How do you know 'their' refers to 'elephants' and not the other nouns?* (*their* is plural, so it cannot refer to the singular nouns – Zambia, hotel, Mfuwe Lodge – or the uncountable noun – fruit. You also need to check the sentence makes sense if you replace the pronoun with the noun you think it refers to. *Their* cannot refer to *trees* because the sentence would make no sense.)

Ask students to work alone before comparing answers with a partner. Encourage students to explain to each other why they think the noun they identified is correct. Remind students they might have to read quite far back to find what is being referred to. Check answers as a whole class.

ANSWERS

2 antennae
3 trout / fish
4 other animals
5 (young) crabs
6 Arctic tern
7 research
8 elephants

GRAMMAR FILE Student's Book page 113
Refer students to this page for more explanation and practice of pronoun referents.

ANSWERS
See page 130 of this book for answers.

8 This exercise focuses on the relationship between the noun and pronoun by identifying how they agree.
Before reading, you may like to check students understand the role of each word in the box as a whole class. Ask *Which word in the box …*
- *refers to a singular noun?* (it – the others are plural)
- *refers to the object in a sentence?* (them)
- *shows possession* (their)
- *shows that the following word(s) is / are another way to talk about something already mentioned?* (these)

Ask students to work alone before comparing with a partner. Check as a whole class and for each answer, ask them what noun the pronoun refers to (1–4 refer to the emperor penguins, and 5 refers to migration).

ANSWERS

1 they   2 These   3 them   4 their   5 it

What do you think?

9 This exercise encourages students to respond personally and critically about the lesson topic. It helps generate ideas they could use in Speaking Part 3 or Writing Task 2.
Check students understand the meaning of *how popular* (to what degree something or someone is liked) by providing an example answer, and the meaning of *raise their young* (bring up their children). Encourage students to expand their answers as much as possible. After speaking, you may like to pair students with another partner to report and compare their ideas. Monitor for interesting answers and highlight these in whole-class feedback, along with any useful vocabulary used by students.

EXAM CHALLENGE page 76

ANSWERS

Speaking
1–3 Students' own answers

Listening
1 See page 138 of this book for answers and page 141 for the audioscript.
2 Students' own answers

Writing
1 Students' own answers
2 See page 109 of the Student's Book for the model answer.

Reading
1 See page 138 of this book for answers.
2 Students' own answers

UNIT 8　　Producers & consumers

Introduction (page 77)

Featured topic vocabulary
Nouns: exporter, importer, production, trade
Verbs: export, import

Optional lead-in
Before students open their books, you may like to introduce the topic by doing the following:

a Write on the board: *France, Canada, Italy, and China export a lot of it. The USA, Germany, and Japan import a lot of it. It's often free. What is it?* Write students' ideas on the board.
b Tell students to open their books and check their ideas.
c Tell them to close their books again. Write on the board: *You need _____ litres of oil and _____ litres of water to make 1 litre of bottled water.*
d Ask students what numbers they think should go in the gaps. Write their ideas on the board.
e Tell them to open their books and check their ideas.

What do you think?
Check students understand of the infographic by asking:
- *Which country in the infographic exported the most water?* (France)
- *Which countries import the most water?* (USA, Japan)

Before students discuss, you may need to clarify *trade* (buying and selling between people or countries).

Group students in threes. Ask students to discuss questions 1–3 first in their groups. Get feedback and discuss question 4 as a whole class. Ask students to discuss question 5 in their groups, and meanwhile draw two columns on the board for advantages and disadvantages. Get feedback as a whole class and write students' ideas in the two columns.

Optional activity
Ask students to research one product that is either imported or exported in large quantities in their country. Encourage them to find out information such as:
- how much is exported / imported per year
- how important it is to the economy
- why it is imported / exported
- where it is mainly imported from or exported to
- which companies are the biggest exporters of this product.

Ask students to report their findings in the next class.

SPEAKING Recognizing question types (page 78)

EXAM FOCUS: PART 3

Lesson aims
1 Develop students' ability to recognize four types of Part 3 questions: prediction, speculation, comparison, and evaluation.
2 Enable students to speak about consumer products by expanding their topic vocabulary.
3 Prepare students to respond according to the question type using key phrases for predicting, speculating, comparing, and evaluating.

Key language
Types of purchase: impulse buys, branded goods, services, electronic goods, white goods, gifts
Collocations: comparison website, online review, special offer, personal recommendation, browse a catalogue, look at / try a sample, out-of-town shopping centre

Featured topic vocabulary
Nouns: brand, export

Topic focus

Optional lead-in
You may like to engage students with the topic of shopping by personalizing it for your school's city or town. Depending on the size of the place, you could ask questions such as:
- *Which is your favourite shopping centre / mall in (name of the place)? Why?*
- *Which is your favourite area of (name of town / city) for shopping? Why?*
- *Do you have a favourite shop in (name of town / city)? What do you like about it?*

1 This exercise engages students with the topic by encouraging them to reflect on their own personal attitude to shopping.

Before students begin, write on the board *What kind of shopper are you?* and underneath write question 1, to do as a whole class example. You may like to clarify the meaning of *brand* (a type of product made by a particular company) in question 5 by giving examples of brands your students are likely to know. Then ask them to complete the exercise alone.

2 Ask students to guess what option in question 1 is true for you. Reveal your answer and model the discussion by explaining your reasons. Encourage them to expand their answers as much as possible.

Vocabulary

3 Ask students to try the exercise before clarifying vocabulary. They may require help with the meaning of:
- *impulse buy* (buying something without planning to do so in advance, and without thinking about it carefully)
- *white goods* (large pieces of electrical equipment in the house like washing machines, tumble dryers, fridges, and freezers).

Ask students to compare answers with a partner before checking as a whole class.

ANSWERS

Impulse buys	packet of crisps (D)
Branded goods	designer handbag (E)
Services	plane ticket (C)
Electronic goods	smartphone (F)
White goods	washing machine (B)
Gifts	box of chocolates (A)

4 This exercise provides students with an opportunity to practise using the new language and check they understand the meanings correctly.

Ask students to work together to discuss each type of product as they decide their answers. Encourage them to explain their ideas to their partner using vocabulary in the table, to help them remember new phrases by using them.

POSSIBLE ANSWERS

1 impulse buys 2 branded goods 3 gifts
4 Electronic goods 5 services 6 white goods

5 Ask students to work in pairs before sharing ideas as a whole class.

POSSIBLE ANSWERS

impulse buys	magazine, soft drink
electronic goods	TV, printer
branded goods	sunglasses, clothes
white goods	fridge, microwave oven
services	insurance
gifts	flowers, tie

6 This exercise expands students' range of topic vocabulary further, with common shopping collocations.

Give students 2 minutes to decide alone, before speaking to their partner. You may like to write some useful sentences starters on the board to encourage them to answer in full sentences, for example:
- *Whenever I buy _____, I make sure I _____ first.*
- *I tend to _____ before I buy anything / any _____.*
- *If I need to get _____, I usually _____.*
- *The last time I bought _____, I checked / read / looked / got / browsed / looked at …*

You may like to check students understand the meaning of the collocations below:
- *comparison website*: a website that checks many other websites for you and shows you all the prices and details so you can get the best deal. Often used to buy things like insurance and flights. Ask students for examples, such as Skyscanner or KAYAK for flights
- *online review*: a text on a website written by people who have already tried a product, to say if it is good or not
- *special offer*: a deal or discount, like 'buy one, get one free'
- *personal recommendation*: when someone you know tells you something is good because they have already tried it and liked it
- *browse through a catalogue*: look at something like a magazine with pictures and details of products for sale
- *look at / try a sample*: try a small bit of a product to test if you like it.

Demonstrate an example answer to encourage students to extend their answers, by explaining the advantages of their choice.

7 This exercise consolidates vocabulary from exercises 3–6 by giving students a chance to put all the language together. Before students begin, you may like to clarify the meaning of:
- *ink cartridge*: provides ink (black or coloured) to printed products
- *tablet computer*: like an iPad. Smaller than a laptop.

You may like to give students an example answer and then ask them which phrases you used from this lesson, to encourage them to use new language. For extra speaking practice, pair students with a different partner when they finish. Tell them to explain to their new partner how their shopping approach is similar to or different from their original partner.

VOCABULARY FILE Student's Book page 128
Refer students to exercise 1 for more practice of phrases about consumer products.

ANSWERS
See page 134 of this book for answers.

Exam skills

8 This exercise raises students' awareness that there are different types of Part 3 questions, and encourages them to notice typical features of four specific types.

Before students begin, ask them *In what part of the exam could you be asked these questions?* (Part 3). Students may require clarification of:
- *function*: purpose – here it is referring to what the question is asking you to do
- *out-of-town*: far from the centre of a town
- *export*: products sold from one country to another country
- *prediction*: saying what you think will happen in the future

- *speculation*: when you do not know the reason why, but you try to guess
- *evaluation*: saying if something is good or not, and why.

You might like to ask students to answer questions 1–4 in pairs before matching them. This may help them to perceive the differences between the questions, through the differences in their answers. Then ask students to complete the exercise in pairs before checking as a whole class. You may like to ask them to highlight the features of each question which helps them identify the type of question (see below).

ANSWERS
1 c – comparison (which is better: X or X)
2 d – evaluation (what are / is the most important X)
3 b – speculation (why do you think some people)
4 a – prediction (will we X in the future)

Note that question 1 also requires students to evaluate, but it is important that they recognize opportunities to demonstrate comparative language and so, for the purposes of the exam training, they should regard this as a comparison question.

EXAM TIP 2·10 Before students listen, ask them to suggest possible answers to the question and write these on the board. After they have answered the question, refer students to page 145 for more guidance on Speaking Part 3.

ANSWER
Practise listening for certain types of question and prepare phrases that you could use for each type.

Audioscript 2·10

In Speaking Part 3, you can be asked a wide range of question types related to the topic in Part 2. For example, you may be asked to predict, evaluate, speculate, or compare. Other questions may require you to talk about change, give opinions, explain, or hypothesize. The different questions will give you the opportunity to show you can use different grammar structures, vocabulary, and phrases. This is why you need to **practise listening for certain types of question and prepare phrases that you could use for each type.**

9 2·11 This exercise develops students' ability to recognize whether a Part 3 question requires them to predict, speculate, compare, or evaluate.

Play the recording as many times as necessary. After listening, ask students to compare their answers with a partner before checking as a whole class. In feedback, ask them to identify which part of each question helped them identify the type.

ANSWERS
1 prediction
2 evaluation / comparison
3 comparison / speculation
4 speculation
5 comparison
6 evaluation / comparison
7 prediction
8 speculation

Audioscript 2·11, 2·12

1 How are town centres likely to change in the next ten years?
2 Which products make us the happiest?
3 Is it better to save money or spend it? Why?
4 Why do people buy things they don't need?
5 How are shopping habits of men different from those of women?
6 What products are the most difficult to buy?
7 What will happen if levels of consumption continue to rise?
8 Some people say we should give children fewer gifts. Why is that?

Key phrases

10 2·12 This exercise prepares students to respond in Part 3 according to the question type, using key phrases for predicting, speculating, comparing, and evaluating.

Before listening again, give students time to read a–h. Stop the recording after each question and check their ideas after hearing each one. Drill the response in bold after each question by modelling and getting students to repeat all together.

ANSWERS
1 h 2 b 3 g 4 a 5 f 6 d 7 e 8 c

11 This exercise provides students with an opportunity to become more familiar with the phrases and check they understand the meanings correctly.

You may like to ask students to copy the table into their notebook if they require more space. Ask them to work alone before comparing answers with a partner. Check as a whole class. You may like to drill the phrases again as you check each answer.

Stress that these phrases are for speaking, and are mostly too informal for writing.

ANSWERS

Prediction	My guess is that (there'll be), they're likely to become
Speculation	It's probably because, Maybe it's because
Comparison	They're totally different, both are important
Evaluation	The main thing is, more than anything

Exam practice

12 This exercise tests how successfully students have developed the skills focused on in exercises 8–11.

Encourage students to draw on what they studied in this lesson by asking:
- *How can you identify different types of Part 3 questions?*
- *What phrases can you remember, to respond to each type of question confidently and appropriately?*

Encourage students to listen to each other by asking them to make a note of three things they liked in their partner's responses and two points they think could be improved. You may like to give them a second chance to reply, in order to improve their performance.

LISTENING Choosing options from lists (page 80)

EXAM FOCUS: SECTION 3

Lesson aims

1 Develop students' ability to focus on multiple options simultaneously, despite hearing them in a different order, to enable them to choose items from a list.

2 Enable students to recognize and use words to describe money and value in relation to products, people, and experiences.

3 Reduce the impact of test-related stress on students' performance in the Listening test, by encouraging them to reflect on techniques for dealing with it.

Key language

Money and value adjectives: *priceless, worthless, wealthy, good value, rich, valuable, a waste of money, wasteful, pricey, poor*

Featured topic vocabulary

Nouns: *colleague, antique, fortune, income, materialism, possession*

Verbs: *borrow, refuse, afford*

Adjectives: *branded, materialistic*

Topic focus

1 This exercise engages students with the topic of the lesson by asking them to reflect on their personal attitude towards money and value. The questions are taken from various surveys used by academic researchers to find out how materialistic we are. The questions used are later referred to in recordings 2•14, 2•15, and 2•16.

You may like to clarify the meaning of *colleague* (a person that you work with), *borrow* (take for a short time and then give back), and *refuse* (say no).

2 Ask students to discuss with a partner before getting feedback as a whole class. Weaker classes may require clarification of *say about you* (what type of person you are). Adjectives which may be useful to reformulate what students are trying to express include: *generous, stingy, selfish, materialistic, jealous, sensible, frivolous*, and *frugal*.

Language note: This exercise also provides students with an opportunity to revise their use of conditional sentences. Sentences 1–4 are examples of the second conditional:

If + past, ... *would* + verb (= used for hypothetical or imagined situations).

It is not necessary to draw explicit attention to the use of conditionals in these questions, as it may detract from the main aim of engaging students in the topic. However, you may like to collect examples of good sentences as well as mistakes, as these could be used in a later lesson to focus on improving students' accuracy.

Vocabulary

3 This exercise enables students to recognize vocabulary to describe money and value in relation to products, people, and experiences.

Encourage students to try the exercise before clarifying vocabulary, as this can be done while checking answers. You may like to draw the three columns on the board, to write the answers on the board. They may require clarification of:

- *worthless*: without value
- *good value*: not expensive in relation to what you receive in return
- *valuable*: if you sold it, you would get a lot of money
- *pricey*: expensive, and perhaps more expensive than you might expect.

Ask students to work alone before comparing with a partner. Check answers as a whole class and drill the pronunciation of each word as they are added to the table.

Language note: You may like to draw students' attention to the negative suffix *-less* of *priceless* and *worthless*, and positive suffix *-ful* of *wasteful*. Ask them if they know any more words with these suffixes to help them see patterns in their vocabulary learning, e.g. *pointless, meaningless, heartless, fearless, careless, careful, joyful, beautiful*, and *mindful*.

ANSWERS

Products only: priceless, worthless
Products or experiences: good value, valuable, a waste of money, pricey
People: wealthy, rich, wasteful, poor

4 This exercise develops students' ability to use the vocabulary from exercise 3 and familiarizes them with more phrases related to money and value.

Students may require clarification of:

- *antique*: an old and often valuable object, such as furniture or jewellery
- *fortune*: a lot of money
- *afford*: to have enough money to pay for something
- *income*: the money you earn, usually from work.

Ask students to work alone before comparing with a partner. Check answers as a whole class.

ANSWERS

1 priceless   6 wealthy
2 pricey   7 good value
3 worthless   8 valuable
4 wasteful   9 a waste of money
5 rich   10 poor

5 This exercise provides students with an opportunity to practise using the new vocabulary, to help them remember it.

Students may require clarification of the meaning of *designer* (made by a famous designer or having a famous brand name). Give examples of designers your students are likely to know. Focus on the example in the speech bubble and encourage them to expand their answer as much as possible.

UNIT 8 PRODUCERS & CONSUMERS

Share ideas as a whole class by writing *meal, watch, tickets, suit,* and *artwork* on the board. Ask for example sentences and write the adjectives they use for each one on the board.

> **Optional activity**
> a Divide the class into buyers and sellers and give the sellers three pieces of paper each. Tell them they have to sell their pieces of paper to the buyers for as much money as they can.
> b They sell each piece of paper to a different buyer.
> c Buyers have to purchase three pieces of papers for as little money as they can. Buyers and sellers should both keep a record of each transaction by tearing each piece of paper they sell in two and writing the price they agreed on both pieces.
> d The winner is the buyer who made the most money and the seller who spent the least. Those who don't sell / buy three pieces of paper are disqualified.

VOCABULARY FILE Student's Book page 128
Refer students to exercises 2–4 for more practice using adjectives to describe money and value.

ANSWERS
See page 134 of this book for answers.

Exam skills

6 This exercise raises students' awareness of the approach required to choose multiple items in a list.

Focus on the instructions in the blue box, and avoid being drawn into clarifying options A–G as this can be done in the following exercise. Students may require clarification of *does it matter* in question 3 (is it important). Ask them to work alone before checking as a whole class

ANSWERS
1 letters   2 three   3 No

7 This exercise encourages students to use key words to focus on multiple options simultaneously despite hearing them in a different order.

Students may request clarification of vocabulary such as *possessions* (the things that you own), *materialism* (the belief that money, possessions, and physical comforts are more important than spiritual values), and *evolution* (the gradual development of plants, animals, etc. over many years, from simple to more complicated forms). Try to simply guide them to work out what type of word it is at this stage, and focus on what they do understand. Providing a definition does not help students prepare for the likely event of facing unfamiliar vocabulary in the exam. After listening, you may like to use the audioscript to answer any questions they had about vocabulary.

ANSWERS
A happy, important
B possessions
C meaning, 'materialism'
D human motivation
E objects, unhappy
F how long, researchers, materialism
G evolution

EXAM TIP 2•13 Before students listen, ask them to suggest possible answers to the question and write these on the board. After they have answered the question, refer students to page 146 for more guidance on choosing options from a list.

ANSWERS
Because the answers may not be mentioned in order.

Audioscript 2•13
In addition to basic multiple-choice questions, you may have to choose more than one option from a list. This can be difficult **because sometimes the answers may not be mentioned in order**. For this reason, you should consider all the options on the list as you listen. As usual, preparation is important. Make sure you read all the options before the recording starts and underline key words that you should listen for.

8 2•14 Before students listen, encourage them to focus on the need to keep all the options in mind as they listen, by concentrating on the highlighted key words. Play the recording again if necessary, but remind students they will only hear it once in the exam. After listening, ask them to compare their answers with a partner before checking as a whole class. Ask students to justify their answers by explaining what they heard that helped them choose. Ask them to turn to the audioscript on page 171 of the Student's Book to find the parts of the tutorial which match the answers.

ANSWERS
B, C, and F

Audioscript 2•14
Part 1
Tutor: So, how did the preparation go? I think I asked you to do the materialism survey.
Julie: Yes, it was fine.
Ben: Yes, OK.
Tutor: Perhaps you're both wondering why I gave you the survey to do. Well, similar questions have been used in research to find out how materialistic we are. Later we'll look at the survey in more detail but first we need to discuss some related themes. Now, **can one of you explain what we mean by 'materialism'?**
Julie: Yes, er, it's about how much stuff we buy.
Tutor: Partly, Julie, yes, it's about how we value our ownership of things. Now, why do you think sociologists are interested in this?
Julie: They want to find out what motivates us.

Tutor: OK, but individual motivation is more a question for psychologists who study how our brains work. How could materialism affect society generally?
Ben: Maybe it's related to happiness.
Tutor: OK, go on, Ben.
Ben: Er, well, I think materialism is a social thing – it's everywhere and it probably affects our happiness generally and our social relationships.
Tutor: That's right, and sociologists have studied the connection between the objects we possess and happiness ever since we started building large shopping centres in the 1980s. Erm, I'll give you the findings of the research in a minute. In the meantime, let's hear your views. Julie, do you think materialism makes us unhappy?
Julie: No, I don't. According to that survey we did, I'm quite materialistic but I feel happy when I buy things. People might not be happy if they don't have nice things.
Ben: But how long are you happy for? You get one thing and you just want more.
Tutor: OK, that idea has a name. It's called 'adaptation theory'. The theory basically suggests that we adapt quickly to what we have and we start wanting more.
Julie: But it's important to have some things. We can easily say possessions are not important because, basically, we're wealthy, but possessions seem a lot more valuable when you don't have any. We all need houses, a phone, a family car … and the nicer the house, the better! Who wants to live in a bad area?
Tutor: That's all true. But perhaps it's not so much about the house itself as about our basic need for security or freedom. We all have basic needs, but that's not the same as wanting more and more possessions.
Julie: OK, so what does make us happy, then?

Exam practice

9 2•15 Students have a chance here to test the skills developed in exercises 6–8.

Ask students to compare answers with a partner. Check as a whole class.

ANSWERS
A, D, and G

Audioscript 2•15
Part 2
Ben: I think happiness is about people.
Julie: Yes, I agree but that's my point. People want to know you when you have nice stuff. If I had a pool in my garden, an outdoor bar, I'd have crowds of people coming round every night to dance and have fun. It'd be great!
Ben: Right. But then they'd go away so you'd only have a relationship with them as long as you have stuff. I think lasting relationships depend on other things.
Tutor: Such as?
Ben: Well, close relationships like you have with your family depend on the time you spend together. People work so much to get money to buy things that they sometimes never see their family.
Julie: But you want to provide your family with a nice life, don't you? Children always want toys and games.
Ben: Maybe, but I think there's a balance. When I was growing up, I had a wonderful house, nice clothes, a new phone – all that stuff – but I hardly ever saw my dad. I only saw him when he was giving me things. I think I would've preferred it if he'd worked less – you know, if we'd spent more time together, doing things.
Julie: You say that now but I bet if I'd taken away your phone when you were younger, you would've been upset!
Ben: Yes, but only for a while whereas I still think about my dad. Memories of people stay with you forever. If you think about a holiday you went on with your parents or your latest smartphone – which one creates more important memories?
Julie: The holiday, I suppose. But are you saying happiness is about memories?

10 2•16 This exercise revises a different type of listening question, to continue to build on skills developed in previous units.

Ask students to work alone to predict what type of words might fill the gaps. Share ideas as a whole class and write students' predictions on the board. After listening, ask them to compare answers with a partner. Check as a whole class and compare their predictions to the answers.

ANSWERS
1 envious   4 trusting
2 happy   5 experiences
3 worried

Audioscript 2•16
Part 3
Tutor: OK, well, I think it's time to look at some of the research about what makes us happy. Do you remember the research by Professor Howell that we looked at in the last tutorial?
Ben: Yes, hang on, I think I've got something about that in my notes. Er, yes, here we are. He said that people were happiest when they're in control … and when they have good relationships with others.
Tutor: Yes, it was a little more complicated, Ben, but that's certainly a key part of it.
Julie: OK, but you can shop with other people and talk about what you bought. That's a kind of relationship.
Tutor: Er, I agree, Julie, but how do we feel when we talk about our possessions?
Ben: I think people feel bad sometimes. I mean, they don't say it, of course, but they're going to compare their things with what their friends bought.
Tutor: Mmm, yes. Research has in fact shown that people who have materialistic values often have bad relationships.
Julie: So how do researchers know who is materialistic?
Tutor: Well, think about that survey you did. In fact, look at questions 5–7. Question 5 is about being generous – that's the opposite of materialism – and question 6 is about being envious, a characteristic of materialistic people, and question 7?
Ben: That must be about how much you value your possessions.

Tutor: That's right. These researchers also did a happiness survey with the same people and the results showed that there's a strong negative correlation, or connection, between materialism and being **happy**. Why might that be?

Ben: Perhaps people who value possessions are **worried** that people will take them away from them, or they'll lose them or they won't be able to afford them in the future. Perhaps they stop **trusting** people.

Tutor: Yes, that could be part of it.

Julie: So are we saying that we can't buy things any more? Would it be better if we didn't have money?

Ben: No, I think you could spend it on other things, like **experiences**.

Tutor: All right, so why might it be better to spend your money on a holiday, for example?

Ben: Well, life experiences can be enjoyed together and shared. You aren't comparing each other, so it brings you closer together.

Julie: OK, I think I see your point. I shouldn't spend all my money on things …

What do you think?

11 This exercise develops students' ability to critically analyse their own feelings in relation to the world around them. It also helps to generate ideas for Writing Task 2 and Speaking Part 2, and revises vocabulary from the unit so far.

Before speaking, encourage students to use vocabulary studied in this lesson and in the speaking lesson, by giving them 1 minute to look back over the unit to try to remember as much as possible. Then tell them to close their books and ask students what language they can remember. After speaking, you may like to pair students with a different partner to summarize in what ways they are similar or different to their original partner.

Study skills

This exercise aims to reduce the impact of test-related stress on students' performance in the Listening test, by encouraging them to reflect on techniques for dealing with it.

Group students in threes to discuss the first question as a lead-in to the topic of stress. In feedback, find out which are the three most common issues in the class and write these on the board. Discuss the second question as a whole class and write students' ideas on the board. Ask them to discuss the third question in their groups before sharing ideas as a whole class. Write students' suggestions for solutions in a different colour next to each matching problem. If they run out of ideas, feed in your own suggestions and ask them how effective they think your ideas are.

WRITING Connecting ideas (page 82)

EXAM FOCUS: TASK 2

Lesson aims

1 Develop students' ability to structure discussion essays by separating opposing views into separate paragraphs.

2 Enable students to write topic sentences for discussion essays which introduce one side of an argument.

3 Expand students' range of linking words and phrases to connect sentences and show sequence, contrast, and examples.

Key language

Linking words: *for example, for instance, as a case in point, firstly, to begin with, secondly, finally, lastly, on the other hand, however, furthermore*

Featured topic vocabulary

Collocations: *make a decision, make a choice, have the power to do something, economic impact*

Nouns: *flavour, choice*

Topic focus

Optional lead-in

You may like to ask students what their favourite supermarket is in your school's town / city, and why. If they are studying away from their native country, you could also ask how supermarkets are different in comparison to their country.

1 This exercise engages students with the lesson topic of consumer choice, and helps generate ideas for Writing Task 2 which they can later compare to the model.

Take a class vote and write the numbers in favour of a and b on the board.

2 Ask students to discuss with a partner before sharing ideas as a whole class. Encourage them to expand their answers by asking if they think this is true for themselves.

Exam skills

3 This exercise encourages students to analyse the question to determine the approach required.

Ask students in what part of the exam they would find this type of question (Writing Task 2). Ask them to go back to pages 32–33 and decide what category of essay question they think this is (discussion essay).

ANSWERS

No, it doesn't require you to give your opinion; you should present two (*both*) points of view.

EXAM TIP 2•17 Before students listen, ask them to suggest possible answers to the question and write these on the board. After they have answered the question, refer students to page 147 for more guidance on Task 2 essay questions.

ANSWER
Because they require different approaches.

Audioscript 2·17
If a Task 2 essay question asks about opinions, check whether you have to write a discussion essay or personal opinion essay. This is important **because they require different approaches**. In a discussion essay, you should give a balanced response, by giving one view and then the opposite view. You can give your own personal opinion in the conclusion, but it's not required by the task. In a personal opinion essay, on the other hand, you must make your own opinion clear, right from the introduction. Then, in the body section, you focus on giving reasons for your opinion and, perhaps, reasons why the opposite view is wrong.

4 This exercise prepares students for exercise 5 and illustrates the idea of having two points of view. Students may have difficulty understanding the concept of opposing viewpoints. If so, write: *Choice is good because* … on the board and ask them which options can complete the sentence. Then replace *good* with *bad* and repeat.

Ask students to work alone before comparing with a partner. Check as a whole class. Highlight the importance of thinking of ideas for both sides by asking why this candidate has brainstormed both positive and negative points.

ANSWERS
b, c, and e

5 This exercise develops students' ability to structure discussion essays by providing them with a model of how to separate opposing views into separate paragraphs. It also illustrates how to structure a paragraph in this type of essay with a simple reason + example structure.

Before starting the exercise, you may like to focus on the structure by asking how many paragraphs there are (two). You may like to draw attention to the fact that these paragraphs are longer than in the previous unit (page 73). Ask students why this is (because there are fewer 'body' paragraphs). Tell them to read the first line of each paragraph to decide which one focuses on choice as positive (the first) and which one on choice as negative (the second). Ask them what is included after each gap (an example), and stress that this helps them choose which statement fills the gap. Ask them to compare their answers with a partner before checking as a whole class. You may like to reinforce the aim of the lesson by asking students afterwards *Why is this a good example of a discussion essay?* (it discusses both sides / the opposing sides of the argument are separated into clearly defined paragraphs / linking words in the topic sentences clearly show the two paragraphs contrast / there are a number of points made to support the point of each paragraph, and each point clearly links back to the topic sentence / examples are given to illustrate each point).

ANSWERS
1 c   2 b   3 e   4 f   5 d   6 a

Key phrases
6 This exercise expands students' range of linking words and phrases to connect sentences and show sequence, contrast, and examples.

Demonstrate by doing the first question as a whole class. Students may require clarification of the meaning of *furthermore* (introduces an extra point) and *as a case in point* (introduces an example). Ask students to work alone before comparing with a partner. Check as a whole class by asking students to take turns to come to the board and write an answer each.

ANSWERS
1 Finally
2 Secondly
3 Firstly
4 On the other hand
5 For example, For instance

> **Optional activities**
> Ask students to test each other by having one student read one of the linking words and have a second student provide a synonym without looking. You may also wish to have students write these on slips of paper and play a matching game like pelmanism (a memory game requiring players to match cards through memory recall) or snap (a card game requiring quick observation of matching cards).

7 This exercise checks students understand the meaning of the linking words and helps students remember them.

Ask students to work alone before comparing with a partner. Check as a whole class.

POSSIBLE ANSWERS
1 However   4 Finally
2 To begin with   5 For example
3 Furthermore

VOCABULARY FILE Student's Book **page 128**
Refer students to exercises 5 and 6 for more practice using linking words.

ANSWERS
See page 134 of this book for answers.

Exam skills
8 This exercise raises students' awareness of the importance of guiding the reader by introducing the point of view represented in the paragraph and clarifying that several points will be made.

You may like to write the two topic sentences on the board to highlight the answer in whole-class feedback. You may also like to draw a circle around the plural *-s* of *reasons* and *consequences*.

ANSWERS
… there are several reasons why choice can be beneficial
… being able to choose can also have many negative consequences

9 This exercise enables students to write topic sentences for discussion essays which introduce a series of points and clarify for the reader that an opposing view will later be explored.

Focus on the example sentences and ask how the candidate has varied their language (high levels – too much / consumption – consuming / bring – have).

Alternative for weaker classes: you may like to allow students to work in pairs, but insist that both students write the answer. In whole-class feedback, help them to reformulate any unnatural or incorrect language, and write good examples on the board.

> POSSIBLE ANSWERS

2 Some people think shopping online will probably continue to become more popular.
However, others believe (that) people are likely to continue going to shops.
3 To some extent, electricity has transformed our lives. However, electricity has also had negative effects.

Exam practice

10 You may like to demonstrate planning the structure by doing question 1 as a whole class. Write a detailed plan on the board, based on students' ideas. You may feel that writing a whole body section is not a good use of class time, so you could do the first paragraph of one of the essays as a whole class and then ask students to do the second paragraph independently or for homework. Or you could ask half the class to do the first paragraph and the other half the second. Encourage students to look at the model plans in the back of the book on pages 109–10 if they require help.

Alternative for weaker classes: you may like to allow students to work in pairs to share ideas, but ensure that both students write.

> POSSIBLE ANSWERS

1 On the one hand, high levels of consumption bring many benefits. Firstly, they create a range of jobs. For example, opportunities are created in retail and in factories. Secondly, they increase levels of tax. For instance, in the UK 20% of a product's price goes to the government in Value Added Tax and this is one of the government's biggest sources of income. Lastly, trade makes the world more peaceful. For example, Europe has been peaceful since the establishment of the Common Market and trade interests often dominate diplomacy.
On the other hand, consuming too much can have negative effects. To begin with, it uses up limited resources, particularly oil and wood, which cannot easily be replaced. Furthermore, shopping isn't healthy. For instance, some people become addicted to it and end up spending far too much money and going into debt. Finally, not everyone has money to shop. Consequently, poor people are excluded and they may resent those who have more.

2 Some people think there are many reasons why the internet could replace shops. To begin with, it is argued that the internet is more convenient. For example, you don't have to leave the house to shop and things can easily be delivered. Secondly, it is cheaper to shop online. For instance, you can compare prices more easily and as online companies don't need to run shops, they can offer goods at lower prices. Finally, there is a greater variety of goods to choose from and customers can choose from a greater range of colours or brands.
However, others believe there are also several reasons why the internet is unlikely to replace shops. To begin with, it's not as much fun. For example, you cannot try on clothes or enjoy the bright and stimulating shop environments when shopping online. Furthermore, you cannot inspect items. In particular, you cannot touch them to see their weight or check them for faults and this may result in many goods having to be returned to suppliers. Finally, it is unsociable; for instance, you do not usually talk to, or interact with, anyone when shopping online but when you go out you can have breaks in cafés with friends.

3 To some extent, electricity may be considered the greatest discovery. Firstly, it has made possible the emergence of modern factories. For example, without it we would not have car plants or robotic assembly lines. Secondly, it has made digital technology possible. Computer technology in the office or home is the most obvious example of this but we should not forget all the equipment in hospitals that also relies on digital technology. Lastly, it has made our lives more convenient. For instance, we no longer have to rely on fires for light as we can use electric lighting.
However, there are also several reasons why electricity may not be not the greatest discovery. To begin with, the age of digital and electronic machines has brought problems, too. For example, as we can now work until late using electric light, or at home with a laptop, people work too much. Furthermore, there have been negative effects on health. For instance, television and computer gaming has led to problems with sleep and mental health issues. Finally, other major discoveries have been important, too. For example, car or plane engines have also transformed our modern world, making travel easier than ever before.

READING Summary completion page 84

Lesson aims
1 Develops students' ability to read for the main idea in a passage by focusing on topic sentences.
2 Enable students to complete summaries of a passage by predicting the missing part of speech and scanning for the correct word.
3 Improve students' use of modal verbs to talk about ability in the past, present, and future.

Featured topic vocabulary
Nouns: *three dimensions, precision, financial capital, distribution, technical limits*
Verbs: *reproduce, rebuild*

Topic focus
1 Ask students to discuss in groups of four, before taking a class vote.

ANSWER
2

2 Encourage students to look at the details they can see in the photograph to help them. Remind them of the importance of the skill of prediction in the exam.

Exam skills
3 This exercise raises students' awareness of the importance of topic sentences in understanding the main idea of a paragraph.

You may like to write the first sentence on the board to ensure students only read this. Otherwise, focus on the instructions by asking *When should you stop reading?* (at the end of the first sentence) *How do you know you've reached the end of the first sentence?* (at the first full stop). It is important to make sure they do not read any more or the aim of the exercise is lost.

ANSWER
b

EXAM TIP 2•18 Before students listen, ask them to suggest possible answers to the question and write these on the board. After they have answered the question, refer students to page 148 for more guidance on using topic sentences.

ANSWER
Questions where you choose the best heading or questions where you complete a summary

Audioscript 2•18
In order to understand the main idea of a passage, you don't always need to read the complete passage. Often, you need to read just the topic sentences of each paragraph. This strategy is particularly useful for **questions where you choose the best heading or questions where you complete a summary**. But it can also help you to predict the missing word for a gap or help you to find the paragraph of a passage that contains the most useful information.

4 This exercise encourages students to read more efficiently by highlighting how focusing on topic sentences can have the same result as reading whole paragraphs.

It is important to raise students' awareness of the point being made here, by asking them what this exercise shows.

ANSWER
Yes, the answer should be the same. The rest of the paragraph develops the idea in the topic sentence.

5 This exercise develops students' ability to read for the main idea in a passage by focusing on topic sentences. They have already discussed how to use topic sentences to match headings on page 64 so they should be familiar with the idea. Here they are developing their awareness of how to use topic sentences to navigate a text and locate relevant paragraphs.

After reading, ask students to compare their answers with a partner and justify their choice by pointing out how the topic sentences helped them. Check the answer as a whole class, and then ask students which topic sentences talk about advantages and which ones point to disadvantages.

ANSWER
1

Optional activity
You may like to extend this by referring students back to a text from an earlier unit. You could do the following:
a As a whole class, ask students what they can remember about the overall meaning of the text.
b Tell them to read only the topic sentence of each paragraph to decide if the meaning can be understood by reading these alone.
c You may like to repeat this by allocating a different text from the book to each group of students, and ask them to do the same again before reporting back to another group.

6 This exercise demonstrates the first step of completing a summary: scanning a text to locate the relevant part.

Tell students not to worry about the gap for now, as this is probably the first thing they will focus on. Encourage them to highlight the key words they need to scan for. You may like to put them under time pressure by making it a competition to find the paragraph first. Start a stopwatch as you allow students to turn to the text and time how long it takes them.

ANSWER
D

Teaching tip: Students often focus immediately on the missing information and start looking for this before they have precisely located the area which the sentence refers to.

Highlight to students that looking for a specific word requires a different type of reading compared to finding the correct section of a text. If they immediately start looking for a word before they have found the correct part of the text, then they are probably using the wrong type of reading. This will slow them down and potentially stop them finding the correct part of the text. You may like to illustrate this by asking students if they would use the same type of paintbrush to paint their living room as they would use to paint a portrait.

7 This exercise focuses on the second step of completing a summary: predicting the part of speech of the missing word.
Alternative for weaker classes: you may like to guide students by writing the sentence on the board and highlighting *money* and *large houses*. Raise their awareness of why this step is important by asking them how this will help them to find the missing word (they can read more efficiently by scanning for a specific type of word).

ANSWER
Noun

8 This exercise takes students through the final step of completing a summary: scanning a small area of a text for a specific part of speech.
After students have found the missing word, ask if they read this paragraph in the same way they read the whole text in exercise 6. (No, because they are reading much more closely here, focusing on word level. This would not be an efficient way to read the whole text in exercise 6.)

ANSWER
skills

Exam practice

9 Remind students of the steps they should follow by asking them to look back at exercises 3–8. Write on the board *What advice would you give a friend who was doing IELTS if he / she didn't know how to complete a summary?* Write students' ideas on the board.
After completing the exercise, ask students to check in pairs and discuss if they followed their own advice written on the board. Ask them to check if they agree with their partner on the part of speech that is missing, and to check they have chosen words which match the part of speech they predicted. Check answers as a whole class.

ANSWERS
1 (large) factory
2 costs
3 industrial pollution
4 equipment
5 jobs
6 regulate
7 illegal

Grammar

10 This exercise checks students understand the difference between modal verbs about ability in the past, present, and future.
Write the modal verbs on the board and ask students which one is for past, present, or future. Write their answers next to the verbs. Ask them to complete the exercise alone before comparing with a partner. Check answers as a whole class by writing the question number next to each modal verb it matches.

Language note: A common mistake with modal verbs is the addition of *to* afterwards. Highlight to students that after *can* or *could* we use the infinitive without *to*

ANSWERS
1 can
2 won't be able to
3 could
4 will be able to

GRAMMAR FILE Student's Book page 118
Refer students to this page for more explanation and practice of modal verbs.

ANSWERS
See page 131 of this book for answers.

11 This exercise improves students' use of modal verbs by giving them an opportunity to practise talking about ability in the past, present, and future.
Demonstrate by focusing on the example and expanding the answer to talk about the present and future as well.
Alternative for weaker classes: you may like to ask them to do this as a written exercise first to prepare them to speak. Otherwise, ask students to take turns in pairs to talk about a topic each.

What do you think?

12 This exercise develops students' knowledge by encouraging them to think critically about how production and industry are changing. It helps generate ideas they could use in Speaking Part 3 or Writing Task 2.
Check students understand the meaning of *goods* (products) and *technical limits* (what might not be possible because the technology is not able to do it). Encourage them to expand their answers as much as possible. After speaking, share interesting ideas you heard while monitoring and if possible, focus on how students successfully expanded their answers.

EXAM CHALLENGE page 86

ANSWERS

Speaking
1–3 Students' own answers

Listening
1 See page 137 of this book for answers and page 141 for the audioscript.

Writing
1 Students' own answers
2 See page 110 of the Student's Book for the model answer.

Reading
1 See page 138 of this book for answers.
2 Students' own answers

UNIT 9   Media & travel

Introduction

Featured topic vocabulary
Travel nouns: *accommodation, amenities*
Travel collocations: *book accommodation, holiday planning*
Media nouns: *online review, social network, mobile device, social media*
Media collocations: *post a review, post updates*

Optional lead-in
Before students open their books, you may like to introduce the infographic by writing gapped sentences on the board, such as:

- *83% of travellers use _____ for most of their holiday planning.*
- *Travellers now consider an average of _____ hotels when booking holiday accommodation*
- *_____% of travellers post updates on social networks during their holiday.*

Ask students to work in pairs to predict what information could go in the gaps. Tell them to open their books and check.

Alternatively, ask students to find any photos on their mobile devices taken on a day trip or a holiday. Ask:
- *Where did you take the photo?*
- *Did you share the photo on social media?*
- *Did the photo get many positive comments?*

What do you think?
Focus on the infographic and ask students which numbers they find most surprising. Put students into pairs to discuss the questions. You may like to get feedback immediately after each question rather than asking them to discuss all five questions together. Allocate a time limit per question, allowing less time for questions 1–3, more for question 4, and substantially more time for question 5.

SPEAKING Narrating

EXAM FOCUS: PART 2

Lesson aims
1 Improve students' use of sequencing markers to structure a narrative.
2 Develop students' use of narrative tenses (past simple and past continuous).
3 Enable students to speak about events in the news by expanding their range of verbs related to news stories.
4 Improve students' pronunciation of regular past tense verbs to ensure the verb ending is heard.

Key language
Phrasal verbs: *break out, break into sth, take place, run over sb, go off, run off, come across sth, crash into sth*

Featured topic vocabulary
Nouns: *violence, thief (thieves), pedestrian*
Verbs: *rescue, discover, survive, attack, scream, approach*

Topic focus

Optional lead-in
You may like to replace stages 1–3 below by focusing on current news stories. Go to a news website which ranks stories by popularity (a search for *most popular news stories* should reveal such a list) or take a recent local or national newspaper into the class. Show students the photos and headlines from three or four main stories, in no particular order, and ask them:

a which they think would be the most popular
b which is the most important.

If using an online source, you can then reveal which was most popular by looking at the online ranking. If using a newspaper, you can tell students which the editor thought was most important by revealing which was closest to the front page.

1 Focus on the pictures and ask students to discuss in groups of three. Get feedback as a whole class to find out which one is most popular in the class.

2 Ask students to discuss in groups of three and justify their answer. Take a vote to decide the answer as a whole class and write their choice on the board. Then tell students the correct answer and ask why they think this was the case.

ANSWER
The order of popularity on the Yahoo! news website was:
1 B   2 A   3 C

3 This exercise encourages students to think critically about the topic of news media. You may wish to elicit some of these differences:
- Online news stories are often listed by popularity or are selected for the user according to past preferences
- In newspapers, by comparison, there is normally more editorial control
- Online news also tends to be a little briefer
- They include video
- Online news can be updated more frequently
- Online news has briefer and arguably more trivial content, perhaps because it 'competes' for users' attention against many other links.

Ask students to discuss in groups of three before getting feedback as a whole class. Write their ideas on the board, reformulating their language as necessary.

Vocabulary

4 This exercise expands students' range of phrasal verbs related to news stories. Mention that phrasal verbs, and other idiomatic expressions, should be avoided in IELTS academic writing but that using such language is desirable in the speaking.

Encourage students to try the exercise alone first before clarifying any vocabulary. They may need help understanding words in the questions, such as *thieves* (people who steal things) and *violence* (violent behaviour that is intended to hurt or kill someone). Tell students to check with a partner. Check answers as a whole class and clarify the meaning of each verb as it is used:
- *take place*: happen
- *go off*: make a noise (alarm) or explode (bomb)
- *come across (sth)*: discover by accident
- *run over (sb)*: hit someone who is walking when you are in a car or truck (by accident or deliberately)
- *crash into (sth)*: hit something with your car or truck, like a wall or tree
- *break into (sth)*: enter a place without a key, e.g. by breaking a window
- *run off*: escape
- *break out*: start suddenly.

ANSWERS
1 take place
2 go off
3 come across sth
4 run over, crash into
5 break into, run off
6 break out

5 This exercise enables students to understand how the new vocabulary might be used within a sentence.

Alternative for weaker classes: you may like to guide them by asking if these sentences are talking about the past, present, or future (past). Students may require clarification of vocabulary such as *pedestrian* (a person walking in the street and not travelling in a vehicle) and *species* (type of animal). Ask students to work alone before comparing with a partner.

Check answers as a whole class and highlight that stories are mostly told in the past simple

ANSWERS
1 broke into, went off, ran off
2 broke out, took place
3 ran over, crashed into
4 came across

VOCABULARY FILE Student's Book page 129
Refer students to exercises 1 and 2 for more practice of phrasal verbs.

ANSWERS
See page 134 of this book for answers.

Exam skills

6 Tell students neither the pictures nor the sentences are in the correct order. First, ask students to match the sentences with the pictures and write the letters in the spaces. Check their answers and then ask them to discuss the order of the events.

POSSIBLE ANSWER
1 A fire broke out. (picture C)
2 The family screamed for help. (picture B)
3 The firefighters arrived. (picture A)
4 The family was rescued. (picture E)
5 The fire was put out. (picture D)

EXAM TIP 2•19 Before students listen, ask them to suggest possible answers to the question and write these on the board. After they have answered the question, refer students to page 145 for more guidance on Speaking Part 2.

ANSWER
the past continuous

Audioscript 2•19
In Speaking Part 2, you may be asked to describe a series of events or, in other words, to 'narrate'. For example, you may be asked to describe something that happened to you or something that you saw. This provides a good opportunity to use a range of regular and irregular past tenses. A good way to give background to your narrative is by using the **past continuous** tense, as in *I was walking down the street near my home when* … You can then continue with the past simple tense to describe what happened.

---

7 This exercise expands students' knowledge of sequencing markers.

Check the meaning by asking:
- *Which phrase will you use last?* (in the end)
- *Which two have a similar meaning?* (then and next)
- *Which one means 'after a short time'?* (soon)

Refer students back to exercise 6 to remember the story. After speaking, you may like to ask them to work with another partner to tell the story again to improve their confidence, but this time without looking at their books.

Grammar

8 This exercise provides students with a model of a narrative of a past event.

Students may require clarification of the word *plot* (what happens in the story). Tell students not to worry about the gaps for now. Encourage them just to skim the text to get the main idea. Ask students to compare their answer in pairs before checking as a whole class.

ANSWER
c

9 Before students begin, check they understand the meaning and form of past simple and past continuous (see language note below). Tell students to work alone before comparing answers with a partner. Check answers as a whole class. Highlight the use of *while* before question 3 and 11 as this is often used with past continuous to describe something happening simultaneously. Ask students if the verbs in questions 3, 4, 6, and 11 are short or long actions (long).

Language note: You may like to check students understand the meaning and form of past simple and past continuous by doing the following:

a Write on the board *I was driving along a country road when I crashed into a tree*.

b Draw a box around *was driving* and *crashed*, and ask students which one refers to the main event (crashed) and which one describes the background (was driving). Ask which action was longer (driving).

c Ask how we form past continuous (*was / were* + *-ing* verb) and write this on the board. Ask how we form past simple (*-ed* for regular verbs, but irregular verbs each change in different ways). The verb *to be* is different as it does not require the auxiliary *didn't* or *did* for negatives and questions.

ANSWERS
1 read
2 got lost
3 was walking
4 was working
5 drank
6 was carrying
7 ran out
8 became
9 died
10 discovered
11 was crossing
12 rescued
13 took
14 think

GRAMMAR FILE Student's Book page 119
Refer students to this page for more explanation and practice of narrative tenses.

ANSWERS
See page 131 of this book for answers.

10 This exercise develops students' ability to use a variety of regular and irregular verbs in narrative tenses.

Before students begin you may like to check their pronunciation of the verbs, particularly *read, drank, ran, became, took*, and the difference between *walking* and *working*.

11 2·20 This exercise improves students' pronunciation of regular past tense verbs to ensure the verb ending is heard. After listening, ask students if they know why some words end in a /t/ sound and others with a /d/ sound. Guide them to an understanding by asking them to put their hands on their throats to try and feel the difference. After sounds that vibrate (called *voiced*) like /v/ in *discovered*, the ending should be /d/ because this also vibrates. After sounds that do not vibrate (called *voiceless*) like /k/ in *worked*, the ending should be /t/ because this also does not vibrate. The third ending /ɪd/ is used when the word ends in a /t/ or /d/ sound already, and so an extra syllable is added.

ANSWERS
/d/ discovered, survived, arrived, rescued, screamed (all have a voiced consonant sound before the *-ed* ending, which vibrates if you put your hand against your throat)
/t/ worked, attacked, crashed, photographed (all have a voiceless consonant sound before the *-ed* ending, so there is no vibration if you put your hand against your throat)
/ɪd/ reported, visited, posted

Audioscript 2·20
discovered, reported, crashed, arrived, screamed, visited, attacked, survived, worked, rescued, posted, photographed

12 This exercise encourages students to focus on their pronunciation while also providing extra practice using narrative tenses.

Ask students to work in pairs, but tell them they should both write. Then ask them to tell their story to another pair, and compare how many of the same verbs they used.

Exam practice

13 Ask students what they have learnt which can help them answer this type of Part 2 question (phrasal verbs, sequencing markers, past simple and past continuous, and pronunciation of past simple endings). Write their answers on the board. You may like to demonstrate by giving an example answer and ask students to make a note of anything you use which matches their ideas written on the board. Ask them to do the same when they listen to each other. Give students an opportunity to repeat their answer to try and improve the second time.

> **Optional activity**
> If there is an interesting story currently in the news, you may like to ask students to keep a 'news log', to follow how the story progresses over the next week or two. They should regularly check different news sources, and see how the story is covered differently by different media channels, and report back any new perspectives on the story to the class.

LISTENING Understanding connected speech page 90

EXAM FOCUS: SECTION 2

Lesson aims
1 Enable students to decode connected speech by identifying word boundaries.
2 Expand students' vocabulary related to tourist city sights, to enable them to understand descriptions of places.
3 Raise students' awareness of how to maximize a range of resources to prepare for the test.

Key language
City sights: *street market, harbour, monument, mall, art gallery, fountain, cathedral, mosque, main square, city wall, public gardens, statue*

Featured topic vocabulary
Nouns: *street vendor, skyline, conservationist, runway, archway, walkway*
Verb: *construct*

Topic focus

Optional lead-in
You may like to introduce the topic by writing the six cities in exercise 1 on the board and asking students if they have visited any of these places. If you have internet access, you can also find images of the cities online and ask students to guess which cities they are or to match them. Ask students what they think all six cities have in common (they are in the top 20 most visited cities in the world).

1 This exercise introduces the topic of travel and expands students' knowledge.

Ask students to work in pairs. After checking answers as a whole class, ask them if they have visited any of these cities.

ANSWERS
1 c 2 e 3 b 4 f 5 a 6 d

2 This exercise gives students an opportunity to show what topic vocabulary they already know.

After discussing in pairs, get feedback as a whole class. Write examples of topic vocabulary used by students on the board. Ask them which city they would most like to visit.

3 Group students in fours and ask each group to think of other cities that are popular with tourists. You might like to introduce an element of competition by allocating points for each correct answer.

ANSWERS
Top 20 Most Visited Cities in the world (Ranked by millions of visitors, according to *Forbes* magazine – June 2013):
1 Bangkok (Thailand) 15.98
2 London (UK) 15.96
3 Paris (France) 13.92
4 Singapore (Singapore) 11.75
5 New York (USA) 11.52
6 Istanbul (Turkey) 10.37
7 Dubai (UAE) 9.89
8 Kuala Lumpur (Malaysia) 9.20
9 Hong Kong (China) 8.72
10 Barcelona (Spain) 8.41
11 Seoul (South Korea) 8.19
12 Milan (Italy) 6.83
13 Rome (Italy) 6.71
14 Shanghai (China) 6.50
15 Amsterdam (Netherlands) 6.35
16 Tokyo (Japan) 5.80
17 Vienna (Austria) 5.37
18 Taipei (Taiwan) 5.19
19 Riyadh (Saudi Arabia) 5.05
20 Los Angeles (USA) 4.84

Vocabulary

4 This exercise expands students' knowledge of words they may hear in descriptions of cities.

Highlight that not all the words in the box are shown in the photos. Ask students to discuss in pairs before checking as a whole class. You may like to write the vocabulary on the board in order to mark the stress on the words as you check the answers. Model and drill the pronunciation of words that students may find difficult such as *cathedral, statue, monument,* and *harbour*.

ANSWERS
A mosque   D street market
B harbour   E mall
C city wall   F monument

Language note: The word *mall* is increasingly used in the UK, but is more commonly found in American English. In the UK, *shopping centre* is often used instead. The word *mosque* refers to the place of worship for Muslims, while a *cathedral* is a place of worship for Christians, and is much larger than a church.

5 This exercise improves students' accuracy by using the correct verb form in common structures related to travel.

Before students begin, ask them how the verb *visit* could change (*visits / visiting / visited*). Ask students to work alone before comparing with a partner. Highlight the target structures by writing each one on the board as you check the answers as a whole class:
- *enjoy + -ing*
- *prefer + to + verb*
- *have + past participle*
- *can + verb*
- *if + verb*

UNIT 9 MEDIA & TRAVEL 111

ANSWERS

1 visiting
2 to visit
3 visited
4 visit
5 visit

6 This exercise helps students remember new vocabulary and provides them with extra practice of Part 1 style Speaking questions.

Encourage students to use the structures from question 5 in their answers, to promote accuracy in their use of verbs. Monitor to check students are using the correct verb forms. Correct any mistakes after they have finished speaking. Also listen for students' use of vocabulary from exercise 4, and share good examples in feedback.

VOCABULARY FILE Student's Book page 129
Refer students to exercises 3–5 for more practice of phrases related to city sights.

ANSWERS
See page 135 of this book for answers.

Exam skills

7 2.21 This exercise raises students' awareness of the difficulties caused by connected speech.

Play the recording as many times as necessary. Ask students to compare answers before checking as a whole class.

ANSWERS

1st sentence	7 words
2nd sentence	6 words
3rd sentence	6 words
4th sentence	8 words

Audioscript 2.21
1 The main square's got a lovely fountain.
2 Does the gallery open at nine?
3 Let's look around that new mall.
4 You can take a photo of the harbour.

EXAM TIP 2.22 Ask them to suggest possible answers to the question and write these on the board. After they have answered the question, refer students to page 146 for more guidance on recognizing individual words.

ANSWER
The words in a sentence often seem 'connected' together.

Audioscript 2.22
In the Listening test, you often have to write down individual words that you hear. This is difficult because, in natural spoken English, **the words in a sentence often seem 'connected' together**. You can't easily hear where one word ends and another begins! Also, the sound of the individual words sometimes changes when they're spoken with others. This means you might not recognize them. With practice, however, you can improve your ability to recognize individual words and work out which are important.

8 2.23 This exercise enables students to decode connected speech by identifying word boundaries.

Play the recording as many times as necessary. Ask students to compare their answers with a partner before checking as a whole class. Raise their awareness of the difficulties in identifying word boundaries by asking them why they think the person who wrote sentences 1–3 made these mistakes (1 because *great* finishes with the same sound that *town* starts with, so they merge together; 2 the plural -s and contracted -s sound the same; 3 the issue here is a confusion between syllables and words). Ask students what can help them to know the correct words (the context. If it is a talk about sightseeing, it is more likely that the word is *history* not *stories*).

ANSWERS
See audioscript below.

Audioscript 2.23
1 It's a really great town.
2 You'll soon see history's everywhere.
3 Is that the war monument?

9 2.24 This exercise demonstrates the importance of decoding connected speech correctly.

Focus on the instructions by asking how many words students can write (no more than three). Before listening, ask them to work in pairs to predict what type of words might be missing. After listening, ask them to compare answers with a partner before checking as a whole class. Ask students to identify what problems might be caused by connected speech in the answers:

1 The /t/ at the end of *bright* is hardly heard because the /k/ at the start of *colours* is in a similar mouth position.
2 *Nice* ends with the same sound that *statues* begins with, so the two connect.
3 This should not cause problems.
4 The *a* connects with *salt* because it is a vowel, and the /t/ of *salt* is pronounced as a glottal stop to enable the speaker to leave the tongue in the same place to pronounce the /l/ at the beginning of *lake*.
5 This should not cause problems.
6 The /t/ at the end of *tourist* is hardly heard because the /s/ of *tourist* connects the /s/ at the beginning of *sights*.
7 Because *two* ends with a vowel sound and *hours* begins with a vowel sound, there is a /w/ inserted in between the words.
8 Like the example in exercise 8, *great* can sound like *grey* because the /t/ is dropped because the /k/ of *clubs* is in the same area of the mouth.
9 The /k/ at the end of *fantastic* can sound like a /g/ because of the /g/ sound at the beginning of *golden*. The /n/ at the end of *golden* can sound like /m/ because of the mouth position of /b/ at the start of *beaches*, which is in a similar part of the mouth to where /m/ is produced.

ANSWERS

1 bright colours
2 nice statues
3 (completely) straight
4 salt
5 a tour bus
6 tourist sights
7 2 hours
8 great clubs
9 golden beaches

Audioscript 2·24

Hi, I'm Aimee and this is my audio diary. I'm in Mexico City now. From where I'm standing, I can see the grand Monument to the Revolution, in Plaza de la República. Anyway, I think it's really worth coming here. I just love the life in the streets – everyone's so busy. There are lots of street vendors, families, and young people walking around. I adore the many **bright colours** of the buildings as well – they're pretty. The churches are beautiful, too, and have some really **nice statues** inside. There are some interesting things I've learnt about the city. One of the most fascinating facts is that it's sinking! If you look up at the skyline, you'll see the many towers are not **completely straight**. It looks really strange, but apparently it's because Mexico City was constructed on a **salt** lake. Builders and conservationists are constantly trying to limit the effects. Anyway, there are many good ways to get around the city. Today, I'm travelling on **a tour bus**. I really recommend it and it stops at all the best **tourist sights**. And when you're tired of the city, which won't be soon, there are many options for further travel. Tomorrow, I'm going on a **two-hour** flight to Cancún. I'm really looking forward to dancing in the **great clubs** and spending time on the fantastic **golden beaches**!

Exam practice

10 ⊙ 2·25 Students have a chance here to put together everything studied in this lesson and revise the techniques for labelling a map.

Remind students to analyse the map carefully by noticing what features they can see around each option. Discuss as a whole class what can be seen on the map. Highlight that they need to answer both question 1 and 2, but explain that the answer to question 1 is heard before the answers to question 2.

ANSWERS

1 C   2 B, D, and E

Audioscript 2·25

Thank you for downloading this audio guide. We hope you'll enjoy your visit to Dubrovnik. First of all, if you're travelling by plane, don't miss out on the wonderful views as you fly past Dubrovnik to land. Try to book a seat on the left-hand side of the plane because then you'll get the best views of Dubrovnik itself as you head along the coast towards the airport. You will also get great views of all the islands along the coast.
When you arrive at the airport, a bus should be waiting to take you to the city. You can enjoy a coffee in the airport café while you're waiting.
When you reach Dubrovnik, get off the bus at the stone pillar gate, a big archway at the western end of the city walls. Once through that, you'll be in the old city. Now, you can walk along the plaza, a walkway that takes you through the old town, which is lined on each side with two-storey mansions with Venetian-style shutters. You'll see the 15th-century church of St. Saviour on the left and then you'll soon come to the ancient Onofrio's fountain where they say you can drink the clean water. At the end of the street you will find Luza Square. If you need accommodation, there are plenty of private apartments in this area. As you'll see, there are no cars at all along the streets, and it's worth spending an hour or two enjoying the chatter of voices, the live jazz, and the noise of the swallows as they sing and fly between the old buildings. The place has quite a sleepy feel to it and, in fact, there aren't many lively cafés but, later, the place does come to life a little bit …

11 ⊙ 2·26 Students have a chance here to put together everything studied in this lesson and revise the techniques for gap fills.

Before listening, remind students to predict what type of words they think are missing. After listening, discuss as a whole class what problems could be caused by connected speech, particularly in questions 1, 2, and 5:

1 Because *war* ends with a vowel sound, it is hard to hear what word the /f/ of *photo* belongs to.
2 The /d/ at the end of *remained* connects with the vowel at the beginning of *open*.
5 The /k/ at the end of *public* disappears because of the /g/ at the beginning of *gardens*.

ANSWERS

1 War Photo
2 remained open
3 clock tower
4 ferry boat ride
5 public gardens
6 the beach

Audioscript 2·26

In this section of the guide, we'll suggest some places to visit. First, we recommend going to a lovely little gallery called **War Photo** Limited. This small gallery is ranked the third most popular tourist attraction in Dubrovnik. Go inside and you'll see a small exhibition that tells you much about the city's recent history. Opposite the gallery, there's a coffee bar that **remained open** during the war at the end of the twentieth century and also shows interesting photos of the period. After that, we recommend going to the old city walls. Climb the steps and you can enjoy the view out across to the green islands and the sailing boats. The walk along the walls is about 2 kilometres. One of the first things you'll see standing tall over the city is the beautiful **clock tower**. Next, for a little trip, why not go to the harbour and enjoy a 10-minute **ferry boat ride** to the quiet island of Lokrum? There, you can sit in the **public gardens** and enjoy the view of the beautiful old harbour. Later in the evening, if you like to party, there's a popular club on **the beach** where you can dance until the early hours of the morning …

What do you think?

12 This exercise provides students with an opportunity to practise using vocabulary from this lesson, and helps generate ideas which could be useful for Speaking Part 2.

Tell students to note down a minimum of four places. Encourage them to use vocabulary from exercise 4, *would* + infinitive, and to expand their answer by giving reasons for their choices.

13 You might like to encourage students to respond to each other's suggestions by writing some useful phrases on the board, such as:
- *That sounds* + adjective.
- *I've never been there but I've heard of it.*
- *I've never heard of that.*
- *I'm not sure that's my cup of tea.*
- *That's right up my street.*

Study skills

This exercise raises students' awareness of how to maximize a range of resources to prepare for the test.

Group students in threes to discuss. Focus on the first question. You might like to give each group a big piece of paper to brainstorm their ideas. After writing at least one idea for each resource, tell students to exchange their paper with another group and discuss if there are any ideas they would like to steal. Tell them to do the same again by exchanging with another group. Ask students to add ideas to their paper from the other groups' papers. Ask them to discuss the second question before sharing ideas as a whole class.

WRITING Conclusions

EXAM FOCUS: TASK 2

Lesson aims
1 Develop students' ability to write effective conclusions for essays.
2 Expand students' range of compound nouns related to the media.

Key language
Collocations: *positive reaction, viral campaign, well informed, access information, readily available, to raise money*

Media compounds: *news story, news content, news media, news network, news broadcast, web page, web content, web users, TV programme, TV network, TV broadcast*

Topic focus

Optional lead-in
You may like to introduce the topic by asking students:
- *Have you ever found something in the street that belonged to someone else? What did you do?*
- *Have you ever lost something that someone else later found and gave back to you? What did you do to say thank you?*
- *Is it ever OK to keep something you found? What about if you are very poor?*

1 This exercise engages students with the topics of change in news reporting and the power of social media.

Discuss as a whole class and write students' ideas on the board.

2 Ask students if any of their ideas on the board were correct, and circle these.

3 This exercise provides students with an opportunity to respond personally to the story.

Students may need clarification of *viral* (shared by a lot of people online on sites like Facebook, so it spreads quickly). After discussing in pairs, ask them to share ideas as a whole class.

Optional activity
The featured story is a good example of news that seems trivial but in fact illustrates a wider phenomenon: it is essentially a feel-good story but illustrates the power of social media. Being able to place stories in wider contexts is an important skill that will help students think of examples to support their arguments in Writing Part 2 and Speaking Part 3. You may wish to draw students' attention to similarly significant stories. Write up headlines you have chosen, for example:
- *Journalist arrested for phone hacking*
- *Government report leaked*
- *Celebrity to sue for invasion of privacy*

Once you have dealt with difficult lexis, ask student to complete a sentence starting *This is an example of . . .* for each headline. In groups, students can then read their sentences in no particular order (or you can collect them and read them out) and the other class member(s) can try and match their sentences with the original headlines.

Vocabulary

4 This exercise expands students' knowledge of compound nouns related to the media in order to help them write about this topic. It also introduces a range of synonyms which they can use to paraphrase language when they write their conclusions (e.g. *news media*, *news networks*).

Highlight that each word can be used more than once in different combinations (e.g. you can use *news* to create both *news story* and *news content*, etc). Students may require clarification of words such as *network* (a system of connected people or things) and *broadcast* (send out programmes on television or radio). Ask students to work in pairs before checking answers as a whole class.

POSSIBLE ANSWERS
news story, news content, news media, news network, news broadcast
web content, web users, web page
social media, social network
TV programme, TV network, TV broadcast

VOCABULARY FILE Student's Book page 129
Refer students to exercise 6 for more practice of compound nouns related to media.

ANSWERS
See page 135 of this book for answers.

5 This exercise helps students activate and memorize new vocabulary.

Encourage students to expand their answers as much as possible and to use new topic vocabulary. To get whole-class feedback, take a vote to find out which social media site is most popular in the class: a *Facebook*, b *Twitter*, or c *an alternative to these two sites*. Ask students who vote for option c which site they use.

Exam skills

6 This exercise helps students engage with the essay questions that will be used as models in the lesson, and reminds them of the importance of analysing the question in determining the structure of an essay.

Ask students to discuss in pairs before checking the answer as a whole class. Ask students which part of the question helps them to know this (to what extent do you agree or disagree). Students may require clarification of *informed*. Encourage them to guess from the context, and ask if they know any other word that looks like *informed* (information). Ask why it is important to know what type of question it is (so you can know what kind of answer to write).

ANSWER
Question 1

7 This exercise prepares students to focus on writing conclusions by providing a model essay structure.

Ask students to compare and justify their answer with a partner, before checking as a whole class. Ask how they know which question it answers (the thesis statement clearly states a position, and while the first topic sentence presents a concession, the other two topic sentences argue in favour of one clear position).

ANSWER
Question 1

8 This exercise raises students' awareness of the importance of reformulating their thesis statement and topic sentences when writing a conclusion.

Focus on the small numbers in the conclusion and then refer students back to exercise 7. Raise students' awareness of the structure of a conclusion by asking *From looking at this example, what should you include in a conclusion?* Tell them that the Exam tip will help them understand number 3.

ANSWERS
a 1   b 2

EXAM TIP 2·27 Before students listen, ask them to suggest possible answers to the question and write these on the board. After they have answered the question, refer students to page 147 for more guidance on essay conclusions.

ANSWER
a personal comment, like a prediction about the future

Audioscript 2·27
In a conclusion, you should include a summary of your main points and a sentence that directly answers the question – even if you've already stated this in the thesis statement. You may also wish to include **a personal comment that is not connected to the essay question but which is relevant to the essay topic. This could be a prediction about the future.** In an essay about energy use, for example, you could predict how people's lives might change.

9 This exercise enables students to write a conclusion effectively by paraphrasing vocabulary and structures used elsewhere in the essay.

Before students begin, you may like to refer them back to exercise 4 and check as a whole class which words match phrases in this exercise. Do an example as a whole class, and with weaker classes, consider doing more than one example. The repetition of the same structure should familiarize students with this useful phrase.

ANSWERS
2 social networks are replacing traditional friendships
3 web users control web content
4 recorded video content will replace live television broadcasts

10 This exercise improves students' ability to structure a conclusion logically.

Refer students back to the question again in exercise 6, and then refer them to exercise 8 to use this structure as a model. Ask them to compare their answer with a partner before checking as a whole class. Ask them to identify which part (a, b, or c) is most likely to refer to the thesis statement (b), a topic sentence (c), and a personal comment (a). Students may request clarification of *readily* (quickly and without difficulty), although they should be encouraged to try and deduce the meaning first from the sentence.

ANSWER
b   c   a

UNIT 9 MEDIA & TRAVEL

Exam practice

11 Remind students of the key information from the lesson by asking:
- *What three things should you include, and in what order?* (paraphrase of the thesis statement, a summary of the topic sentences, and a personal comment)
- *What phrase can you use to reword the thesis statement?* (This essay has argued that …)
- *What could you think about for ideas about what to include in the personal comment?* (the future)

Alternative for weaker classes: allow students to work in pairs, but stress that both students in the pair should write. After writing, ask students to exchange their conclusion with another pair and try to identify the structure of their writing.

POSSIBLE ANSWER

In conclusion, digital communications can support positive change in several ways. They can make people aware of global issues, allow people to co-operate with each other effectively, and they also provide opportunities to collect and distribute money swiftly. No doubt they will become increasingly powerful agents of change in the future.

READING Yes / No / Not Given page 94

Lesson aims

1 Develop students' ability to identify opinions, in order to answer *Yes / No / Not Given* questions.
2 Raise students' awareness of the difference between *Yes / No / Not Given* and *True / False / Not Given* questions.
3 Expand students' range of vocabulary related to advertising to improve their comprehension skills.

Key language

Advertising nouns: *advert, (hash)tag, campaign, brand, logo, blog, trending list, review, slogan, search engine ranking*

Brand collocations: *national branding, rebranding campaign, control branding, successful rebranding, have an effect on branding*

Topic focus

Optional lead-in

You may like to introduce the topic of place branding by taking magazine or newspaper adverts into class or finding advertisements for holiday destinations online and getting students to discuss which ones they think are the most effective and why.

1 This exercise introduces the topic of national branding and prepares students for the text by illustrating the meaning of branding (a particular image or identity regarded as an asset).

You may like to begin by asking students if anyone has visited New Zealand. If a student has, you could ask them to describe what it was like. If not, ask them what type of holiday they think they would have in New Zealand, based on what they can see in the advert. Discuss as a whole class.

2 This exercise engages students by personalizing the topic of place branding.

You may like to ask students if they know what advert (if any) their country is using at the moment. Ask them to discuss in pairs before sharing ideas as a whole class.

Vocabulary

3 This exercise expands students' range of vocabulary related to advertising to improve their understanding of texts on this topic.

To check students understand the vocabulary you may like to ask:
- What famous logos or slogans do you know?
- Can you think of any strong brands?
- What types of things might be included in a campaign?
- What types of things do people write blogs / reviews about?
- Where do you see adverts?
- What type of stories most often trend?
- Why is it important for companies to have a high search engine ranking?
- Can you draw a hashtag? (#)

ANSWERS

1 g   2 h   3 j   4 i   5 b   6 a   7 e   8 f   9 d   10 c

4 This exercise checks students' understanding of new vocabulary and provides an opportunity to clarify any difficult words.

You may like to draw two columns on the board, headed *companies* and *public*, and ask students to copy it into their notebooks. Demonstrate by asking students for an example for each, and writing it into the correct column on the board. Tell them to do the same with the rest. Check answers as a whole class.

ANSWERS

Usually created by companies: 1, 3, 4, 5, 9
Usually created by the public: 2, 6, 7, 8, 10

VOCABULARY FILE Student's Book page 129

Refer students to exercise 7 for more practice of nouns related to advertising.

ANSWERS

See page 135 of this book for answers.

116 UNIT 9 MEDIA & TRAVEL

Exam skills

5 This exercise focuses on the importance of the conclusion in identifying the author's opinion.

Make sure students' attention is focused on the correct paragraph. Ask them to compare their answer with a partner before checking as a whole class. If they have difficulty, focus their attention on the word *key* (because then they know that what is coming next is something important), the *-er* suffix of *users*, which shows they are people, the comparison of *more powerful than*, which means *advertising slogans* cannot be the correct answer.

ANSWER
(patriotic) social media users

6 This exercise develops students' ability to infer an author's opinion based on other opinions expressed in a text.

Raise students' awareness of the importance of inferring the opinion by asking:
- *Does the author talk about what the government should spend money on in this paragraph?* (No)
- *Does this paragraph mention tourists?* (No)
- *So how can you answer these questions based on this paragraph?* (Because if the author says something else is more effective than advertising slogans, then it would be contradictory to say we need more advertising slogans. The author thinks the internet is powerful and authentic, so it would be contradictory to state that it is not useful for tourists.)

ANSWERS
1 & 2 disagree

EXAM TIP 2·28 Before students listen, ask them to suggest possible answers to the questions and write these on the board. After they have answered the questions, refer students to page 148 for more guidance on *Yes / No / Not Given* questions.

ANSWER
Yes / No / Not Given questions test your ability to identify opinions rather than facts. You can often find the author's main opinion in the final paragraph.

Audioscript 2·28

Yes / No / Not Given questions are different to *True / False / Not Given* questions. **Yes / No / Not Given questions test your ability to identify opinions rather than facts. You can often find the author's main opinion in the final paragraph.** Understanding this can help you to predict or guess whether they agree with the statements in *Yes / No / Not Given* questions.

Exam practice

7 Students have a chance here to put together the skills developed in exercises 5 and 6.

Remind students that in order to choose *No*, what is written in the text must contradict the sentence given. Also highlight that there is often something in the text which looks connected to a *Not Given* sentence, but in fact does not express that specific idea. Highlight that students need to identify the author's opinions even if they are not the opinions directly expressed in these sentences, because these clues could enable them to infer the answer. After completing the exercise alone, ask them to compare with a partner and justify their answer by referring to the relevant part of the text. Check answers as a whole class.

ANSWERS
1 No – the author says it's 'not surprising' that so much is spent.
2 Yes – the author gives three examples of successful campaigns.
3 No – the campaigns were unsuccessful.
4 Yes – the author says 'it is becoming increasingly difficult for authorities to control the brand'.
5 Not Given – 'all other sources of information' are not mentioned.
6 No – the example is being used to show the opposite.

8 This exercise revisits the skill of completing a summary but does so using a pool of words, which is another common exam format. Knowledge of the text is required to complete the summary, but students with a good knowledge of word class may find they can predict some answers correctly. It is therefore a good idea to emphasize prediction skills.

Ask students if they can remember how they should approach a summary:
- find the relevant part of the text by scanning for synonyms which match the summary
- predict what type of word is missing.

Invite students to do the above, covering the word pool. Then instruct them to look for words in the pool that match their prediction.

Finally instruct them to read more closely around the relevant part of the text to confirm the correct option. They shouldn't find the same words in the pool and in the text so they are trying to match ideas.
- Check if this matches any of the available words in the box.

Ask students to work alone before comparing with a partner. Check answers as a whole class.

ANSWERS
1 adverts
2 social media
3 support
4 pictures
5 countries
6 believable

What do you think?

9 This exercise generates ideas which could be useful for Speaking Part 3 and Writing Task 2 and provides students with an opportunity to practise using vocabulary from this lesson.

In a multilingual class, you may like to group students from the same country together first, to share ideas, even if this means students are in differently sized groups. Then they can regroup with students of other nationalities to report a summary of their discussion. In a monolingual class, group students in fours to discuss as they may find it difficult at first to generate ideas. Encourage them to expand their answers as much as possible, and feed in ideas as necessary.

10 This exercise develops students' knowledge and provides a further opportunity for students to respond personally to the topic of the text.

Ask students to remain in their groups. If they seem to have little idea about these countries, you may like to allocate one country per group to research for homework. They can then regroup in the following class and report their findings.

> **Optional activity**
> You may like to develop students' knowledge by getting them to research predictions about the future of tourism in their own country. You could also ask them to find out how much is spent on advertising in their country, and how much their country's tourism industry is worth.

EXAM CHALLENGE

ANSWERS

Speaking
1–3 Students' own answers

Listening
1 See page 138 of this book for answers and page 141 for the audioscript.
2 Students' own answers

Writing
1 Students' own answers
2 See page 110 of the Student's Book for the model answer.

Reading
1 See page 139 of this book for answers.
2 Students' own answers

UNIT 10   Science & progress

Introduction   page 97

Featured topic vocabulary
Nouns: science, progress, invention, timeline
Verbs: invent, affect, extend

Optional lead-in
To introduce the topic, you may like to do the following before students open their books:

a Write the words *camera, telephone, internet, biro, antibiotics* on the board and ask students to put them in the order in which they were invented.

b Ask them to add three more inventions to the list which they think are very important.

c Tell them to open their books and check if the order is correct and if any of their suggestions are included in the infographic.

What do you think?
You may like to ask students to do the following:

a Discuss questions 1 and 2 in pairs, before sharing feedback as a whole class.

b Then discuss questions 3–5 in pairs, and take a vote to find out which invention has most affected the class as a whole.

Students may have difficulty extending the timeline. There have been lots of developments in the fields of mobile technology, robotics, genetics, and nanotechnology but few specific inventions. You may wish to accept ideas such as iPhone or YouTube. Real inventions could include 3D printers, driverless cars, or electric charging stations for cars.

SPEAKING   Comparing past and present   page 98

EXAM FOCUS: PART 3

Lesson aims
1 Raise students' awareness of common errors in Speaking Part 3 to avoid giving answers that are too short, too personal, or irrelevant.

2 Enable students to compare the past to the present using *used to*, and improve their pronunciation to distinguish between *used* and *use*.

3 Expand students' range of vocabulary needed to discuss progress in a country.

4 Enable students to ask the examiner for clarification if the question is unclear.

Key language
Nouns: housing, income, community, civic engagement, satisfaction, safety, work-life balance, life expectancy, wealth, support network, purity, leisure, security, standard of accommodation

Optional lead-in
You may like to introduce the topic in a personalized way by searching the internet for old photos of the town or city where your students are studying. Print off the photos and stick them on the board or display them on the electronic whiteboard. Ask them how they think life has changed in their town / city since the photos were taken, and whether these changes benefit the people or not.

Topic focus
1 This exercise introduces the topic of area of progress and illustrates the range of sub-topics involved.

Focus students' attention on the photos and ask them to discuss in pairs what they can see in the photos and answer the question. You may need to clarify the meaning of *income* (money you earn for doing a job).

ANSWERS
A income   B education   C health

2 This exercise provides students with an opportunity to show what they already know about this topic.

Students may require clarification of the phrase *indication of progress* (something that shows life is getting better for people). You may like to give an example by highlighting the most familiar indication of progress, wealth. Write up some statistics indicating economic growth or show students a graph. For example, as is widely reported, the economist Angus Maddison in *The World Economy: Historical Statistics* (2004) suggested average income per person grew from approximately $1,000 to $7,000 dollars from 1900 to 2000. Ask students if this is a good thing. Elicit the idea that wealth can also damage the earth through excessive consumption, etc.

Now ask students to discuss Task 2 in threes or fours before sharing ideas as a whole class.

Vocabulary
3 This exercise expands students' range of vocabulary related to progress by enabling them to identify areas and measures of progress.

You may like to clarify the meaning of *assess* (make a judgement about the nature or quality of something). Encourage students to try the exercise before clarifying any other vocabulary, as it may become clear to them once they are more familiar with the definitions.

ANSWERS
1 c 2 e 3 k 4 h 5 a 6 i 7 b 8 g 9 f 10 d 11 j

Optional activity
To consolidate the vocabulary, you may like to get students to write the words and definitions separately, on small pieces of card or paper. They can then use them as flashcards to test each other, or as revision by physically matching the cards in the next class.

4 This exercise focuses on other useful topic vocabulary which could help students speak about progress in a country.
Encourage students not to underline too much. Tell them to work alone before checking with a partner. In whole-class feedback, take the opportunity to drill any words they had difficulty pronouncing.

POSSIBLE ANSWERS
a qualifications, studying, skills
b issues, public concern
c rooms per person, basic facilities
d crimes
e wealth, money, paying taxes
f feeling good, life
g life expectancy, feeling fit
h social support network
i air pollution, water purity
j working less, more leisure time
k unemployment, salary, job security

VOCABULARY FILE Student's Book page 130
Refer students to exercises 1–3 for more practice of vocabulary related to the topic of social progress.

ANSWERS
See page 135 of this book for answers.

5 Tell students to discuss in pairs, but explain they can write different answers if they don't agree. When checking as a whole class, ask *Which country has the highest level of ...?* for each one and take a vote for each. Note that in English it is not correct to say *highest level of ...* for areas that don't have a numerical value such as environment, community, and housing. You might therefore like to use appropriate collocates: *cleanest* environment, *strongest* communities, *best* housing. Write the answers with the most votes on the board, before revealing the correct answers.

ANSWERS

Sweden	environment
Iceland	community
USA	housing, income
Denmark	life satisfaction, work-life balance
Finland	education
Japan	safety
Switzerland	jobs, health
Australia	civic engagement

6 This exercise gives students an opportunity to respond personally and critically to the topic.
Highlight that they should work alone here and not discuss yet.

ANSWERS
A Ireland   B Russia   C South Korea   D Mexico

7 Encourage students to expand their answers as much as possible, by asking them if they'd like to live in their chosen countries. You may wish to use the opportunity to practise the second conditional: *I don't think I'd enjoy living there because ...*

Grammar

8 2·29 This exercise provides students with a model Part 3 response and demonstrates how to describe changes using *used to*. It also focuses on the form of *used to*.
Play the recording as many times as necessary, students may require clarification of *accommodation* (somewhere to stay or live; here it means house or apartment, but it can also refer to somewhere temporary like a hotel).

ANSWERS
1 used to   3 didn't use to
2 didn't use to   4 used to

Audioscript 2·29
In the past, the population was much smaller than today and I think people **used to** have larger homes. However, the standard of accommodation **didn't use to** be so high. Lots of people shared bathrooms and many people didn't have electricity ... Our country **didn't use to** export much and now it sells things to the whole world. This has meant that workers earn more money than they **used to** and the standard of living has generally gone up ...

9 This exercise clarifies the meaning of *used to* and raises students' awareness that it can be used for situations and actions.
Ask students to think about it alone before checking with a partner. Discuss as a whole class.

ANSWERS
a 4   b 3   c 1   d 2

10 2·30 This exercise improves students' pronunciation to ensure a distinction is heard between *used to* (for past habits) and the main verb *to use*.
Before focusing on this exercise, you may like to ask why they think it was difficult to hear the differences in exercise 8. Ask them to discuss in pairs before modelling it for students again. Check answers as a whole class and drill each sound as you check.

ANSWERS
1 No, the /d/ sound becomes silent.
2 No, the /uː/ sound becomes a schwa /ə/.
3 The *s* in the first *use* is an /s/ sound, but the *s* in the second *use* is a /z/ sound.

Audioscript 2·30

In the past, people didn't use to use cars and they used to walk more.

11 This exercise generates ideas students could use in Speaking Part 3, and provides extra practice comparing the past and present.

Focus students' attention on the example in the speech bubble. Tell them to take turns to make a sentence about each topic and to help each other if they run out of ideas. Share ideas as a whole class and write key words on the board, depending on what students say.

GRAMMAR FILE Student's Book page 119
Refer students to this page for more explanation and practice of *used to*.

ANSWERS
See page 131 of this book for answers.

Exam skills

12 2·31 This exercise raises students' awareness of common errors in Speaking Part 3.

After listening, ask students to compare their answers with a partner. Check as a whole class and ask students how they can avoid these common errors.

ANSWERS
1 b 2 a 3 c

Audioscript 2·31
A: How have people's lives changed in your country?
B: My family are richer. My father made some good investments and we have a much nicer house now. It also means I can go to private school and have a lot of holidays.
A: Do you think people are more or less satisfied with their life?
B: More, probably. Yes, more.
A: Is pollution more of a problem today than in the past?
B: Definitely. As a result, lots of people look to leave our country now. They study abroad or, as soon as they can, they get a job in another country. People didn't use to emigrate so much.

EXAM TIP 2·32 Before listening, ask students for their ideas and write these on the board. After they have answered the question, refer students to page 145 for more guidance on Speaking Part 3.

ANSWER
Begin your question with *Sorry* or *Sorry, but* to sound more natural.

Audioscript 2·32
In Speaking Part 3, the questions are sometimes complicated so it's important you listen carefully and answer the question you're actually asked. Unlike in Part 1, you can ask the examiner for clarification if you don't understand. Try to remember some phrases to help you, and **begin your question with *Sorry* or *Sorry, but* to sound more natural**.

13 2·33 This exercise enables students to ask the examiner for clarification if the question is unclear.

If students do not suggest this skill as a tip to avoid problems a and c, then tell them this is an important way to ensure what they say is relevant. Before doing the exercise, you may like to ask them what phrases they already know and write these on the board. After listening, drill the pronunciation of each phrase as you check the answers.

ANSWERS
1 mean 2 rephrase 3 what

Audioscript 2·33
1 Sorry, but what do you **mean** by community?
2 Please could you **rephrase** the question?
3 Sorry, I'm not sure **what** you mean.

Exam practice

14 This exercise reminds students what they have studied by asking what common errors they should avoid in Part 3 (making answers too short, too personal, or not answering the questions), and what they should say if they need clarification.

Encourage students to simulate an exam situation by sitting opposite each other and timing the mock test. In whole-class feedback, draw their attention to any good use of clarification phrases.

LISTENING Following exam instructions page 100

EXAM FOCUS: SECTION 4

Lesson aims
1 Raise students' awareness of common errors in the Listening test to avoid losing marks unnecessarily.
2 Improve students' use of *can* and *may* to describe possibility both generally and in the future.
3 Expand students' ability to understand and use key phrases to discuss cause and effect.
4 Encourage students to work independently using online study resources.

Key language
Discussing effects: *consequently, lead to, account for, as a result, which means that*

Featured topic vocabulary
Nouns: *obesity, junk food, laboratories, equipment, profit*
Adjectives: *effective, inaccurate, legal, statistical, depressed, saturated, reliable*
Verbs: *correlate, cause*

> **Optional lead-in**
>
> Before students open their books, you may like to engage them with the topic by writing gapped sentences from exercise 1 on the board and ask what words could be missing, for example:
>
> a A _____ dropped from a tall building can kill someone. (coin)
>
> b Eating _____ can make a country win more Nobel prizes. (chocolate)
>
> c A full moon can make people go _____. (mad)
>
> Write students' ideas on the board. Tell them to open their books and check their ideas.

Topic focus

1 This exercise introduces the topic of myths and falsity in reporting and encourages students to focus on relevant vocabulary.

Students may require clarification of *Nobel prize* (one of the top prizes given to people who make an important difference in science or culture) and *full moon* (draw a picture of a half moon and then a full moon). After they have discussed in pairs, share feedback as a whole class.

2 2·34 Ask students for their opinions first, to compare their ideas to the recording.

ANSWER
None of them is true. Accept students' ideas about which might be true.

Audioscript 2·34

It's amazing how readily the public accept some things as facts. Take, for example, the commonly held idea that a coin dropped from a great height might kill someone. While people may think a coin dropped from a tall building would pick up enough speed to kill a person on the ground, **this just isn't true**. The non-aerodynamic nature of a coin, as well as its relatively small size and weight, would keep this from happening. A person on the ground would most certainly feel the impact, but the coin wouldn't kill anyone … Not so long ago, an interesting study looked at the correlation between a country's consumption of chocolate and how many Nobel prizes a country had won. It seems that in countries that have won a lot of Nobel prizes, people eat a lot of chocolate. In other words there is a strong correlation between chocolate-eating and prize-winning. However, **this simple observation would need a lot more testing before a causal connection could be proved** … Finally, an idea that's been around for centuries is that a full moon can make people go mad. In fact, the English words 'lunacy' and 'lunatic' come from the word 'lunar' – connected to the moon. But despite the general consent of mythology and numerous studies, **this notion has no scientific support**.

Key phrases

3 This exercise expands students' ability to understand key phrases to describe cause and effect.

Students may ask for clarification of *saturated fats* (a type of fat that is bad for you). Ask them to try the exercise first before clarifying the words in bold. Ask them to work alone before comparing answers with a partner. Check as a whole class and clarify any vocabulary issues. You may also like to check the pronunciation of *consequently*, by marking a stress bubble above the first syllable.

ANSWERS
1 d 2 a 3 b 4 e 5 c

4 This exercise gives students the opportunity to use the key phrases to discuss cause and effect with a degree of personalization.

Focus students' attention on the five sentences in exercise 3. Ask which three phrases for cause and effect are followed by a subject and which two are followed by a noun phrase. Students may find this difficult so elicit some examples in open class first. Give them a few minutes to prepare their ideas alone before telling a partner. Monitor for good examples which you can write on the board to share with the class.

Grammar

5 This exercise improves students' understanding of the difference between *can* and *may* to describe possibility, generally and in the future.

Demonstrate by writing sentence 1 from exercise 3 on the board and highlighting *can*. Discuss as a whole class what it means (junk food is sometimes expensive in poor countries). Ask students to work with a partner to look at the other sentences. Check answers as a whole class.

ANSWERS
can means possible now / generally possible
may means possible in the future

6 This exercise provides an opportunity to check students have understood the difference in meaning correctly.

The main point to stress is that we don't use *can* for future possibility. If you feel you need to explain why *may* is not possible for 1 and 4, then you could make the point that we use *may* when we are not certain if something is true, whereas *can* usually means *sometimes*. In the first question, *may* is not possible because we are certain that smoking sometimes causes cancer. In the last question, *may* is not possible because the absence of article means we are talking about media reports in general; not specific reports. You may also like to raise students' awareness of the form, by asking what type of verb comes after a modal verb (infinitive without *to*).

ANSWERS
1 can 2 may 3 may 4 can

7 This exercise improves students' use of *can* and *may* and generates ideas they could use in Speaking Part 3 or Writing Task 2.

Focus students' attention on the example in the speech bubble. Give them a few minutes to prepare their ideas before speaking. After speaking, you may like to ask students to turn to a new partner to say their sentences again, to help them remember the structure.

GRAMMAR FILE Student's Book page 118
Refer students to this page for more explanation and practice of *can* and *may* for possibility.

ANSWERS
See page 131 of this book for answers.

Exam skills

8 This exercise raises students' awareness of the dangers of common errors in the Listening test.

Ask students to check in pairs before comparing ideas as a whole class.

Alternative for weaker classes: discuss as a whole class, so that you can prompt them with questions such as *What about multiple-choice questions?*

ANSWER
Common errors students might make include writing more than the instructed number of words, not using the correct code (e.g. questions 37–40), incorrect spelling, choosing the wrong number of options, transferring answers into the wrong spaces, using words instead of a code.

9 This exercise demonstrates how marks can be lost, to prevent students from falling into these traps.

After they have checked with a partner, ask students how they would feel if they were this student, to elicit that it is frustrating to lose marks unnecessarily. As many students do lose marks in these ways, you may want to make the point that students can gain marks by simply following instructions carefully.

ANSWERS
31 the words do not fit the gap
32 wrong verb form
33 incorrect spelling
34 too many words are used
35 not enough options have been chosen
36 the answer is written in the wrong space
37 two answers have been chosen (rather than one)
38 no answer has been attempted
39 the wrong letter / code is written
40 words are written instead of a letter / code

EXAM TIP 2·35 Before listening, ask students for their ideas and write these on the board. After they have answered the question, refer students to page 146 for more guidance on avoiding common errors.

ANSWERS
Make sure that your answers fit the gaps grammatically / check that they are spelt correctly / guess any answers you weren't sure about.

Audioscript 2·35
A few simple steps can help you to avoid common errors in the Listening test. First, it's important to read the instructions carefully so that you answer in the correct way. Make sure you know how many answers will be given in each recording as sometimes you'll hear the answers to more than one set or you may have to turn the page to find some of the questions. At the end of the test, you'll have time to transfer your answers to the answer sheet. Use this time to **make sure that your answers fit the gaps grammatically and to check that they are spelt correctly. You can also guess any answers you weren't sure about!**

Exam practice

10 2·36 This exercise encourages students to focus on avoiding losing marks and to develop good habits for the exam. It also provides an opportunity to practise their Section 4 Listening skills.

After listening, do not check the answers. Move directly on to exercise 11.

Audioscript 2·36
Over one hundred years ago the science fiction writer H. G. Wells said that he believed that statistical thinking would be as important as the ability to read and write in the modern scientific and technological society. This is arguably true, but have we become good at interpreting statistics? The answer is almost certainly not.

In today's lecture, I'd like to look at some of the most common mistakes you find when people use and interpret data and we'll see why so many scientific myths are reported to us. The most common error is the confusion between 'correlation' and 'cause'. In the media, you see this a lot in reports on **health studies**. Typically, a scientific study indicates that whenever X happens, Y happens, too. This is called 'correlation'. But by the time it's reported in the media the story has become that X is the cause of Y. But just because two things occur together, it doesn't mean that one caused the other, even if a cause and effect relationship seems to **make sense**.

Let's take an example. People have often held the belief that there's a connection with success in elementary school and eating **breakfast**. We are perhaps therefore led to believe that eating a healthy breakfast causes students to be more successful. However, other factors are coming into play here, as students not eating breakfast also often **missed classes** or were late. So arguably, it could be the lateness or the absence that affects performance rather than missing breakfast. On retesting the idea, it was found that, when other factors were left out, eating breakfast only helped those who were not eating enough in the first place.

How, then, do scientists establish cause when they do experiments? Let's say we want to prove that eating five portions of fruit and vegetables a day lowers the risk of cancer. We have to make sure that other factors such as physical activity, hours of sleep, and genetic make-up play no part. Researchers do this through a controlled study, a method of research in which two similar groups of people are exposed to two different conditions. Once we do this, we can then compare the outcome for differences. Any significant difference could be related to the conditions as the groups were relatively similar.

Unfortunately, controlled studies still have a number of limitations. The first is ethics. It would be problematic to make one group of people smoke and to force someone addicted to smoking not to smoke, and in fact **laws stop scientists from doing such studies**. There's also the issue of paying enough people to take part in the study for a long enough time to make the study meaningful. The sample size has to be large and the experimental condition has to last a long time, creating **great expense**. Plus, of course, there may not be enough people who are genetically similar to create a large enough group to study.

There are many other sources of error and these are listed on your handouts, but there's one further problem I'd like to discuss now and that's a lack of critical thinking on the part of the people reporting the data. This issue is becoming more and more serious as journalists with poor statistical training increasingly attempt to deal with data. Furthermore, **journalists are under ever-growing pressure** to write interesting articles, and so they may take a number or a set of data and make their own interpretation quickly without thinking carefully.

One recent example of poor critical thinking comes from a statistic related to depression in England. Two leading newspapers reported that the number of prescriptions for anti-depressant drugs had gone up significantly and concluded that this also meant that the number of depressed people must have risen as well. In fact, **the number of depressed people could be exactly the same**. It's probably true that doctors are simply writing more frequent prescriptions to the same people but that **each prescription is for a lower quantity of medication**. And of course, when journalists make mistakes, the effects can be far-reaching. Take, for example, fish oil tablets. These are now the best-selling food supplement and **sales have increased** to around $2.5 billion after parents around the world were told by journalists that they increased academic performance. However, what the original study actually showed was that brain activity increased when people took the tablets. Basically, they saw that parts of the brain had become more active when they looked at it in a scanner. But scientists did not confirm that this part of the brain was connected to school results. In fact, results of the academic tests showed that concentration and **test results did not improve at all** and later tests have proved that the connection isn't significant. The problem is that it takes time for scientists to disprove such claims and when they do their evidence is often not reported in the media because it's less interesting than the myth. And this of course means that the myth continues to persist.

11 This exercise familiarizes students with the answer sheet so that they may avoid losing marks when they transfer their answers.

After completing the answer sheet, tell students to compare answers with a partner and review each other's work for any common errors, before checking as a whole class.

ANSWERS

31	health studies	36	A
32	make sense	37	N
33	breakfast	38	D
34	miss classes	39	I
35	C & E	40	N

What do you think?

12 This exercise provides students with an opportunity to respond personally to the topic of the practice listening text and helps generate ideas which could be useful for Speaking Part 3.

Students may require clarification of the word *reliable* (that can be trusted). Weaker classes may find this challenging, and may require prompting with questions such as *Do you watch the news on TV? / Which channel? / Why do you like this news channel? / Do you think they always tell the full truth? / Is it possible to tell the full truth?* Once they seem to understand the concepts, ask them to discuss in pairs.

Study skills

This exercise encourages students to work independently using online study resources.

After students have discussed in pairs, get feedback as a whole class and write any useful websites on the board. In case they don't have any suggestions, you may like to familiarize yourself with sites like:

- www.bbc.co.uk/worldservice/learningenglish

WRITING Describing processes

EXAM FOCUS: TASK 1

Lesson aims
1 Enable students to summarize a process by writing an overview statement.
2 Develop students' ability to effectively review their writing by systematically checking for common grammar, vocabulary, or punctuation errors.
3 Enable students to use the passive to describe a process.
4 Improve students' use of sequencing words to show the staging of a process.

Key language
Sequencing words: next, then, firstly, now, lastly, after that, meanwhile, subsequently, secondly

Featured topic vocabulary
Nouns: invisibility, tracking, fitting room, illusion
Verb: disappear
Adjectives: virtual, complex

Topic focus

> **Optional lead-in**
>
> To introduce the topic, you may like to do the following before students open their books:
>
> a Print pictures from the internet of unusual or funny inventions and ask students to guess what the inventions were designed to do, e.g. a baby mop, flask tie, and cutting board bird feeder are among the 30 unusual inventions listed on www.boredpanda.com/funny-inventions.
>
> b Then ask students if they can think of some more useful inventions. Write their ideas on the board.

1 This exercise introduces the concept of an invisibility cover to prepare students to analyse the process involved, and it establishes the topic of inventions of dubious value.

Students may require clarification of *invisibility* (no one can see you), *disappear* (to become impossible to see), *tracking* (following someone, but not always physically. You can track someone using a signal.), *virtual* (not real), *fitting room* (a place in a shop to try on clothes). After students have made their choice, ask them to discuss with a partner and explain their decision.

Grammar

2 This exercise reminds students of the form of the passive.

Write the example sentence on the board and underneath write *The invisibility cover reflects the image*. Ask students to discuss with a partner what the difference is between the two sentences, before checking as a whole class. Focus on the example in sentence a and ask students to work alone to complete the exercise. Tell them to compare their answers with a partner before checking as a whole class.

ANSWERS

b is processed   e is projected
c is seen   f is recorded
d is sent

3 This exercise demonstrates the role of the passive in describing processes.

Focus students' attention on the diagram and ask them to work in pairs, before checking as a whole class.

ANSWERS

2 b   3 d   4 e   5 a   6 c

4 This exercise checks students' understanding of the passive and highlights its importance in answering this type of Task 1 question.

Ask students to discuss in pairs before discussing as a whole class. They may be tempted to choose answer a, because this is sometimes the case in other uses of the passive. For example, in newspaper reports, the passive is useful if someone was killed but we do not know who did it. However, in a process, it is possible that we know who or what does the action, but this is simply not the main interest.

ANSWER

b

GRAMMAR FILE Student's Book page 120

Refer students to this page for more explanation and practice of the passive.

ANSWERS

See page 131 of this book for answers.

> **Optional activity**
>
> To provide students with further practice using the passive, you may like to ask them to write three sentences to describe how they think the locating tracking device and / or the virtual fitting room device work.
>
> **Alternative for weaker classes**: you could work as a whole class and write their ideas on the board as students speak, reformulating their ideas where possible to use the passive.

Key phrases

5 This exercise improves students' use of sequencing words to show the staging of a process.

Remind students of the order of the invisibility cover process by asking where the step *the image is sent to a computer* would come in exercise 3 (it would be between f and b, which are steps 1 and 2). Ask them to work alone before comparing with a partner. Check answers as a whole class. If students ask why their incorrect answers are wrong, focus their attention on the next exercise.

ANSWERS

next
now
after that
subsequently
secondly

6 This exercise focuses attention on the meaning of the sequencing words, as well as the punctuation needed to use them.

In a weaker monolingual class, you may like to consider allowing students to discuss this in their own language. Students may be unaware of the rules related to punctuation. If so, guide them by telling them to think about the comma.

ANSWERS

meanwhile can only be used to describe parts of a process that happen at the same time, not in sequence
and is a coordinating conjunction and so should have no punctuation before or after it
firstly introduces the first stage of the process
then is not usually used before a comma
lastly introduces the last step in this particular process

7 This exercise checks students' understanding of the sequencing words and provides them with a model, once completed.

Ask students to work alone before comparing with a partner. Check as a whole class and clarify why students' errors are not possible, for example:
- *at first* or *in the end* are not possible because we use these in a story but not in a process
- *next* is not possible because it is not a coordinating conjunction
- *and* is not used at the start of a sentence in academic writing
- *meanwhile* is not possible because it cannot be simultaneously processed and sent
- *now* is not a coordinating conjunction.

ANSWERS
1 Firstly   4 After that
2 and   5 where
3 Then   6 Lastly

> **Optional activity**
> If you chose to do the optional activity after exercise 4, you can now work together as a class to turn those sentences into a paragraph. Focus students' attention on what they wrote on the board, and ask them how they could join the ideas using sequencing words. Add their suggestions to the sentences on the board.

Exam skills

EXAM TIP 2•37 Before students listen, discuss as a whole class and write students' ideas on the board. After they have answered the questions, refer students to page 147 for more guidance on writing 'overview statements'.

ANSWER
It requires a different approach to how you write an overview statement for describing data. Try to comment on a feature of the process as a whole that makes it interesting.

Audioscript 2•37
When you describe a process, try to include an 'overview statement'. This is difficult because **it requires a different approach to how you write an overview statement for describing data**. With a process, there's no mention of trends, numbers, or possibly no comparisons. Instead, **try to comment on a feature of the process as a whole that makes it interesting**. For example, it may be particularly complex or have a surprisingly large number of stages.

8 This exercise enables students to summarize a process by demonstrating how to write an overview statement.

Before students begin, ask them what the paragraph is summarizing (the invisibility cover). Tell them to work alone before comparing with a partner. Students may require clarification of *complex* (complicated / involving many different stages). Check as a whole class.

ANSWERS
1 diagram   4 suggests
2 general   5 achieve
3 complex

9 Stress to students that it is not 'cheating' to copy parts from the model – in fact, it is a good way to improve. Help them to begin by doing the first sentence as a whole class. Allow them to work in pairs if they prefer, but insist that both students must write. After writing, ask students to compare with a partner / another pair, to see how similar their summaries are. Then refer them to the model answer to compare.

POSSIBLE ANSWER
The diagram shows how a robotic vacuum cleaner functions. We can see two parallel processes, one of navigation and the other of cleaning. In general, the chart reveals how the machine manages to perform a range of tasks normally done by humans.

10 This exercise develops students' ability to effectively review their writing by systematically checking for grammar, vocabulary, or punctuation errors.

Ask students to work alone before checking with a partner. Tell them to also discuss with their partner which mistakes from 1–10 they commonly make in their own writing. An underscore (_) indicates where the common errors are in the examples. Check answers as a whole class.

ANSWERS
1 P   2 P   3 G   4 G   5 G   6 G   7 V   8 V   9 V   10 G

11 This exercise raises students' awareness of the impact of surface level errors on the reader, and encourages them to review their writing thoroughly.

Tell students they are now the teachers, and this is the role they need to take when they finish writing in the exam, in order to check their answer carefully. Ask students to work alone before comparing with a partner. You may like to write the corrected parts on the board before the class and cover with paper, before revealing them one at a time to make feedback more efficient.

ANSWERS
First[1] the room size and the time needed to clean are calculated. Next, the machine moves to [10]middle of the room and begins moving around in a spiral pattern until it hits something [2]when this happens, it reverses, rotates, and moves forward until [6]finds a clear path. It avoids steps using four sensors on the bottom of the unit and if the battery power get[5] low, the vacuum finds the charger and connects itself. Meanwhile, dirt [3]removed from the floor by two spinning brush[4]. At the same time, two dirt sensors check how much dirt is being kicked up and tell the cleaner to go back over [7]durty areas again. [9]At last, the dirt bin is [8]automatic emptied into a large container.

UNIT 10 SCIENCE & PROGRESS

Exam practice

12 Remind students of the skills developed in this lesson by asking:
- *What verb form do we often use to describe a process? Why?* (passive, because we are more interested in what happens, not who does it)
- *What sequencing words can you remember?* (Write students' ideas on the board. Refer them back to exercise 5 to see if they have forgotten any.)
- *What should you include in an overview statement?* (a feature of the process as a whole that makes it interesting).

Alternative for weaker classes: allow students to work in pairs to write, but make sure both students write at the same time.

MODEL ANSWER
See exercise 2 in the WRITING FILE on page 139 of the Student's Book for a model answer.

13 This exercise encourages students to spend time reviewing work after writing.

Tell students not to correct the errors but simply to identify them. If students are given an opportunity to self-correct, they are often able to, and this illustrates the benefit of reviewing and editing your writing. Tell students to pass the papers back to the original pair and encourage them to try to self-correct.

WRITING FILE Student's Book pages 139–40
Refer students to page 139 for another Task 1 process question, accompanied by a sample essay. Refer students to page 140 for two more examples of Task 1 questions featuring diagrams, both with sample answers.

READING Labelling page 104

Lesson aims
1 Enable students to label graphics by interpreting information.
2 Expand students' topic-related vocabulary.
3 Develop students' ability to speak about scientific issues.

Key language
Scientific verbs: *design, discover, experiment, invent, predict, prove, research, test*
Scientific nouns: *design, discovery, experiment, invention, prediction, proof, research, test*
Verbs: *construct, reflect, pick up (on camera)*
Adjectives: *upright, individual*

Topic focus

1 This exercise introduces the topic of public scepticism (doubting that something is true) over scientific claims.

Focus students' attention on the photo and ask what they can see. Tell students that some people argue about this photo, and ask if they know why. Then focus on the instructions.

They may require clarification of *constructed* (made), *upright* (standing up), *reflected* (like in a mirror or a still lake), *pick up things on a camera* (identify). Ask students to discuss in pairs before checking answers as a whole class.

ANSWERS
1 c   2 a   3 b

2 Ask students to discuss in pairs before checking briefly whether the class mostly believes it happened or not. Be careful to avoid debate of this question taking over the whole lesson, as students can become quite animated talking about this.

Vocabulary

3 This task expands students' knowledge of scientific nouns and verbs. Most of the items in this activity appear in the text so this task will support students' comprehension, but the language is particularly useful for academic discussion in general.

Demonstrate by prompting students to give you the correct answer to the first one and write it on the board.

ANSWERS

Verb	Noun
design	design
discover	discovery
experiment	experiment
invent	invention
predict	prediction
prove	proof
research	research
test	test

4 Focus students' attention on the instructions by asking *Can you write all the words in the same way as in the book?* (no, you need to change some of them). Do sentence 1 as an example.

Students may ask for clarification of the *Higgs boson particle*, and without going into too much detail, you may like to explain that it was an important scientific experiment in 2012 which involved finding a particle that gives mass to other particles.

ANSWERS
1 prove   5 research
2 predict   6 experiment
3 design   7 invent
4 test   8 discovery

5 This exercise gives students an opportunity to respond personally and practise using some of the vocabulary.

Monitor for good use of the vocabulary and share any examples in whole-class feedback.

VOCABULARY FILE Student's Book page 130
Refer students to exercises 4–6 for more practice of vocabulary related to science.

ANSWERS
See page 135 of this book for answers.

UNIT 10 SCIENCE & PROGRESS

Exam skills

6 This exercise prepares students to work on the skill of labelling diagrams.

Focus students' attention on the graphs. Remind them which way we normally read graphs in English by asking if the dates go from left to right, or right to left (left to right).

ANSWER
fewer

7 This exercise develops students' ability to translate data from a verbal form to a graphic form, to be able to label diagrams.

Focus students' attention on the gaps in the graphs and encourage them to predict what is missing. Focus their attention on the correct part of the text, stressing that the answers only come from paragraph A.

ANSWERS
1 Conservative Americans
2 35%
3 78%
4 Europeans

EXAM TIP 2•38 Before students listen, discuss as a whole class and write their ideas on the board. After they have answered the question, refer students to page 148 for more guidance on labelling graphics.

ANSWER
scanning

Audioscript 2•38
You may be given a series of two or more graphics and be asked to complete labels for them or to choose the correct graphic. The first thing you should do in these cases is consider how they're different. For example, one may point to a square object and another to a round object, or one will refer to a certain century and another to a different century. If you have to complete labels, first study the visual information to help you to predict answers. The missing labels will quickly tell you the type of information you need – often a number or a name. You can then **scan** the passage and underline sentences which contain possible answers.

Exam practice

8 Refer students back to the graphs in exercise 6 and ask them to think about the advice in the exam tip. Ask:

- *How are the graphs different?*
  (Conservative Americans v Europeans)
- *How did you know what types of words were missing?* (the percentage sign means you need a number / because of the verb *trust*, the missing word needs to be a type of person)

Tell students to think about these skills as they analyse the graphics on page 105.

You may need to clarify the following vocabulary:

- *autism*: a mental condition which makes it difficult to communicate or form relationships
- *consensus*: an opinion that all members of a group agree with
- *conspiracy theorists*: people who believe that a secret plan is responsible for a particular event
- *epidemic*: a large number of cases of a disease happening at the same time
- *IQ*: Intelligence Quotient (a measure of level of intelligence)
- *vaccine*: a medicine that can stop you getting a disease

After completing, ask them to compare answers with a partner, before checking as a whole class.

ANSWERS
A scientific knowledge (line 34)
B freedom (line 42)
C communities (line 43)

9 This exercise revises the skills required to answer *Yes / No / Not Given* questions.

Remind students of the skills involved by asking:

- *What are the key words in the instructions to explain the difference between Yes / No / Not Given?* (*agrees, contradicts,* and *impossible to say*)
- *What should you do before reading?* (underline key words)

After completing, ask students to compare answers with a partner and justify their choices. Check answers as a whole class

ANSWERS
1 No
2 Not Given
3 Not Given
4 Yes
5 Not Given
6 Yes

10 This exercise revises the skill of identifying the main point. Remind students where they can look to often find the author's overall opinion (final paragraph). Also, ask them *Can you choose an answer even if the author does not actually say this?* (yes, because you can infer meaning).

ANSWER
C

What do you think?

11 This exercise encourages students to engage with the text and respond personally to develop their knowledge and critical thinking skills.

You may like to focus students' attention on the correct part of the text by writing the final sentence on the board: *This is a great shame because science is based on evidence and the scientific community should largely be beyond suspicion.*

Alternative for weaker classes: you may need to ask guiding questions to get them started, such as:

- *Are there any situations when it is right to be suspicious of scientists?*
- *Is having evidence enough? Are there any questions that science cannot answer?*

> **Optional activity**
> You may like to ask students to research a conspiracy theory of their choice and present it to the class. Or, you may like to find a video of 'unexplained' photographs online and ask students to decide which is the most difficult for science to explain.

EXAM CHALLENGE

ANSWERS

Speaking
1–3 Students' own answers

Listening
1 See pages 137–138 of this book for answers and page 141 for the audioscript.
2 Students' own answers

Writing
1 Students' own answers
2 See page 111 of the Student's Book for the model answer.

Reading
1 See page 139 of this book for answers.
2 Students' own answers

Answer key

Grammar File

It and there (page 113)

1A
1 There 2 it 3 There 4 There 5 there 6 It 7 It

1B
Students' own answers

2
1 There are many negative effects (associated) with car ownership.
2 It is easy to speak English.
3 It is very dry in the south of the country.
4 There are not / aren't many people who vote in local elections.
5 There are several cinemas in larger towns.

Pronoun referents (page 113)

1
1 employees at the best companies
2 200 engineers and accountants interviewed by Herzberg
3 200 engineers and accountants interviewed by Herzberg
4 a time when they felt exceptionally positive about their job
5 researchers
6 200 engineers and accountants interviewed by Herzberg

2
1 they 2 this 3 This 4 He 5 they 6 those 7 it

Much / many / a lot of (page 114)

1A
1 aren't many
2 isn't much
3 isn't much
4 aren't many

1B
Students' own answers

2
1 Correct
2 She eats a lot of food.
3 We create a lot of waste.
4 It costs a lot of money to maintain the roads.
5 Correct

Comparisons (page 114)

1A
1 less than
2 fewer
3 less
4 less, than
5 fewer, than

1B
1 I weigh more than I thought.
2 I walked farther / further than I expected.
3 I try to swim more every week.
4 I want to sleep more than eight hours.
5 There aren't as many people in the park on weekdays as there are at the weekends.

2A
1 better
2 happier
3 more motivated / motivated more
4 higher
5 more technological

2B
good: *better, best*
busy: *busier, busiest*
bad: *worse, worst*
excellent: *more excellent, most excellent*
little: *less, least*
boring: *more boring, most boring*
far: *farther / further, farthest / furthest*
small: *smaller, smallest*
long: *longer, longest*
different: *more different, most different*

Adverbs (pages 115–116)

1
1 Maybe I'll do a Master's degree.
2 My family certainly won't be happy.
3 I like to do my homework well.
4 I find learning languages really difficult.
5 Some people are never satisfied.
6 Personally, I think private education is wrong.
7 I often get up before my parents do.

2
1 Hopefully
2 extremely
3 a little
4 from time to time
5 Unfortunately
6 completely
7 absolutely
8 at all

Gerunds and infinitives (page 116)

1A
1 to live, Living
2 dancing, to find / finding, cycling
3 To get
4 to travel, to ski / skiing

1B
Students' own answers

Uses of *that* (page 116)
1A
1 Many people believe that war will end.
2 One benefit of consumerism is that economies grow.
3 –
4 The subject that I liked the most was art.
5 People that play computer games become addicted easily.
6 –
7 I'm so hard-working that I sometimes forget to have lunch.

1B
Students' own answers

'Real' conditionals and time clauses (page 117)
1A
1 will have to, happens
2 have, don't have
3 pass, might / may / could study
4 take, am
5 grows
6 have
7 become

1B
Students' own answers

2A
1 unless
2 when
3 unless
4 when
5 while
6 whenever

2B
1 I won't learn to drive if I don't get a car.
3 Young people become obese if they don't exercise.

'Unreal' conditional (page 118)
1A
1 met, would tell
2 changed, wouldn't be
3 could take, would you take
4 had, would travel
5 wasn't / weren't, might / would enjoy
6 had, would be
7 would be, had
8 increased, could / might / would reduce

1B
Could is used in sentence 3 because it talks about an unreal possibility. Using *could* in sentence 2 would change the sentence to *If I could change my job, I would be happier* (= if it were possible to change my job).

2A
1 c 2 a 3 f 4 d 5 e 6 b

2B
1 would
2 could, would
3 could
4 could, would
5 could, would

Modal verbs (page 118)
1
1 could
2 can
3 will be able to
4 can't
5 couldn't
6 can't
7 will not be able
8 can / could

2A
1 can / may
2 can
3 can
4 may
5 may
6 can / may
7 can
8 can

2B
Sentences 1, 4, 5, and 6

Describing the past (page 119)
1A
hid, did, died, dried, drank, kept, told, cut, ate, tended / ended, drew, won

1B
1 did, tended
2 kept, died
3 told, kept
4 drew / won, drew / won
5 cut, ate

2
1 used to go
2 used to put
3 were camping
4 was
5 were sleeping
6 started
7 woke up
8 realized
9 were
10 were

The passive (page 120)
1
1 P 2 P 3 A 4 P 5 P 6 A

2A
1 is spent
2 is spent
3 are bought
4 spend
5 cost
6 spend
7 is spent

2B
The past simple tense would be used.

2C
1 My luggage was lost on holiday.
2 The streets are cleaned every day.
3 A lot of money will be saved.
4 My wallet was stolen.
5 The parcels are delivered at the end of the week.
6 The carnival will be held in March next year.

Vocabulary File

Unit 1 Education & learning (page 121)

1
1 geography
2 law
3 psychology
4 engineering
5 business / management
6 (English) literature
7 biology
8 medicine

2
2 high court judge, lawyer
3 mind, people's behaviour
4 maths, structure, materials, processes, design
5 leader, organizations
6 reading, books, thrillers, horror stories
7 doctor, physics, chemistry, human
8 doctor, heart specialist

3
1 natural, geographical, urban, maintain, build, rural
2 legal, charge, bureaucratic, case, authority
3 hospital, personality, case, conscious, relationships
4 charge, relationships
5 personality, relationships, authority, chairman
6 poem, author, reader
7 natural, organic, biological
8 hospital, surgery, biological

4
Possible answers:
1 erosion, terrain, migration
2 crime, verdict, evidence
3 mental health, patient, therapy
4 electricity, particle, energy
5 money, brand, service
6 novel, genre, review
7 organism, lifecycle, species
8 medication, pill, operation

5
a 2, 4   b 1, 6   c 3, 5, 7, 8

6
1 greatest achievement
2 under pressure
3 private school
4 levels of stress
5 school grades
6 compulsory education
7 ambition for

7
Students' own answers

8
Movement up: rise, increase, grow
Movement down: fall, decline
Big change: significant, dramatic, major
Small change: slight, minor

9
1 in   2 from, to   3 by   4 to

Unit 2 Health & medicine (page 122)

1
1 simple
2 demanding
3 effective
4 convenient
5 dull
6 ideal
7 expensive
8 beneficial
9 repetitive

2
Positive: comprehensive, handy, gorgeous, gentle, superb
Negative: dreadful, trivial

3
2 dreadful
3 trivial
4 comprehensive
5 gorgeous
6 superb
7 gentle

4
Noun: -ment, -es, -ness, -tion
Verb: -ate, -ed, -es
Adjective: -ate, -ive, -ful, -ic, -al, -able, -ed, -y
Adverb: -ly

5
1 regional
2 consumption
3 adequate
4 sustainable
5 individually
6 distribution
7 Sleeplessness

6
Noun: -er, -cy, -ility
Adjective: -istic, -less
Adverb: -ally

7
1 convenient
2 demand
3 effective
4 ideal
5 significant
6 beneficial
7 thoroughly
8 consider

8
Students' own answers

Unit 3 Society & family (page 123)

1
for sth: account, search
from sth: benefit
of sth: convince sb
to sth: react, lead
with sth: associate sth

2
1 convince sb of sth
2 search for sth
3 lead to sth
4 account for sth
5 associate sth with sb or sth
6 benefit from sth
7 react to sth

3
1 associated with
2 account for
3 convinced of
4 benefited from
5 react to
6 led to
7 search for

4
1 responsibility
2 laws
3 housework
4 customs
5 immigration
6 opportunities
7 income
8 well-being

5
Students' own answers

6
1 Looking closely at the results leads *to* some surprising conclusions.
2 I read an article *about / on* the effects of old age on family members.
3 Her motivation *to return* to work was linked to gender equality
4 The rationale *behind* living together was the fact that people were financially dependent on each other.
5 The analysis *of* behaviour is often carried out using studies of twins.
6 Research *into* living alone often focuses on the psychological impact of living alone.

7
Students' own answers

8
1 d   2 f   3 c   4 e   5 g   6 a   7 h   8 b

9
Students' own answers

Unit 4 Population & the environment (page 124)

1
overcrowding U
depopulation B
lack of green spaces U
congestion U
lack of facilities R
exhaust emissions U
poor public transport R
uncontrolled migration B
unemployment B
household waste B

2
1 lack of facilities
2 overcrowding
3 uncontrolled migration
4 poor public transport
5 exhaust emissions
6 household waste
7 congestion
8 depopulation
9 unemployment
10 lack of green spaces

3
1 access, doctors, hospitals, schools
2 small, too many people
3 Slums, control, move to cities
4 walk, cycle
5 air pollution, high, cities
6 recycle, waste, home
7 traffic jams, bad, several hours, travel
8 fewer people
9 enough work, fail, jobs
10 city, hardly any parks, open areas

4
1 flood
2 desertification
3 climate change
4 extinction of species

5
1 increasing population
2 Food shortages
3 increasing consumption
4 extinction of species

6
1 c   2 h   3 a   4 b   5 g   6 d   7 e   8 f

Unit 5 Culture & entertainment (page 125)

1
Biography: fact, life events, relationships, real events
Detective story: police, fact, crime, psychology, betrayal, murder
Fantasy: creatures, imaginary lands and species, monsters
Horror story: creatures, monsters, frightening
Romance: relationships, betrayal, love
Sci-fi: space, extra-terrestrials, planets, creatures, imaginary lands and species, monsters, frightening

2
Students' own answers

3
1 plane
2 nightclub
3 hotel
4 theatre
5 cinema
6 stadium

4
1 reasons   2 examples   3 effects

5
1 origin, root, owing to
2 illustrates, in the case of, including
3 therefore, hence, so

6
1 outcome
2 In the case of
3 origin
4 Owing to
5 for instance, such as, for example, including

7
1 attain, fulfil
2 upgrade, raise
3 contribute, present

ANSWER KEY 133

8
1 create, give, provide, present
2 achieve, raise, improve
3 achieve, attain, fulfil

9
Students' own answers

Unit 6 Careers & success page 126
1
1 inspiring, intelligent, fair, imaginative, passionate, supportive, competent
2 inspiring, intelligent, fair, determined, passionate, ambitious, forward-looking, honest, dependable, extroverted, sociable
3 inspiring, determined, passionate, courageous, competent

2
1 inspiration
2 depends
3 ambition
4 passionate
5 Competency
6 supportive
7 fairly
8 Determination

3
1 part time
2 bonus
3 pension
4 flexitime
5 training
6 holiday
7 boss
8 public holidays
9 Praise

4
1 consequence of
2 advantage of
3 drawback of
4 way to
5 reason for
6 explanation for

5
1 dress
2 drive
3 curiosity
4 educational background
5 Family background
6 looks
7 intelligence

6
Students' own answers

Unit 7 Nature & biology page 127
1
1 changeable
2 steady
3 pleasant
4 chilly
5 sunny
6 mild
7 cool
8 dry
9 windy
10 overcast
11 wet
12 humid

2
sunny, pleasant, mild, steady, dry, cool, changeable, windy, wet, humid, chilly, overcast

3
1 S/I 2 R 3 S/I 4 S 5 S/I 6 S/I 7 S 8 R

4
1 11 kilometres
2 9.3 metres
3 Canada
4 Victoria Falls
5 half the size
6 Angel Falls
7 the Netherlands
8 almost non-existent

5
1 flood a, food shortage c, volcano b
2 asteroid c, drought a, earthquake b
3 disease b, erosion c, climate change a

6
Students' own answers

Unit 8 Producers & consumers page 128
1
1 impulse buys, chewing gum, chocolate
2 White goods, washing machines, dishwashers
3 gifts, toys, clothes / perfume / chocolate / shoes
4 branded goods, clothes, shoes
5 electronic goods, laptop, tablet
6 services, financial advice

2
1 priceless
2 wealthy
3 rich
4 very poor
5 wasteful

3
Students' own answers

4
2 valuable
3 a waste of money
4 pricey
5 good value

5
1 lastly
2 additionally, moreover
3 first
4 whereas
5 such as

6
1 such as
2 First
3 whereas
4 Additionally / Moreover
5 Lastly

Unit 9 Media & travel page 129
1
1 went off
2 ran off
3 broke out
4 broke into
5 took place
6 ran over
7 came across
8 crashed into

2
1 discovery, breakthrough, invention, innovation
2 speeding, jam, congestion, motorway
3 robbery, speeding, blackmail, murder, hacking

3
1 harbour
2 monument / statue
3 mall / main square
4 public gardens
5 mall / street market
6 art gallery / cathedral
7 fountain
8 city wall

4
1 ships, fish restaurants
2 dedicated, memory, Second World War
3 shops, stores
4 open, green space
5 buy, local food, snacks, clothing, souvenirs
6 sculptures, paintings, priceless artefacts
7 splashing, water
8 stretches, 4 kilometres

5
Students' own answers

6
1 c 2 e 3 g 4 h 5 a 6 b 7 d 8 f

7
1 advert
2 broadcast
3 programme
4 search engine ranking

Unit 10 Science & progress page 130

1
1 housing
2 Work-life balance
3 Incomes
4 health
5 education
6 jobs
7 Communities
8 environment
9 Civic engagement
10 Safety

2
1 sanitation
2 leisure time
3 earnings
4 elderly
5 grades
6 employment
7 neighbourhood
8 pollution
9 public concern
10 violence

3
Students' own answers

4
1 design
2 discovery
3 experiments
4 inventions
5 predict
6 proof
7 research
8 tests

5
1 predicted
2 designer
3 Testing
4 discovered
5 prove
6 Experiments / Testing
7 invented
8 Research

6
Students' own answers

Study Skills File

Vocabulary page 131

1
Students' own answers

2
Possible answers:
A 2 B 3 C 3, 4 D 1, 4

3
Possible answers:
1 D 2 C 3 B 4 A

4, 5
Students' own answers

Speaking page 132

1
Students' own answers

2
Possible answers:
A 2, 3 B 3 C 4 D 1

3
Possible answers:
1 D 2 A 3 B 4 C

4, 5
Students' own answers

Listening page 133

1
Students' own answers

2
Possible answers:
A 1, 2 B 1 C 3 D 4

3
Possible answers:
1 D 2 A 3 C 4 B

4, 5
Students' own answers

Writing (page 134)

1
Students' own answers

2
Possible answers:
A 4 B 2, 4 C 2 D 1, 3

3
Possible answers:
1 C 2 A 3 B 4 D

4, 5
Students' own answers

Reading (page 135)

1
Students' own answers

2
Possible answers:
A 3 B 4 C 2 D 1, 3

3
Possible answers:
1 A 2 D 3 B 4 C

4, 5
Students' own answers

Writing File

Task 1: Description of trends (page 137)
3 1, 2, 3, 4, 5, 7, 9

Task 1: Comparison (page 138)
3 2, 4, 8, 9, 10

Task 1: Description of a process (page 139)
3 1, 3, 4, 5, 7

Task 1: Description of a diagram (page 140)
3 2, 4, 5, 7, 9, 10

Task 2: Personal opinion essay (1) (page 141)
3 1, 4, 5, 9, 11

Task 2: Discussion essay (page 142)
3 1, 2, 4, 5, 7, 9

Task 2: Personal opinion essay (2) (page 143)
3 6, 7, 9, 10

Task 2: Explanation essay (page 144)
3 2, 3, 4 (Note: this would not be expected in an effects essay), 7, 8, 10

IELTS Practice Test

Listening
Section 1

1 Stephen Morgan
   He spells out his name. The two alternative spellings of the first name are 'Stephen' and 'Steven', but his is the first one.
2 14 Sycamore
   The number 14 sounds different from the number 40. He spells out the name of the road.
3 LM6 8PB
   British postcodes are a mixture of letters and numbers. The letters P and B sound similar to each other but are clearly different from each other.
4 07438 972 118
   For phone numbers, 0 is usually pronounced 'oh'. The word 'double' is used for repeated numbers.
5 economics
   He says that he is in the second year of a three-year degree course in economics, so the subject he is studying is economics.
6 sports shop
   He says that he worked for two months as a shop assistant in a sports shop. The noun *retail* refers to the business sector of shops in general.
7 waiter
   He says that he was employed by a restaurant as a kitchen assistant, but when he arrived to start the job, they needed another waiter as they were a bit short of them, so that's what he did.
8 evening work
   She says there might be some evening work involved in the job at the café because it stays open in the evening and there is a shift system (different employees working for different time periods during the day and night).
9 computer skills
   She says that the job requires computer skills, and he says that he has those skills.
10 electronic goods
   She says that the store is looking for people to work in the electronic goods department, serving customers.

Section 2

11 exam results
   The head teacher will give general information about the school, such as the most recent exam results that the students have achieved.
12 lunchtime(s)
   The speaker says they've just introduced different arrangements for lunchtimes so that they can avoid overcrowding and make it easier for everyone to eat their meals without having to wait too long; the deputy head teacher will give details about that change and other changes.

13 behaviour
The speaker says that the deputy head teacher will also give you details of the school's new guidelines and policies concerning behaviour.

14 current student
The speaker says that the final talk will be given by a current student at the school.

15 websites
The final speaker will be showing the parents how their children will be using certain websites a bit later in their first year for homework and other school work.

16 A
The music department is in the far left-hand corner for the parents, as they look behind them, and the healthy eating scheme is in the opposite corner from the music department (the right-hand corner as the parents look behind them).

17 H
When the parents leave the hall through the doors at the back, they will find the refreshments on their right when they're outside the hall.

18 G
At the far end of that area (the area containing both refreshments and noticeboards), there is a reception desk, where parents can meet the person who runs the parents' association.

19 D
If parents turn left before they get to the reception desk, they go into the corridor where the majority of the teaching staff are. To the left of that corridor, they'll find maths, science and IT, in that order, so maths is the first one on the left as they go along the corridor.

20 E
The head teacher and other senior members of staff will be at the far end of that corridor (the corridor where the teachers are).

Section 3

21 B
Holly says she finds it hard to imagine now just how many people bought the paper a few decades ago and describes the sales figures as *incredibly high*. Liam says the sales figures are *Amazing* and *Way beyond what I would have thought*.

22 L
Liam says that he finds it hard to believe that they didn't at least to try to charge for it online from the start, but Holly says that putting the paper online free of charge was something that couldn't be avoided and she can see why they did it in the context of the time.

23 H
Holly says she thinks it is extraordinary that the paper has been so influential and that she hadn't realized that a single paper could have so much influence. Liam says that this fact was what he expected to find and he already knew about the paper's influence.

24 H
Holly says that she was actually shocked by some of them, and she hadn't realized how satirical and critical they could be; but Liam disagrees by saying *I don't know about that* and that he felt that they weren't so different in tone from a lot of the cartoons in the paper today.

25 A
Liam says that its politics can't be said to have changed much: *In my view, it's been pretty consistent in that area all the time*. Holly agrees and says: *Although the issues have changed, its general position has remained the same.*

26 C
Liam says that he found its coverage of famous people interesting – the way it hasn't really got involved in the so-called celebrity culture that's grown over the last few decades. Holly says: *It certainly hasn't jumped on that bandwagon; hasn't 'dumbed down', as they say.*

27 E
Liam says: *It was also interesting to look at its handling of social issues. It has a strong reputation for that today but, in fact, it was always an important feature that distinguished it from other papers.* Holly says: *It was campaigning on social issues just as much then as it does now.*

28 B
Liam is going to focus on the way a lot of British people form their opinions of other people on the basis of which newspaper they read. He says that British people decide what sort of person someone is and make assumptions about people because of the paper they read.

29 A
Holly says that she is going to look at why people might change from reading one paper to another as they get older, why some people do not stick with the same paper all their adult lives and at the kind of life changes that result in a change of paper.

30 C
Liam says that he particularly enjoyed the project because the main focus was on one particular paper, rather than all of them, which would have been too big a topic; Holly agrees that this has enabled them to look at one thing in depth rather than just a superficial view of a lot of them.

Section 4

31 underground railway
Tower Subway contained an underground railway, one of the world's first, but it didn't last for long. After three months, it closed and then Tower Subway re-opened as a pedestrian tunnel.

32 public competition
After the Special Bridge or Subway Committee was formed, a public competition was set up to choose the best design.

33 tall
A traditional fixed bridge was not possible because it would have prevented ships with tall masts from gaining access to the port facilities in that part of the river.

34 raised

35 (water)pipes / pressurized water
… these engines produced pressurized water … This was sent via pipes …
The boiler was in the engine rooms, which were at the far end of the south side of the bridge.

36 Bridge Operator
The levers were operated by the Bridge Operator, who was situated at the bottom of the tower on the south side.

37 (driving) engines
The engines that opened the bascules were in each of the two piers, each of them operating one of the two bascules; and these two engines were called the driving engines.

38 red flags
In the daytime, red flags were used to signal to ships, and these were placed on both bridge piers.

39 black ball
In the daytime, ships had to display a black ball high up in the ship.

40 24 hours / twenty-four hours
Signals are no longer used, and today ships have to give 24 hours' notice that they will require the bridge to be opened.

Reading
Reading passage 1
1 his grandmother
(second paragraph) His task is to take some money by train to his grandmother, who lives in the big city Berlin.

2 asleep / sleeping
(third paragraph) Emil falls asleep. When he wakes up, his money has gone.

3 boys
(third paragraph) The story describes his meetings with a group of boys in Berlin and how Emil and the boys catch the criminal who took the money.

4 statue
(second and third paragraphs) Emil is anxious about a crime he's committed – he drew a moustache on the face of the town statue of an important person. He does not want to involve the police because he fears exposure as the criminal who daubed the statue (he thinks they will realize he is the person who drew on the statue).

5 D
(fourth paragraph) In detective fiction the detective is usually a clever adult, but in this book children are the detectives. However, the children are as clever as adult detectives and they manage to do a very difficult job that adult detectives usually do.

6 A
(fourth paragraph) The writer says that children like fiction which appeals to a child's desire for power and independence, and in which its heroes are capable of acts beyond a child's usual capabilities (are able to do things real children cannot do).

7 C
(fifth paragraph) One reason why the book broke new ground (did something new at the time) was that it was one of the first books for children that gives us a full picture of a child in a single-parent family of very little means (with very little money).

8 FALSE
(sixth paragraph) The book only has one narrator. What is unusual is that the narrator doesn't just tell the story, but also gives the reader witty one-page commentaries on people appearing in the story, which involve the narrator thinking aloud for our benefit and talking directly to us.

9 NOT GIVEN
(sixth paragraph) We are told that in the original novel in German, the boys whom Emil meets talk using Berlin slang; but the writer does not say whether or not any readers found this hard to understand.

10 TRUE
(sixth paragraph) The local dialect in the book seems to confirm the resourcefulness of the boys; it helps to show how clever they are and how they are capable of dealing with things themselves. In other children's books, this kind of urban speech usually indicated that a character was bad or stupid.

11 TRUE
(sixth paragraph) The film was innovative (had features that were new at the time) in the realistic acting of child actors and the use of 'synch' sound on location on the streets of Berlin.

12 NOT GIVEN
(last paragraph) We are told that Kästner's life had similarities to Emil's – he lived in a small town like Emil's and his father also died when he was young – but we are not told whether or not Kästner based the story on things that happened in his own life.

13 FALSE
(last paragraph) Kästner was approached by the head of a Berlin publishing house, Edith Jacobsen, and it was she who suggested the idea. He didn't write it and then send it; he was asked to write it.

Reading passage 2
14 iv
The paragraph describes the context of the building of Park Hill, which was the major post-war shortage of housing in the city. The shortage of housing resulted from the destruction of many streets by bombs during the Second World War, the fact that a lot of housing was considered to be in too bad condition for people to live in and that land for building houses was in short supply (there was not much of it). The development was needed because of this shortage of housing.

15 viii
The paragraph describes how the people who created Park Hill were inspired by housing projects in other parts of Europe that they went to see, particularly by the work of Le Corbusier. It also says that they wanted to avoid what

they considered to be modern architecture's failures when creating the development.

16 ix
The paragraph consists mainly of details of what the development contained for the use of its residents.

17 ii
The paragraph describes the efforts made to make sure that residents would feel at home in the development – it included things from the houses and streets the people used to live in and that were therefore familiar to the residents.

18 v
The paragraph describes what people living in the development said about it soon after it opened and the response of experts in the field of architecture when the development was new.

19 i
The paragraph is about how Park Hill got into a poor condition, got a very bad reputation, and became a place full of problems after being successful at first.

20 street-decks
Paragraph C: *Park Hill's flats had interlinked 'street-decks' – communal areas on each storey ... The decks were as broad as real streets and wide.*

21 front doorsteps
Paragraph C: *The flats all had traditional front doorsteps.*

22 roof line
Paragraph C: *... their height varied, from four storeys to thirteen, in order to maintain a roof line that remained level ...*

23 (a) survey
Paragraph D: *A survey of residents conducted by the housing department a year after the flats had been officially opened was overwhelmingly positive ...*

24 (the) concrete
Paragraph F: *The concrete used for building Park Hill proved not to be suited to the damp climate of Sheffield and it became damaged.*

25 problem families
Paragraph F: *The council was accused of dumping problem families there ...* It was believed that families who were considered to cause problems for other people were sent to live there by the council because they did not want to give them homes in other places and they did not care about the result for other residents.

26 deliverymen
Paragraph F: *Deliverymen found that they often had to dodge milk bottles and other missiles ...* When people were delivering things at Park Hill, objects were thrown at them and they had to try to avoid them.

Reading passage 3

27 G
The author says that revulsion to robots may just be a temporary phenomenon and that we are capable of empathy for them. He ends by saying: *Eventually, human-like robots will make us love them, too.*

28 E
The author describes the roots in our evolutionary past ... between 60,000 and 40,000 years ago. This was when the modern mind came into being and he describes in this paragraph what this development of the brain involved.

29 A
The author compares people's emotional response to non-living objects such as dolls and toy soldiers and cars, which they feel affection for (they like them very much), with their response to human-like robots, which make us less comfortable and create a feeling of revulsion (the feeling that something is disgusting and horrible).

30 B
Robots like the Geminoid F have movements that show something of the mechanism beneath their 'skin' despite having human-like bodies, and people didn't respond well.

31 D
Saygin's research reveals a conflict between parts of the brain that interpret movement and appearance. In paragraph D Saygin says: *The brain look(s) for its expectations to be met – for appearance and motion to (match).*

32 C
According to the text, Charles Darwin noted that we react most adversely to species (animals) with eyes, nose and mouth arranged like our own.

33 A
Paragraph F: The text says MacDorman is one of the scientists who points to the importance of cultural factors (causes) to explain the 'uncanny valley' effect.

34 affection
Paragraph B: *The term comes from the dip in a graph with two parameters: affection and human-likeness. As human likeness increases, so does our affection. As soon as the resemblance becomes too great, though, affection drops below zero – hence the 'valley'. If the resemblance to a real human becomes very strong, the amount of affection we feel for a robot goes down.*

35 language
Paragraph E: *Researchers believe that the modern mind developed probably thanks to the evolution of language.*

36 photographs
Paragraph F: *... the 'uncanny valley' effect has been observed in our response to still photographs of humans that have been altered slightly ...*

37 YES
Paragraph A: *We humans have evolved to relate emotionally to non-living objects, which is strange when you think about it.*

38 NOT GIVEN
Paragraph B: The author explains what the term 'unhappy valley' means, but he does not talk about whether or not people find it hard to understand the term.

39 NO
Paragraphs F: *The phenomenon may therefore be more complex than Saygin's research suggests.*

40 YES
Paragraph G: *Eventually, human-like robots will make us love them, too.*

Writing

Writing task 1 – model answer
The chart shows how the number of shops in various categories changed in the first six months of 2013. In general, we can see that the growth in shop numbers varied considerably depending on shop type, with some types of shop doing very well during the period shown and others performing badly.

Shops selling low-value items that are not available on the internet saw the biggest increase in numbers. Over the six months, the number of charity shops increased dramatically by nearly 100 and the number of convenience stores also grew, though by only 50.

However, the period saw a large number of shop closures with photography shops being hit particularly badly. Their number declined by around 130 over the period. The number of DVD rental shops declined almost as rapidly with over 100 closing. It wasn't only technology-related shops that performed badly. Women's clothing also saw over 100 of its outlets disappear. In conclusion, it is worth noting that all these shop types, including banks, offer goods or services that can easily be bought online.

Writing task 1 – comments
Task achievement
Does the answer include all the relevant information?
The answer focuses on the main features of the chart and gives a general summary concerning the main trends over the period.

Coherence and cohesion
Does the answer flow well, with clear and logical organization of information and paragraphs?
The answer contains appropriate paragraphing – the first paragraph summarizes the information and the general changes; the following paragraph groups the shops into appropriate categories.

Lexical resource
Is there a range of appropriate and accurate vocabulary?
There is a good range of appropriate vocabulary, particularly words and phrases for describing statistical changes, for example *increased dramatically*.

Grammatical range and accuracy
Is there a good range of appropriate and accurate grammatical structures?
There is good use of appropriate grammatical structures, particularly ones for making comparisons, for example: *the biggest increase in numbers, almost as rapidly*.

Task 2 – model answer
These days schools are often compared according to how well they perform in a few core subjects. But is it useful to compare schools in such narrow categories? In general, I think this is a negative development and we should value a broader range of subjects.

Admittedly, it useful to be able to compare schools, and by limiting our comparisons to a few key subjects that all schools teach we make these comparisons simpler. It is also easier to compare schools in different countries by giving students tests in subjects that have 'right' or 'wrong' answers, such as maths and spelling, and so such subject areas provide a useful measure of comparison. For example, the *PISA* testing system has recently been able to rank schools worldwide by giving students in all countries the same tests in maths, science, and literacy.

However, the result of this is that schools dedicate an increasing proportion of their time to education in these subject areas and neglect other subjects. This is a problem because we need students who have a variety of creative and technical skills, too, as well the global knowledge to make informed decisions. Many modern economies, for example, depend on design skills and innovation which all require creative skills and are not encouraged by mechanical testing. Furthermore, we risk alienating students who do not excel at the core subjects. Some students have creative talents and ability in specific areas such as computing, design, or drama but by failing to allocate resources to these areas we run the risk that they may lose interest in education and so fail to achieve their full potential.

In conclusion, it is important that we find a way of giving schools credit for developing all the skills required in our modern economies and for nurturing all kinds of talent. If we fail to do so, we run the risk of damaging both economies and the individual lives of our young people.

Task 2 – comments
Task response
Does the answer cover everything in the question and answer it fully?
The answer includes everything required in the question – it discusses both the value of rating in core subjects and the disadvantages in doing so, but most importantly it maintains a clear position on the issue throughout the response as is required by the question.

Coherence and cohesion
Does the answer flow well, with clear and logical organization of points and paragraphs and good linking?
The answer flows well, with a clear introduction and conclusion. It is appropriately divided into paragraphs – the first paragraph deals with a view that differs from the view of the author, whereas the second two paragraphs construct the argument. Linking words and phrases such as *Furthermore* and *In conclusion* are used appropriately.

Lexical resource
Is there a range of appropriate and accurate vocabulary?
A good range of vocabulary suitable for the topic is used, for example: *global knowledge, informed decisions*.

Grammatical range and accuracy
Is there a good range of appropriate and accurate grammatical structures?
There is a good grammatical range, including a range of complex sentence forms, for example: *by failing to allocate resources to these areas we run the risk of …*

IELTS Practice Test Audioscript

Audioscript 2·39
SECTION 1
You will hear a young man who wants to find a temporary job talking to someone at an employment agency. First, you have some time to look at questions 1–7.
You will see that there is an example that has been done for you. On this occasion only, the conversation relating to this will be played first.
Stephen: Hi, I'm looking for a temporary job.
Agent: OK, please take a seat. I'll get some details from you and see what we can do.
Stephen: Thank you.
Agent: OK, so you're looking for temporary work. Would that be full-time or part-time?
Stephen: Well, I'd be happy with either at this point, but I'd prefer full-time rather than part-time, really.
Agent: OK, well I'll put you down for that, then.
Stephen: Fine.
Stephen says that he would prefer full-time work and the agent says that she will register him for that, so *full-time* has been written in the space. Now we shall begin. You should answer the questions as you listen because you will not hear the recording a second time. Listen carefully and answer questions 1–7.
Stephen: Hi, I'm looking for a temporary job.
Agent: OK, please take a seat. I'll get some details from you and see what we can do.
Stephen: Thank you.
Agent: OK, so you're looking for temporary work. Would that be full-time or part-time?
Stephen: Well, I'd be happy with either at this point but I'd prefer full-time rather than part-time really.
Agent: OK, well I'll put you down for that, then.
Stephen: Fine.
Agent: Right, let's get some details from you. First of all, your full name.
Stephen: Stephen Morgan.
Agent: There are different ways of spelling Stephen. Which one is yours?
Stephen: S-T-E-P-H-E-N.
Agent: OK, thanks. And your surname is Morgan. So that's M-O-R-G-A-N?
Stephen: Yes, that's right.
Agent: OK, fine. I'll just need a few more personal details from you and then we can look at the possibilities. So, next then, I need your address and postcode, please.
Stephen: It's fourteen, Sycamore Avenue, that's S-Y-C-A-M-O-R-E Avenue.
Agent: And it's number fourteen. Right?
Stephen: Yes, that's right.
Agent: OK. And the postcode?
Stephen: LM6 8PB.

Agent: OK, I've got that. Next, I'll need a contact number so that we can get in touch with you if and when something suitable comes up. Please say it slowly.
Stephen: 07438972 double 1 8.
Agent: Right, thanks. That's all the personal and contact details. Now, I just need to fill in a couple more sections for our records here. The first one is your current situation – are you working now?
Stephen: No, I'm a full-time student at university.
Agent: Ah, OK. What are you studying?
Stephen: I'm in the second year of a three-year degree course in economics.
Agent: OK, I've made a note of that. Now, I need to get some information about your availability for work. When would you like to start, that sort of thing?
Stephen: OK, well, I'm looking for something from July to September, during the long summer holiday from university. If I can, I'd like to work for the whole of that period.
Agent: OK, fine. The last thing I need from you is what kind of work experience you already have. Just general information on what type of work you've done will be fine.
Stephen: Well, I haven't done much – I've been studying most of the time. But I worked for two months as a shop assistant in a sports shop – selling sports equipment and clothing.
Agent: OK, so some experience in retail. Anything else?
Stephen: Er, yes, I worked in a restaurant for three months.
Agent: OK, and some experience in catering. What did you do there?
Stephen: Well, they actually employed me as a kitchen assistant, but when I got there, they needed another waiter as they were a bit short of them, so that's what I did.
Agent: OK, I've got all that, and straight away I think there are two or three vacancies that might suit you. One second …
Stephen: That sounds good, I'll make a note of them.

Audioscript 2·40
Before you hear the rest of the conversation, you have some time to look at questions 8–10.
Now listen and answer questions 8–10.
Agent: Right, first of all, there's a café in the town centre that's looking for an extra assistant for the busy summer period. That might work for you. There might be some evening work involved in that – they work a shift system there as they stay open in the evening.
Stephen: OK. That sounds possible.
Agent: Well, they're holding interviews for that next week, so I could fix that up for you.
Stephen: Great – thank you.
Agent: OK. I'll let you know about interview dates and times once I hear back from them.
Stephen: Fine, thanks.

Agent: Also, the tourist information office is looking for people to do administrative work. It doesn't involve giving any advice to the public – it's in an office behind the scenes there. Would that be of interest? It requires computer skills.

Stephen: That's not a problem. Yes, I'd be really interested in that.

Agent: OK, I'll email them your details. What else have we got? OK, finally, the new department store is looking for temporary staff over the summer period – at the moment they're looking for people to work in the electronic goods department, serving customers. Interested?

Stephen: Er, yes, that's another possibility, I guess.

Agent: OK, I'll email them your details, too. So we've got a few possibilities and I'll get in touch with you when I hear something back from them.

Stephen: That's great, thanks very much. I'll wait for your call, then.

Audioscript 2·41
SECTION 2
You will hear a teacher talking to parents at the beginning of a parents' evening at a school. First, you have some time to look at questions 11–15.
Now listen and answer questions 11–15.

Teacher: Good evening, everyone. Welcome to the school – it's great to see so many of you here. My name's Jackie Payne and I'm the Year 7 coordinator and organizer of the parents' evening. As you know, we hold this event every year for parents of new children who've just started. OK, I'm going to kick things off by telling you something about the schedule for the evening.

So, starting in a few minutes, at 7, Mrs Forester, the head teacher, who of course many of you have already met, will be telling you all about things that will be happening at the school over the course of your children's first year here. She'll explain about the tests that they'll take during the year, and how students are divided into different classes for various subjects. She'll also be giving you general information about the school, such as the most recent exam results that our students have achieved, as well as telling you about certain important dates during the school year.

At 7.30, the deputy head teacher, Mr Francis, who again many of you have met, will talk about some of the ways in which the school is run and give you some information about recent changes to the way things are organized. For example, we've just introduced different arrangements for lunchtimes so that we can avoid overcrowding and make it easier for everyone to eat their meals without having to wait too long. He'll also give you details of our new guidelines and policies concerning behaviour. This is generally very good at this school, but we've decided to introduce a few new rules to deal with one or two issues that have come up recently.

The final talk, from 7.45 to 8, will be given by a current student at the school, and she'll be telling you about some aspects of daily life here from the point of view of someone attending it. She'll also talk about the school trips that happen every year, specifically about the ones that your own children will be going on. And she'll be showing you how your children will use certain websites a bit later in their first year. These are connected with doing homework and with research for projects they'll be doing in their lessons, so we feel it's a good idea for you to find out how these work so that you can help your children to navigate their way around, and also for your own information, of course.

Audioscript 2·42
Before you hear the rest of the talk, you have some time to look at questions 16–20.
Now listen and answer questions 16–20.

OK, when the talks have finished, there'll be various things that you can do and people you can meet around this area of the school. Here in the main hall, in the far left-hand corner as you look behind you, there are teachers from the music department, who'll tell you all about what they've been doing in that department and you can find out about instruments your children can learn and concerts they can take part in. In the opposite corner, you'll find information about our healthy eating scheme, with details of the meals and snacks that we provide.

As you leave the main hall through the doors at the back, on your right when you're outside the hall you'll find a variety of refreshments and while you're there you'll be able to chat to other parents. If you continue along that area of the school, on your left you'll find a number of noticeboards with all sorts of displays about what's going on at the school, future events, and lots of interesting news and information to look at.

At the far end of that area, you'll find a reception desk, where you can get information and ask questions about the administrative aspects of the school, and get to know the staff that you're in touch with when you contact the school by phone or email, for example to report that your child is ill and can't come to school. There, you can also register your interest in volunteering to help at the school, perhaps with the organization of events to raise money through the parents' association, and you can have a chat with Helen Graham, who runs that. She'll be very happy to welcome any new volunteers! If you turn left before you get to the reception desk, you'll be going into the corridor where the majority of the teaching staff will be waiting to greet you and answer questions about their subjects. On the left of that corridor, you'll find maths, science, and IT, in that order, and on the right, you'll find languages, history and geography, and art – again in that order. And at the far end of that corridor, the head teacher and various senior members of staff will be waiting to discuss any issues you may want to raise or any queries you may have.

OK? Well, that's more than enough from me! I'd now like to ask Mrs Forester, our head teacher, to tell you about …

Audioscript 2·43
SECTION 3
You will hear two students, Liam and Holly, discussing an assignment they are doing which involves studying the history of a particular British national newspaper. First, you have some time to look at questions 21–24.
Now listen and answer questions 21–24.

Liam: So, how are you getting on with the newspaper assignment, Holly?
Holly: Yeah, pretty well. I think I've done all my research and I'm just about ready to write it up. How about you?
Liam: Yes, same as you. Must say I found it fascinating – there were lots of things I hadn't expected.
Holly: That's true. I mean, for example, the sales figures. It's hard to imagine now just how many people bought the paper a few decades ago.
Liam: Amazing, isn't it? But then of course there weren't all the other news sources back in those days.
Holly: I know, but even so, the figures are incredibly high.
Liam: Way beyond what I would have thought, too. And of course it's very interesting to compare them with the sales since the arrival of the internet.
Holly: Yeah, the way they responded to that – putting the paper online free of charge – was, I guess, something that couldn't be avoided. Every other paper was doing it.
Liam: But the paper came to regret it, and probably still does, because that decision had such a negative financial impact. I find it hard to believe that they didn't at least try to charge for it online from the start.
Holly: Hmm, I can see why they did it in the context of the time. One aspect that did strike me as extraordinary was finding out how influential that paper has been over the ages. It seems to have played a significant role in shaping government policy on occasions …
Liam: Yes, and social attitudes, too.
Holly: I hadn't realized that a single paper could have so much influence.
Liam: Really? I think you'll find that it still does. It's always been the paper read by what they call 'opinion formers' and people in high places, so that was what I expected to find.
Holly: What did you make of its coverage of those major historical events we looked at?
Liam: That was fascinating, to read about such huge events as they were reported at the time when they happened. It was great to read contemporary accounts of things that are now part of history.
Holly: Yeah, I really enjoyed doing that, too – seeing how reporters at the time described these things that we all know about.
Liam: One other thing that struck me was how interesting it was to look at the cartoons …
Holly: Yes, I think so, too. I was actually shocked by some of them. I hadn't realized how satirical and critical they could be. They showed public figures in ways that I don't think you'd be allowed to today.
Liam: I don't know about that. I felt that they weren't so different in tone from a lot of the cartoons in the paper today.

Audioscript 2·44

Before you hear the next part of the conversation, you have some time to look at questions 25–27.
Now listen and answer questions 25–27.
Holly: OK, so that brings us to the section of our report that has to cover major changes in the paper over the last few decades.
Liam: Yes, well, its politics can't be said to have changed much. In my view, it's been pretty consistent in that area all the time.
Holly: Right. Although the issues have changed, its general position has remained the same.
Liam: I found its coverage of famous people interesting – the way it hasn't really got involved in the so-called celebrity culture that's grown over the last few decades
Holly: It certainly hasn't jumped on that bandwagon; hasn't 'dumbed down', as they say. But sport, for example, is a whole different matter. That used to be just a relatively small section and now it's a massive part of the paper.
Liam: And its approach isn't the same either …
Holly: Hmm, instead of dry match reports and articles, as it used to have, it moved into a lot more interviews and opinion pieces.
Liam: Yes, I spotted that. It was also interesting to look at its handling of social issues. It has a strong reputation for that today but, in fact, it was always an important feature that distinguished it from other papers.
Holly: Yeah – it was campaigning on social issues just as much then as it does now.
Liam: Of course, one major feature we shouldn't ignore is the way it looks.
Holly: Definitely. It's unrecognizable today compared with how it looked even twenty years ago.
Liam: Very noticeable, everything about it – size, layout, even the design of the name at the top.

Audioscript 2·45

Before you hear the rest of the conversation, you have some time to look at questions 28–30.
Now listen and answer questions 28–30.
Holly: OK, so now we need to have a general section about British newspapers over the last few decades. What are you planning to say in that?
Liam: I'm going to focus on the way a lot of British people form their opinions of other people on the basis of which newspaper they read. It's one of the ingredients that makes people decide what sort of person someone is. It's a very British thing, that, and I'm going to write about the assumptions that people make of the readers of various papers.
Holly: That's really interesting – nice idea! I'm going to look at the issue of loyalty to a particular paper. I'm going to look at why people might change from reading one paper to another as they get older, whether price changes have any significant impact on sales, that sort of thing. It seems to me that the key point here is that while some people stick with the same paper all their adult lives, others change the paper they read as their own lives change. So I'm going to look at the kind of life changes that result in a change of paper.
Liam: That's a really good idea. Wish I'd thought of it! Anyway, it's been enjoyable doing this project, hasn't it?
Holly: Mmm.
Liam: I think it was great that the main focus was on one particular paper, rather than all of them, which would have been too big a topic to tackle for the whole project.
Holly: Yes, it meant we could look at one thing in depth rather than just a superficial view of a lot of them.

Liam: It's one of the better things we've done on the course.
Holly: Definitely.

Audioscript 2·46
SECTION 4
You will hear a lecturer talking about Tower Bridge in London. First, you have some time to look at questions 31–34.
Now listen and answer questions 31–34.

Lecturer: Tower Bridge is, of course, one of the best-known landmarks in London today. When it was built, it was actually one of many great engineering achievements in Britain in the 19th century – a period when all sorts of inventions and innovations were being made to modernize the country and to solve particular problems of the day.

In this case, the problem was how to provide another way of crossing the river Thames in that area of the river – the East End of the city. That part of London had become a very busy port and it was densely populated. The nearest bridge at the time was London Bridge, to the west of the port area. To provide a way of crossing the river in this part of the city, Tower Subway was built in 1870. This contained an underground railway, one of the world's first, but it didn't last for long. After three months, it closed and Tower Subway was then re-opened as a pedestrian tunnel, with users paying a toll to walk through it. Public demand for another crossing to be built grew, as it was taking both pedestrians and vehicles a long time to cross the river – the sheer volume of traffic and people was so great that people were delayed for hours when trying to use the available crossings.

Eventually, in 1876, the Special Bridge or Subway Committee was formed, to produce a solution, and a public competition was set up to choose the best design. There were over 50 entries, and a considerable amount of controversy over which to select, until in 1884 a design submitted by Horace Jones, the City Architect, was chosen. Construction began in 1886, and it involved five major contractors and 432 construction workers until the bridge was finally completed and opened eight years later in 1894.

The key issue when it came to the design of the bridge was that it wasn't possible to build a traditional fixed bridge in that location as such a bridge would have prevented ships with tall masts from gaining access to the port facilities in that part of the river. So a type of bridge called a bascule bridge was devised. This involved two towers built on piers in the centre of the bridge, with two equal bascules between them. These bascules were pieces that could be raised and separated from each other so that ships could pass through the bridge. On each side of the towers, piers, and bascules, there were two suspension bridges. Between the central towers were high-level walkways for the use of pedestrians when the bridge was open.

Audioscript 2·47
Before you hear the next part of the lecture, you have some time to look at questions 35–37.
Now listen and answer questions 35–37.
Right, now let's have a detailed look at how the bridge was raised for ships to pass through it. This is a slide showing a diagram of the bridge, and here you can see at the far end of the south side of it are the original engine rooms, which you can visit today if you take a tour of the bridge. In here, there was a boiler which was powered by coal. This boiler produced steam, which powered two big engines, and these engines produced pressurized water which was stored in six containers called accumulators. This was sent via pipes to some more accumulators in each of the two piers in the central section of the bridge. When it was time to open the bridge, the Bridge Operator, situated at the bottom of the tower on the south side, pulled a set of levers to set in motion the opening of the bascules. This action started engines in each of the two piers, each of them operating one of the two bascules. Gears attached to these two engines, which were called the driving engines, would then turn, causing the bascules to rise and open. The bascules rose to an angle of 86 degrees, providing enough room for ships to get through the central part of the bridge. Although the process was quite complex, it actually took only about a minute for the bascules to rise to their maximum height.

Audioscript 2·48
Before you hear the rest of the lecture, you have some time to look at questions 38–40.
Now listen and answer questions 38–40.
A number of rules were used for controlling the passage of ships through the bridge at different times. In the daytime, red flags were used to signal to ships, and these were placed on both bridge piers. At night, coloured lights were used – red to show that the bridge was closed and green to show that it was open. Ships going through the bridge also had to display signals. In the daytime, they had to display a black ball high up in the ship, and at night they had to have red lights in the same place.

Well, the bridge today is much the same as it was when it was first built, but the process for raising the bascules has changed quite a lot. The bascules are still operated by hydraulic power but the engines are now driven by oil and electricity, not steam. And the Bridge Operator now works in a different location, in the control cabin in the North Tower of the bridge. The system of signals is no longer used, and today ships have to give 24 hours' notice that they will require the bridge to be opened.